Bitter Lemons

BOOKS BY LAWRENCE DURRELL

NOVELS

Nunquam
Tunc
The Alexandria Quartet:
Justine, Balthazar, Mountolive, Clea
The Revolt of Aphrodite: Tunc and Nunquam
Monsieur *or* The Prince of Darkness
Justine
Balthazar
Mountolive
Clea
The Dark Labyrinth
The Black Book

TRAVEL

Bitter Lemons
Reflections on a Marine Venus
Prospero's Cell
Sicilian Carousel
Spirit of Place: Letters and Essays on Travel

HUMOUR

Stiff Upper Lip
Esprit de Corps
Best of Antrobus

POETRY

Selected Poems 1935-1963
Vega and Other Poems

PLAY

Sappho: A Play in Verse

CHILDREN'S

White Eagles Over Serbia

BITTER LEMONS

Lawrence Durrell

faber and faber

First published in 1957
by Faber and Faber Limited
3 Queen Square, London W.C.1
First published in this edition 1959
Reprinted 1960, 1961, 1962,
1964, 1967, 1970, 1973, 1978 and 1982
Printed in Great Britain
by Whitstable Litho Ltd., Whitstable
All rights reserved

ISBN 0 571 06186 9 (Faber Paperbacks)
ISBN 0 571 06096X (hard bound edition)

To
AUSTEN HARRISON
of
Lapithos in Cyprus

Contents

Preface

———◆———

This is not a political book, but simply a somewhat impressionistic study of the moods and atmospheres of Cyprus during the troubled years 1953–6.

I went to the island as a private individual and settled in the Greek village of Bellapaix. Subsequent events as recorded in these pages are seen, whenever possible, through the eyes of my hospitable fellow-villagers, and I would like to think that this book was a not ineffective monument raised to the Cypriot peasantry and the island landscape. It completes a trilogy of island books.

Circumstances gave me several unique angles of vision on Cyprus life and affairs, for I did a number of different jobs while I was there, and even served as an official of the Cyprus Government for the last two years of my stay in the island. Thus I can claim to have seen the unfolding of the Cyprus tragedy both from the village tavern and from Government House. I have tried to illustrate it through my characters and evaluate it in terms of individuals rather than policies, for I wanted to keep the book free from the smaller contempts, in the hope that it would be readable long after the current misunderstandings have been resolved as they must be sooner or later.

I much regret that the cutting of my overgrown typescript removed the names of many friends to whom I am deeply indebted for material and information on Cyprus; let me briefly make amends by thanking the following for many kindnesses: Peter and Electra Megaw, G. Pol Georghiou, Fuad Sami, Nikos Kranidiotis, Paul Xiutas, and Renos and Mary Wideson.

The poem 'Bitter Lemons' first appeared in *Truth*, March 1, 1957.

'A race advancing on the East must start with Cyprus. Alexander, Augustus, Richard and Saint Louis took that line. A race advancing on the West must start with Cyprus. Sargon, Ptolemy, Cyrus, Haroun-al-Rashid took this line. When Egypt and Syria were of first-rate value to the West, Cyprus was of first-rate value to the West. Genoa and Venice, struggling for the trade of India, fought for Cyprus and enjoyed supremacy in the land by turns. After a new route by sea was found to India, Egypt and Syria declined in value to the Western Nations. Cyprus was then forgotten; but the opening of the Suez Canal has suddenly restored her to her ancient pride of place.'

(BRITISH CYPRUS by W. Hepworth Dixon, 1887)

'But the poor Cypriots are much-enduring people, and God in his Mercy avenges them; they are no more rulers than the poor serfs and hostages are; they make no sign at all.'

'Portents do not speak falsely, for those who have experience of them recognize their truthfulness.'

(THE CHRONICLE OF MAKHAIRAS)

Towards an Eastern Landfall

Journeys, like artists, are born and not made. A thousand differing circumstances contribute to them, few of them willed or determined by the will—whatever we may think. They flower spontaneously out of the demands of our natures—and the best of them lead us not only outwards in space, but inwards as well. Travel can be one of the most rewarding forms of introspection. . . .

These thoughts belong to Venice at dawn, seen from the deck of the ship which is to carry me down through the islands to Cyprus; a Venice wobbling in a thousand fresh-water reflections, cool as a jelly. It was as if some great master, stricken by dementia, had burst his whole colour-box against the sky to deafen the inner eye of the world. Cloud and water mixed into each other, dripping with colours, merging, overlapping, liquefying, with steeples and balconies and roofs floating in space, like the fragments of some stained-glass window seen through a dozen veils of rice-paper. Fragments of history touched with the colours of wine, tar, ochre, blood, fire-opal and ripening grain. The whole at the same time being rinsed softly back at the edges into a dawn sky as softly as circumspectly blue as a pigeon's egg.

Mentally I held it all, softly as an abstract painting, cradling it in my thoughts—the whole encampment of cathedrals and palaces, against the sharply-focused face of Stendhal as he sits forever upon a stiff-backed chair at Florian's sipping wine: or on that of a Corvo, flitting like some huge fruit-bat down these light-bewitched alleys. . . .

The pigeons swarm the belfries. I can hear their wings across the water like the beating of fans in a great summer ballroom. The *vaporetto* on the Grand Canal beats too, softly as a human pulse, faltering and renewing itself after every hesitation which marks a landing-stage. The glass palaces of the Doges are being pounded in a crystal mortar, strained through a prism. Venice will never be far from me in Cyprus—for the lion of Saint Mark still rides the humid airs of Famagusta, of Kyrenia.

It is an appropriate point of departure for the traveller to the eastern Levant. . . .

But heavens, it was cold. Down on the grey flagged quay I had noticed a coffee-stall which sold glasses of warm milk and *croissants*. It was immediately opposite the gang-plank, so that I was in no danger of losing my ship. A small dark man with a birdy eye served me wordlessly, yawning in my face, so that in sympathy I was forced to yawn too. I gave him the last of my liras.

There were no seats, but I made myself comfortable on an up-ended barrel and, breaking my bread into the hot milk, fell into a sleepy contemplation of Venice from this unfamiliar angle of vision across the outer harbour.

A tug sighed and spouted a milky jet upon the nearest cloud. The cabin-steward joined me for a glass of milk; he was an agreeable man, rotund and sleek, with a costly set of dimples round his smile—like expensive cuff-links in a well-laundered shirt. 'Beautiful,' he agreed, looking at Venice, 'beautiful': but it was a reluctant admission, for he was from Bologna, and it was hard to let the side down by admiring a foreign city. He plunged into a pipe full of scented shag. 'You are going to Cyprus?' he said at last, politely, but with the faintest hint of commiseration.

'Yes. To Cyprus.'

'To work?'

'To work.'

It seemed immodest to add that I was intending to live in Cyprus, to buy a house if possible. . . . After five years of Serbia I had begun to doubt whether, in wanting to live in the Mediterranean at all, I was not guilty of some fearful aberration; indeed the whole of this adventure had begun to smell of improbability. I was glad that I was touching wood.

'It is not much of a place,' he said.

'So I believe.'

'Arid and without water. The people drink to excess.'

This sounded rather better. I have always been prepared, where water was scarce, to wash in wine if necessary. 'How is the wine?' I asked.

'Heavy and sweet.' This was not so good. A Bolognese is always worth listening to on the subject of wine. No matter. (I should buy a small peasant house and settle in the island for four or five years.) The most arid and waterless of islands would be a rest after the heartless dusty Serbian plains.

'But why not Athens?' he said softly, echoing my own thoughts.

'Money restrictions.'

'Ah! Then you are going to live in Cyprus for some time?'

My secret was out. His manner changed, and his picture of Cyprus changed with it, for politeness does not permit an Italian to decry another's plans, or run down his native country. Cyprus was to become mine by adoption—therefore he must try to see it through my eyes. At once it became fertile, full of goddesses and mineral springs; ancient castles and monasteries; fruit and grain and verdant grasslands; priests and gipsies and brigands. . . . He gave it a swift Sicilian travel-poster varnish, beaming at me approvingly as he did so. 'And the girls?' I said at last.

But here he stuck; politeness battled with male pride for a long moment. He would have to tell the truth lest later on, in the field, so to speak, I might convict him—a Bolognese, above all!—of having no standards of female beauty. 'Very ugly,' he said at last, in genuine regret. 'Very ugly indeed.' This was disheartening. We sat there in silence for a while until the steamer towering above us gave a loud lisp of steam *fffff*, while beaded bubbles of condensing steam trickled down the siren.

It was time to say good-bye to Europe.

Tugs brayed as we passed the harbour bar. The mist thinned out and quivered on the hills beyond Venice. With such associations how could I forget Catherine Cornaro, the last Queen of Cyprus, who in twenty years of exile forgot perhaps her uneasy reign over the island, finding in the green arbours of Asolo, surrounded by devoted courtiers, a kindlier way of life? She died aged fifty-six in 1510, and her body was carried across the Grand Canal from the family palace. ('The night was a stormy one, with heavy wind and rain. On her coffin lay the crown of Cyprus—outwardly at least Venice insisted that her daughter was a Queen; but, inside, her body lay shrouded in the habit of Saint Francis, with cord and cowl and coarse brown cloak.') It is hard in the early morning radiance of this sky and sea to imagine those flapping torches, the scattering waters flushed by lightning, the wind snatching at cloaks and vestments as the long boats set out with their marvellously clad dignitaries. Who remembers Catherine? Titian and Bellini painted her; Bembo wrote a philosophy of love to amuse her courtiers. In the only portrait I have seen the eyes are grave and beautiful, full of an impenitent life of their own; the eyes of a woman who has enjoyed much adulation, who has travelled much and loved much. The eyes of one who was not narrow enough, or self-seeking enough to trespass on the domain of politics without losing at the game. But the eyes of a true woman, not a phantom.

And then my thoughts turned to another sad relic—the flayed and stuffed skin of the great soldier Bragadino which lies mouldering somewhere among the recesses of *Giovanni e Paolo*. His defence of Famagusta against the Turkish general Mustafa ranks among the great feats of military leadership in the whole of European history. When at last the pitifully small forces of the besieged were forced to parley they agreed to surrender on condition that they were given a safe passage to Crete. Mustafa broke his word, and no sooner was Bragadino in his power than he unleashed upon his person and that of his captains all the pent-up fury of the religious fanatic. Bragadino's nose and ears were cut off, and his body was flayed; then he was set in a slung seat with a crown at his feet and hoisted at the yard of a galley, 'hung like a stork', for all to see. Finally he was dragged to the main square and tortured while 'the drums beat'. But 'his saintly soul bore all with great firmness, patience and faith ... and when their steel reached his navel he gave back to his Saviour, a truly happy and blessed spirit. His skin was taken, stuffed with straw, and carried round the city: then hung on the yard of a galliot and paraded along the coast of Syria with great rejoicings.'

All this was recorded faithfully by Calepio, detail by detail—but it is difficult to read in cold blood. Venice is fading against the hills.

At dusk the mute grey destroyer which had been playing hide-and-seek with us all afternoon heeled abruptly, disconcertingly about and vanished westward into the green ray. We turned from the rail with a sigh, aware that the light was sifting quietly away into the darkness, as casually as the plumes of smoke from the funnel of the ship which carried us. We had become, with the approach of night, once more aware of loneliness and time—those two companions without whom no journey can yield us anything.

It is now that the traveller seeks to renew, if only vicariously, his sense of connexion with the land in letters to be written, documents to be sorted, baggage dispositions to be worked out. It is still warm on deck, and from the glow of light coming from the saloon I am able to return once more to the pages of Mrs. Lewis, who in 1893 made the same voyage as ourselves, and who, in *A Lady's Impressions of Cyprus*, has left us a spirited and observant record of life in the island when British suzerainty was only a few years old. She came within a few years of Rimbaud's visit—the last one. With his talent for tasting every extreme the French poet not only baked himself raw in the oven-like quarries of Larnaca, but succeeded in freezing himself almost insensible on the bony heights of Troodos, building the Governor's summer lodge, with a small team of mules and workmen. What did he think of Cyprus? He does not say. It was simply a place where a few decently paid jobs existed under the British. His two brief visits have left us a few whining references to the heat and the cold—that is all.

In the same span of time a young second-lieutenant conducted a forlorn battle with the War Office which was to result in the first accurate field-survey of the island. Those antler-like moustaches, those stern but shy eyes, were later to become an international symbol for a whole generation—Kitchener! Poet and soldier, their paths must actually have crossed on several occasions. But that is what islands are for; they are places where different destinies can meet and intersect in the full isolation of time. The poet with his grunting mule-team winding laboriously up through the foothills to the lodge he was building: Kitchener bivouacked with his two clerks and the jumble of theodolites, markers and tables, in some worn bell-tent among the olives. They have nothing in common save that they share the same nook in time.

Yet there is one fugitive similarity. The handwriting of both men is remarkable for the conscious control it reveals over a sensibility excited beyond the pitch of the normal. Kitchener's is stronger, less sensitive—but then he had already taken refuge in the Army, behind the double-locked doors of a corporate tradition, behind the moustaches, behind a vocation as exacting as that of the Church. From this he drew the strength which Rimbaud denied himself. The French poet was of a different order of bravery, for he was on the run from the Hound of Heaven. . . .

In Cyprus I stumbled upon many more such echoes from forgotten moments of history with which to illuminate the present. Invaders like Haroun Al Rashid, Alexander, Coeur de Lion: women like Catherine Cornaro and Helena Palaeologus . . . the confluence of different destinies which touched and illumined the history of one small island in the eastern basin of the Levant, giving it significance and depth of focus.

Different invasions weathered and eroded it, piling monument upon monument. The contentions of monarchs and empires have stained it with blood, have wearied and refreshed its landscape repeatedly with mosques and cathedrals and fortresses. In the ebb and flow of histories and cultures it has time and time again been a flashpoint where Aryan and Semite, Christian and Moslem, met in a death-embrace. Saint Paul received a well-merited thrashing there at the hands of the Paphiots. Antony gave the island to Cleopatra as a gift. Aphrodite. . . .

I picked Mrs. Lewis off an overturned bookstall in Trieste.

There had been a riot after a bomb-throwing, and I was hurrying back to my hotel from the observation-ward of the hospital. The street with its wrecked fruit-stalls and booths and smashed shop-windows was perfect illustration of my state of mind. The boat was to sail at midnight. *A Lady's Impressions of Cyprus* stared up at me from a jumble of fruit and books, and a whole drift of smashed second-hand discs. There was no one about, though I could hear the grumble and crash of a crowd down towards the harbour. Military patrols kept roaring by. The gutters were running mournfully with wine which on the black tarmac looked like blood. The whole contents of a toy-shop had been blown into the street, giving it all a carnival air. I stopped guiltily, fearful of incurring the penalties of looting should the police return, and picked Mrs. Lewis up. Her faded green cover with it florals device promised me a Victorian travel-account which might introduce me in a most suitable manner to the Crown Colony of Cyprus. But something more than this. I felt she was a sort of omen.

A book picked up at such a time and in such a place could not turn out to be merely the vague ramblings of some dreadful nursery governess. I glanced at it and was reassured. A first-class ticket from London to Smyrna in 1893, she informed me, cost her exactly £17 2s. 3d. Without more ado, I slipped Mrs. Lewis into my pocket beside my passport and my own ticket from Trieste to Limassol, which had cost me £47. There she would stay until I had time to digest her.

A patrol roared out of a side-street and I thought it wiser to be off with my prize. Hurrying through the misty and deserted streets I felt absurdly reassured by the little book—as if I had put myself into the hands of a trustworthy guide. Nor was my confidence misplaced. Mrs. Lewis offered me a splendid picture of Cyprus with which to compare my own experience and impressions.

We berthed towards sunrise in a gloomy and featureless roadstead, before a town whose desolate silhouette suggested that of a tin-mining village in the Andes. An unlovely straggle of godowns and warehouses, patched and peeling, fronted the shallow and dirty littoral. Here and there along the flat alluvial coastline, with its unhealthy suggestion of salt-pans (I was not wrong: Limassol lies upon a shallow lake), here and there the eye picked out a villa of some style or consequence in a flowering garden. But even at this early hour the sunlight created a dense haze, while the humid air of the little port came out across the still sea to meet us.

We landed by bum-boat and were charged an inordinate fee for unnecessary porterage. In the gaunt customs-house things were not too bad—but in place of the tremendous roaring and gesticulating, of chaffering and swearing, which one had come to expect from the ports of the Levant, there reigned a heavy and stupefied silence. The officials went about their duties with the air of sleep-walkers. It was surprising to find them collected enough to answer questions. I asked in Greek and was answered in English. I asked again in Greek and was once again answered in English. It was a long moment before I recollected why. I was in the presence not, as I thought, of Turks who either knew no Greek, or would not condescend to speak it: no, I was in the presence of *babus*. To lapse into Greek with anyone who was not a peasant would involve a loss of face. It was rather sad. Just to make sure I asked for the names of the customs officials with whom I had been dealing; they looked faintly surprised, but politely gave me Greek names. I wished I knew enough Turkish to see whether any such inhibition reigned among the Turkish officials.

Outside the customs house a mob of expensive-looking taxis had collected, manned by young Cypriots who shouted at me amiably enough. But altogether the atmosphere lacked *brio*. A vague and spiritless lethargy reigned. I was beginning to think that successive occupations had extirpated any trace whatsoever of the Greek genius when I was relieved by the sight of a bus with both back wheels missing, lying on its side against a house. It was just like home. Three old ladies were dismembering the conductor; the driver was doing one of those laughing and shrugging acts which drive travellers out of their minds all over the

Levant; the village idiot was pumping up a tyre; the owners of the house against which the bus was leaning were hanging indignantly out of their drawing-room window and, with their heads inside the bus, were being rude to the point of nausea. Meanwhile, a trifle removed from the centre of the hubbub, and seated perilously on the leaning roof of the machine, with contorted face, perched an individual in a cloth cap who appeared to be remorselessly sawing the bus in half, starting at the top. Was this perhaps some obscure revenge, or a genuine attempt to make a helpful contribution? I shall never know.

A grave-looking priest stood on the outskirts of the crowd, uttering the expression 'Po-Po-Po-Po' under his breath, gently, with compassion. His lack of frenzy betokened that he had not been intending to travel on the bus himself. He was simply an onlooker, studying the tragedy and comedy of the life around him. From time to time he resettled the black bun of hair on his neck, and muttered 'Po-Po-Po-Po' as some new development in the drama became clear, or as the householders reached a new high point of invective.

'Can you tell me the fare to Kyrenia?' I asked him in Greek and was at once aware of two bright surprised brown eyes staring into mine. 'You are English,' he said after a moment's scrutiny. 'Yes.' He seemed taken aback. 'But you speak Greek.' I agreed; he seemed taken even further aback. He drew back like a bowstring before launching a smile of appreciation so dazzling that I felt quite bewildered.

The questions which betoken politeness now followed and it gave me great pleasure to find that I could still, after four years, hold a tolerably steady course through a Greek conversation. My host was even more pleased than I was. He dragged me to a café and filled me with heavy red wine. He himself was leaving for England that night or he would have personally made himself responsible for this paragon, this wonder of an Englishman who spoke indifferent but comprehensible Greek. . . .

Before we parted he drew a piece of brown paper out of his cassock and smoothing it out with an inexpert hand wrote a message on it to his brother in Nicosia who would, he said, be responsible for my well-being until he himself got back. 'You will like Cyprus,' he repeated.

This completed, he led me to the taxi rank and selected a cousin of his, a large contemptuous-looking young man, as a suitable driver to take me to Kyrenia. We parted effusively and he stood in the main street waving his umbrella until we turned a corner of the road. Father Basil.

The cousin was made of different stuff; his biting air of laziness and superiority made one want to kick him. He answered my politenesses with grunts, gazing at me slyly in the mirror from time to time. He chewed infinite gum. He rasped his unshaven chin with his thumb from time to time. Worst of all, he drove badly. But he inadvertently did me a good turn, for as we reached the last point where the road turns inland from the sea and begins its sinuous windings among the foothills, he ran out of petrol. There was a spare can in the boot so that there was no cause for alarm; but the respite, during which I got out on to the road to light a cigarette, was useful in another way—for we had stopped directly under the bluff where the remains of ancient Amathus stand today. (Mrs. Lewis had eaten a watercress sandwich there, while brooding upon its ancient history.)

'What is that place?' I asked him, and hardly bothering to turn his fat and ugly head he replied, 'Amathus' in a voice full of apathetic disdain. I left him whistling tunelessly as I climbed a little way up the bluff towards the site of the temple. The position of the acropolis is admirably chosen, standing as it does above the road at the very point where it turns inland from the sea. Priest and soldier alike would be satisfied by it. From the summit the eye can travel along the kindlier green of a coast tricked out in vineyards and fading away towards the Cape of Cats and Curium. Here and there the great coarse net of the carob tree—a stranger to me. I noticed that some of these trees had been planted in the middle of fields reserved for barley or corn. They were presumably to give the cattle shade against the pitiless heat of August. But altogether the carob is a curious tree with its red flesh; branches torn from it leave wounds the colour of human flesh.

My driver was seated disconsolately by the roadside, but his whole manner had changed. I was at a loss to explain his smiling face until I saw that he had unearthed my little volume of Greek folk-songs from among the newspapers I had left on the back seat. The change in him was quite remarkable. He suddenly turned into a well-educated and not unhandsome young man, full of an amiable politeness. He was prepared, if necessary, to stay here all night. Would I care to explore the ruins thoroughly? There was much to be known about them. It was at this point that Coeur de Lion actually landed.* 'I know this from my brother, who works in the Museum,' he added. As for Amathus, it was up there that Pygmalion. . . . He plunged once more into the boot of the car and emerged with a bottle of *ouzo* and a length of yellow hosepipe which I recognized as dried octopus. We sat beside the road in the thin spring sunshine and shared a stirrup-cup and a *meze* while he told me, not only all he knew about Amathus, but all about himself and his family with an attention to detail which would have been less wearying perhaps were I planning a novel. The only point of interest in this conversation was the continual reappearance in it of an aunt of his who suffered from palpitations of the heart and had to live on the top of Troodos; but the excellent *ouzo* and his general affability transformed the journey—freeing me at a stroke from my irritation and enabling me to look about me with a fresh eye.

We moved slowly inland now along a road which winds steeply through a green belt of vine-country, through little whitewashed villages bespattered by the slogan ENOSIS AND ONLY ENOSIS. I felt that it was too early for me to probe the national sentiments of my host and I avoided comment upon this ubiquitous piece of decoration. From time to time lorries passed, or smart saloon cars, and there was not one which did not earn a greeting from my driver. He lowered his window and shrieked across the intervening space as we passed, only to lean back once more and explain, 'That was Petro, a friend,' 'That was my aunt's cousin,' 'That is a friend of my uncle.' It was admirable practice for my Greek. 'You would like him,' he never failed to add, politely including me in the exchange of courtesies. 'He

* He was wrong.

drinks like a fish. What a drinker!' We passed a succession of topers in this fashion, quietly finishing our own bottle of *ouzo* in sips and discoursing vaguely in the manner of old friends. 'You seem to know everyone,' I said admiringly, and he accepted my compliment with a self-deprecating smile. 'Cyprus is a small island. I think I have relations in every one of the six hundred villages. At *least* six hundred free drinks,' he added meditatively.

'I seem to have come to the right place.'

'We are mad about wine.'

'I'm glad to hear it.'

'And about freedom—our freedom.' Lest the remark might smack of an impoliteness he caught my hand in his own and pressed it warmly, sympathetically, smiling into my eyes. 'Freedom,' he repeated more softly. 'But we love the British. How could we Greeks not?'

'Are things bad here that you are so unhappy with the British?'

He sighed deeply and his sigh exploded into a 'No'; it was as if my question were hopelessly ill-informed, the question of a half-wit or a child. 'We don't want the British to go; we want them to stay; but as friends, not as masters.'

We took a small swig of *ouzo* and finished off the octopus. 'My friend,' he said, disarmingly using the rare, rather formal vocative. 'We do not have to teach you what freedom means—you brought it to Greece, to the Seven Islands. Why do we call you the Phileleftheri—the Freedom-lovers? In the heart of every Greek . . .' His peroration is one familiar to everyone who has ever visited Greece. I must have endured it several thousand times in my life. It is pure anguish—but none the less true and felt. But here in Cyprus I was doubly glad, doubly reassured by having to endure it once more—for it proved that the old sentimental tie was still alive, that it had not been killed by wooden administration and bad manners. So long as this tie held, fragile and sentimental as it was, Cyprus would never become a shooting affray—or so I thought.

Under the stress of all this intellectual by-play, or perhaps under the impetus created by neat *ouzo*, we had begun to drive very fast indeed, screeching round corners and roaring over the crest of hills. And now at last Nicosia was in sight, the frail fountain-points of the Grand Mosque, and the misty outlines of the medieval bastions. Rising across the dry brown plains we could see the slight, deft aerial range of the Kyrenia mountains, chalky grey under the soft spring sunshine. The air was crisp with a vanished rain.

We had moved insensibly into the great bare plain called the Mesaoria in the middle of which the capital lies. It is dusty and unprepossessing in the extreme. 'We will leave it to our left,' said the boy, 'and go up there and over. To Kyrenia.' His hand described the trajectory of a swallow—and indeed the speedometer was touching seventy. The *ouzo* bottle was empty, and with a fine disregard for passing topers he pitched it overboard into the ditch. 'Within the hour', he said, 'you will arrive at the Dome.' Swiftly and expressively his hand built up a series of belfries and cupolas, of towers and turrets. Apparently the hotel was to be an echo of Coleridge.

A Geography Lesson

'Recent research has carried the history of Cyprus back to the early Neolithic age, around 3700 B.C., when the Island seems to have been first settled by an enterprising people whose origins are obscure.'

(*Colonial Report*—Cyprus 1954)

> *If you should come to Kyrenia*
> *Don't enter the walls.*
> *If you should enter the walls*
> *Don't stay long.*
> *If you should stay long*
> *Don't get married.*
> *If you should get married*
> *Don't have children.*

(Turkish Song)

While I was finding my bearings and conducting an initial exploration I lodged with my friend Panos, a schoolmaster, in two small clean rooms overlooking the harbour of Kyrenia, the only port in Cyprus which—diminutive, cleanly coloured, beautiful—has some of the true Cycladean *allure*. It is on the seaward side of the Kyrenia hills opposite the shaggy Turkish coastline whose mountains sink and rise out of the sea, dissolve and reappear with the transparent promise of a desert mirage.

Panos lived with his wife and two small sons in a house which must once have been part of the Church of Saint Michael the Archangel—up forty whitewashed steps, brilliant with sunshine, into a stone courtyard: the obvious site of the ancient acropolis of the town. The belfry of the church towered over us, its bell banging aggressively for every service, the lazy blue-and-white ensign of Greece softly treading the wind above the blue harbour.

The schoolmaster himself was very typical of Greek Cyprus— a round curly head, stocky body, with strong arms and legs; sleepy good-natured eyes. Through him I made my first acquaintance with the island temperament which is very different from the prevailing extrovert disposition of the metropolitan Greek. The styles of politeness were more formalized, I noticed, even between Cypriots. Forms of address were somewhat old-fashioned and lacking in spontaneity; there was a certain thoughtful reserve in conversation, a sense of measure. Hospitality was unobtrusive and shyly offered—as if the donor feared rebuff. Voices were lower and laughter set in a lower key. But the Greek Panos spoke was true Greek, with here and there an unfamiliar word from the *patois* of the island.

Every evening we took a glass of sweet, heavy Commanderia on his little terrace, before walking down the tiny winding lanes to the harbour in order to watch the sunset melt. Here by the lapping water I was formally and civilly introduced to his friends, the harbourmaster, the bookseller, the grocer, who sat by the lapping water sipping *ouzo* and watching the light gradually fade over the stubby bastions of Kyrenia Castle, and the slender points of the Mosque. Within a week I had a dozen firm friends in the little town and began to understand the true meaning of Cypriot hospitality which is wrapped up in a single word—'*Kopiaste*' which roughly speaking means 'Sit down with us and share.' Impossible to pass a café, to exchange a greeting with anyone eating or drinking without having the word fired at one as if from the mouth of a gun. It became dangerous even to shout 'Good appetite', as one does in Greece, to a group of labourers working on the roads when one passed them at their lunch-hour seated under an olive-tree. At once a dozen voices would reply and a dozen hands would wave loaves or cans of wine. . . . After ten days of this I began to feel like a Strasbourg goose.

But these evening sessions by the water were of the greatest value to me in another way, for I was able to get a fair picture of the cost of living in the island, and more important still, the cost of buying a house. The harbourmaster came from Paphos, the bookseller from the mountain villages, while the grocer came from the more cosmopolitan surroundings of Limassol. All of them were lavish with their information, though, somewhat to my disappointment, none of them were topers.

Panos himself was the only one of them who knew that I was something more than a chance traveller, that I planned to stay in the island, and he nobly respected the secret though he went to no end of trouble to obtain information for me about relative prices and conditions elsewhere. Walking by the water, holding his two little boys by the hand, he talked excitedly of the house I would buy and of the vine he would plant for me as soon as I had bought it. 'You will find nothing better than the Kyrenia district,' he said. 'My dear friend, it is not selfishness, though we would like you to be near us. No. It is the greenest and the most beautiful part of the island. Also, though near the capital, you can find quite remote villages within half an hour of shops and cinemas.'

But no schoolmaster can be without a blackboard for long and in his anxiety to present as clear a picture as possible of the island he would inevitably jump down on to the spit of sand under the castle and say, 'Look. I will make it clear.' His sons watched this frequent demonstration with grave pride, each sucking a sweet.

With a certainty born of long practice, for his subject was the history of Cyprus, he sketched in the odd, snouty and rather charmless outline of the island on the wet sand, cross-hatching in the two great mountain ranges which traversed it, and inadvertently falling into the rather bookish manner of exposition which he doubtless employed with his classes. 'The name is obscure; some say the island gave its name to copper which was mined here. Some say it derives from its shape which is that of an ox-hide pinned to a barn-door to dry after being salted. Who can tell?'

Michael and Philip nudged one another admiringly and watched my face to make sure that I was suitably impressed. I was, for Panos' exposition was always precise and economical —obviously the fruit of long practice spent in simplifying his ideas in order to get them into the heads of village children.

'First there were two islands,' he said, lightly touching the two parallel ranges of mountain. 'Then the plain rose from the sea to join them—the Mesaoria—flat as a billiard-table. The winds find a clear thoroughfare to roll from sea to sea across the centre of the island. The two islands are now two groups of mountains, the big Troodos range and the little Kyrenia range.' He continued in his sweet level voice, aiming his disquisition obliquely at his two small sons. By frequent repetition I could see them already quite clearly—the two mountain ranges and the grim, beautiful Mesaoria which linked them. The Troodos range was an unlovely jumble of crags and heavyweight rock, unarticulated and sprawling, hanging along the fringes of the Mesaoria like a backcloth. Such beauties as it had were in its hidden villages, tucked into pockets and valleys among the foothills, some rich in apples and vines, some higher up smothered in bracken and pine; once the green abode of Gods and Goddesses, the Troodos range is now extravagantly bald in many places, its great shoulders and arms thrusting out of the painfully afforested areas like limbs in a suit too small for them. Snow covers it for part of the year when its grim and eagle-patrolled fastnesses match those of the Taurus Mountains across the water, reminding one that the whole island is geologically simply an appendix to the Anatolian continent which has at some time been broken off and set free to float.

The Kyrenia range belongs to another world: the world of the sixteenth-century print. Though it is about a hundred miles long its highest peak is just over three thousand feet. Running as it does along the sea-line its graceful and various foothills are rich with running streams and green villages. It is *par excellence* the Gothic range, for it is studded with crusader castles pitched on the dizzy spines of the mountains, commanding the roads which run over the saddles between. The very names smell of Gothic Europe: Buffavento, Hilarion, Bellapaix. Orange and mulberry, carob and cypress—the inhabitants of this landscape discountenance those other green intruders from the Arabian world, the clear green fronds of palms and the coarse platters of banana-leaves. . . .

But I had already begun to see the island as whole, building my picture of it from the conversations of my host. With him I spent three winters snowed up on Troodos, teaching in a village school so cold that the children's teeth chattered as they wrote; with him I panted and sweated in the ferocious August heat of the plains; suffered from malaria at Larnaca; spent holidays among the rolling vineyards of Paphos in search of vines to transplant; like him I came back always to the Kyrenia range, to cool my mind and gladden my heart with its greenness, its carpets of wild anemones, its castles and monasteries. It was like returning to a fertile island from a barren one—from Cephalonia to Corfu.

I did not need to know where my house would be found; I was sure that it would be here, along the foothills of this delightful range. But how should I find it?

Nothing must be done in a hurry, for that would be hostile to the spirit of the place. Cyprus, I realized, was more Eastern than its landscape would suggest, and like a good Levantine I must wait and see.

Voices at the Tavern Door

'Everyone pulls the quilt over to his side.'

'The hardest crusts always fall to the toothless.'

'Work is hard, no work is harder.'

'So long as he has a tooth left a fox won't be pious.'

(Cypriot Greek Proverbs)

After a few weeks Kyrenia, for all the formalized beauty of its ravishing harbour, its little streets and walled gardens rosy with pomegranates, began to pall. It is difficult to analyse why—for the Spring was on us and the green fields about the village, still spotted with dancing yellow oranges and tangerines, were thick with a treasury of wild flowers such as not even spring in Rhodes can show. But other considerations intruded, changing its atmosphere. The outskirts of the walls, where still the traces of ancient tombs were clear in the rock face of quarries or cuttings, had begun to bristle with cheap little villas and tarmac roads on the pattern of Wimbledon. Here and there houses already bore the alarming name-signs which greet one from the gates of seaside boarding-houses, 'Mon Repos', 'Chowringee', 'The Gables'. The little place was obviously soon to become one of those forlorn and featureless townships hovering on the outskirts of English provincial cities—suburbs without a capital to cling to. There was a building boom on; all land was booming. The regular holiday-makers' season Kyrenia enjoyed had already imposed on it a rash of unpleasant bars and cafés painfully modelled on those of Messrs. Lyons. It was, in fact, enjoying all the deformities and amenities associated with our larger suburbs at home. Its real life as a Graeco-Turkish port of the Levant was ebbing out of it. Or so one felt.

In all this one could see something which marked Cyprus off

from the rest of the Mediterranean—an agricultural island being urbanized too quickly, before its inhabitants had really decided what was worth preserving about their habits and surroundings.

Disturbing anomalies met the eye everywhere: a Cypriot version of the small-car owner, for example, smoking a pipe and reverently polishing a Morris Minor; costumed peasants buying tinned food and frozen meat at the local version of the Co-op; ice-cream parlours with none of the elaborate confectionery, the true Levant delicacies, which make the towns of the Middle East as memorable as a tale from the Arabian Nights; an almost total absence of good fish or any fishy delicacy. As far as I could judge the townsman's standard of living roughly corresponded to that of a Manchester suburb. Rural life remained as a sort of undertow. The peasant was already becoming a quaint relic of a forgotten mode of life. White bread and white collars!

Yet side by side with this crude and graceless world the true Mediterranean *moeurs* lingered—but the two aspects of life seemed totally divorced from one another. Crowded buses still brought black-booted peasants with quaint old-fashioned manners into the town, accompanied by their wives and daughters, many of whom sported permanent waves and shingles. There were gipsies, there were tramps and professional poets, to be sure, but their appearances were fugitive and had the air of being illusory. I could not be sure where they lived, where they came from, these figures from the literature of the past. How had they escaped the cloth cap and boots, the cheap overcoat and brief case which—apart from the hunger and despair—had been the only noticeable feature of the people's revolution in Yugoslavia? It was hard to say—for they were still roughly and talkatively alive. They were still melon-fanciers and tosspots, carrying about with them the rough airs of village life and village ways which one can enjoy anywhere between Sardinia and Crete. Yet there seemed to be something disembodied about them. Somewhere, I concluded, there must be a Cyprus beyond the red pillar-boxes and the stern Union Jacks (floating, mysteriously enough, only over the police-stations) where weird enclaves of these Mediterranean folk lived a joyous, uproarious, muddled anarchic life of their own. Where?

Occasionally I stopped people and asked them where they came from: booted and bandoliered sportsmen drinking brandy and leaning on their guns as they waited for a bus; grave priests or turbaned hodjas; baggy-trousered patriarchs holding swaddled infants; women in coloured head-kerchiefs. I was rewarded by the names of villages which I memorized. Later I would know exactly where to find woven stuff and silk (Lapithos), or carved cupboards and shelves (Akanthou). Kyrenia was the shopping centre for a district.

Meanwhile the British colony lived what appeared to be a life of blameless monotony, rolling about in small cars, drinking at the yacht club, sailing a bit, going to church, and suffering agonies of apprehension at the thought of not being invited to Government House on the Queen's Birthday. One saw the murk creeping up over Brixton as one listened to their conversations. No doubt Malta and Gibraltar have similar colonies. How often they have been described and how wearisome they are. Yet my compatriots were decent, civil folk, who had been brought here, not by any desire to broaden minds cumbered only by the problems of indolence and trade, but by a perfectly honourable passion for sunlight and low income tax. How sad it is that so many of our national characteristics are misinterpreted! Our timidity and lack of imagination seem to foreigners to be churlishness, our taciturnity the deepest misanthropy. But are these choking suburbanisms with which we seem infused when we are abroad any worse than the tireless dissimulation and insincerity of the Mediterranean way of life? I doubt it. Yet Manoli the chemist lived in a perpetual ferment of indignation about British manners, British stand-offishness and so on. His particular hate was General Envy. He would perform a little dance of rage as he saw the old soldier sauntering down the main street, patronizing not only the poor Cypriots but the very morning air by the self-confident sweep of his tobacco-stained moustache. 'Look at him,' he would say. 'I could throw a tomato at him.' Then one day the General asked him how to pronounce the Greek for 'potato' and shyly showed him a shopping list which he had laboriously made out in Greek. After that Manoli would flush with annoyance if ever he heard a word spoken against the old fellow. He became, for Manoli at least, a saint; and yet the General, as all who remember him will agree, was a vile old bore with scarce manners and little enough consideration for the world around him. 'Such a good, kind man,' Manoli would say after the General's canonization, rolling his dark eyes and nodding. 'Such a *worthy* and *respected* man.' This is what happened whenever Briton and Cypriot met, even to exchange the merest civility.

The truth is that both the British and the Cypriot world offered one a gallery of humours which could only be fully enjoyed by one who, like myself, had a stake in neither. Never has one seen such extraordinary human beings as those who inhabited the Dome Hotel; it was as if every forgotten Victorian *pension* between Folkestone and Scarborough had sent a representative to attend a world conference on longevity. The figures, the faces, the hats belonged to some disoriented world populated only by Bronx cartoonists; and nothing could convince one more easily that England was on its last legs than a glimpse of the wide range of crutches, trusses, trolleys, slings and breeches-buoys which alone enabled these weird survivals to emerge from their bedrooms and take the pale spring sunshine of the Kyrenia waterfront. . . . Shadowy and faded plumage of dejected fowls and crows shuffling through the sterile white corridors towards a terrace laid with little tables and religiously marked 'Afternoon Teas'; or the strange awkward figures of honeymooners sauntering hand in hand under the fort—convalescents from a prenuptial leucotomy. Alas! the Cypriots did not see how funny they were. They were merely aghast at their age and the faded refinements which they exemplified.

Conversely the British saw a one-dimensional figure in the Cypriot; they did not realize how richly the landscape was stocked with the very sort of characters who rejoice the English heart in a small country town—the rogue, the drunkard, the singer, the incorrigible. Here and there the patriarchal figure of some booted worthy seemed to strike them for a moment, like a fugitive realization that here was a figure belonging truly to his landscape. But the fitful understanding died there, under the label of 'quaintness', and was dispersed. Perhaps language was the key—it was hard to say. Certainly I was astonished to find how few Cypriots knew good English, and how few Englishmen the dozen words of Greek which cement friendships and lighten the burdens of everyday life. There were, of course, many honourable exceptions on both sides who struck the balance truly. Scholars of wild flowers and students of wine and folklore already had something in common which overstepped the gaps created by lack of knowledge. But generally speaking the divorce was complete, and the exceptions rare; all too many of us lived as if we were in Cheltenham, while some had been there as long as five years without feeling the need to learn the Greek or Turkish for 'Good morning'. These things are trivial, of course, but in small communities they cut deep; while in revolutionary situations they can become the most powerful political determinant.

But I was on a different vector, hunting for other qualities which might make residence tolerable, or might isolate me from my fellows. My attitude was a selfish one, though wherever I saw our national credit prejudiced by an inadvertent word or action I tried to restore the balance if it were possible by soothing ruffled feelings or interpreting the significance of some action which had been misconstrued. It is fatal in the Levant to be too proud to explain.

But this digression has led me away from my topic—the music of a flute, which one day issued from the shadowy recesses of Clito's cavern, and restored my confidence in the belief that topers did, in fact, exist in Cyprus. My dissatisfaction with the existing Coca-Cola bars or pubs had for some time been nagging me, persuading me to try to find a modest tavern whose habitués would correspond more nearly to the sort of people I had come to live amongst. In Panos' world there had been good fellowship and kindness, but also a middle-class restraint and poise which were in the final analysis, wearying. The lives of his friends were lived according to a pattern already familiar to me; the middle bourgeois of France or England live just such lives, among the circumscribed politenesses of people who have face to lose and positions to keep up. Panos' was the world of the quiet scholar of means in a small village. I wanted to see a little further into Cypriot life, to canvass its values at a humbler level.

The feeble insinuations of a shepherd's flute directed my steps to the little wine-store of Clito one fine tawny-purple dusk when the sea had been drained of its colours, and the last coloured sails had begun to flutter across the harbour-bar like homesick butterflies. It had been the first really warm spring day—the water cold and bracing. It was good to feel salt on one's skin, in one's hair, salt mixed with dust between one's sandalled toes. It would be another hour before lamp-light, and by now the harbour walk would be full of people taking their dusk aperitifs. I was on my way to buy a torch battery and a roll of film when the flute intervened.

It was obviously being played by someone with an imperfect command over it; it squeaked and yipped, started a line again, only to founder once more in squeals. The music was punctuated by a series of shattering disconnected observations in a roaring bass voice of such power that one could feel the sympathetic vibrations from a set of copper cauldrons standing somewhere in the innermost recesses of Clito's cave. Bursts of helpless laughter and a laboured altercation also played an intermittent part in the proceedings.

I entered the cave with circumspection and greeted Clito, whom I had seen before. He stood behind his own bar with a faint and preoccupied kindness graven on his thin face, gazing up at the flute-player with the helpless affection of a moth drunk on sugar-water. He held his hand over his mouth to imprison his laughter.

The musician was a large sturdy peasant clad in tall black boots and baggy Turkish trousers of rusty black. He wore a sweat-stained shirt of serge, open at the throat to show a woollen vest which had once been white. He had a fine head and a thick un-trimmed moustache; a blue and somewhat vague eye, and at his belt a finely carved gourd for a water-bottle. On his head he wore a sort of bonnet made from a strip of lambswool. He was gorgeously drunk.

At either elbow stood a sleepily smiling Turkish policeman

with the air of a mute, waiting to help with the body when the service was complete; they both made deprecating noises from time to time, saying 'You shut up, now', and 'That's enough', and so on, but with a helpless lackadaisical air. The fact that both had large glasses of cognac before them seemed to indicate that the law-breaker was not the ogre he sounded, and that this was by way of being a performance repeated regularly. They were used to it. I had no sooner deduced this than Clito confirmed it. 'Every time he has a Name Day in his family he drinks. He's a strange one.' 'Strangeness' in Greek means 'a character'. One indicates the quality by placing one's bunched fingers to the temple and turning them back and forth in the manner of someone trying a door-handle. Clito made the gesture furtively and let it evolve into a wave—towards a chair from which I could watch the fun. 'His name is Frangos,' he said, with the air of a man who explains everything in a single word.

'Who dares to say I am drunk?' roared Frangos for perhaps the ninth time, blowing with the same breath a squeak or two from his handsome brass flute. More guffaws. He then began a splendid tirade, couched in the wildest argot, against the damned English and those who endured them with such patience. The policemen began to look more alert at this, and Clito explained hastily: 'When he goes too far . . . *pouf*! they cut him off and take him away.' With his two fingers he edited a strip of cinema film. But Frangos seemed to me a formidable person to cut off in this fashion. He had shoulders like an ox. One of the policemen patted him awkwardly and was shaken off like a fly. 'Why,' bellowed Frangos, 'do you tell me to shut up when I am saying what everyone knows?' He gave a toot on his instrument and followed it up with a belch like a slammed door. 'As for the English I am not afraid of them—let them put me in irons.' He joined a pair of huge fists dramatically. A couple of timid English spinsters peered nervously into the tavern as they passed. 'Let them fire on me.' He tore open his shirt and exposed an expanse of breast-bone curly with dense black hair with a gold cross nestling in it. He waited for a full half-second for the English to fire. They did nothing. He leaned against the bar once more, making it creak, and growled on, lashing his tail. Renos, the little boot-black sitting next to me, was shaken by giggles; but lest I might find this impolite he explained breathlessly between sobs: 'He doesn't really mean it, sir, he doesn't.'

Frangos took another stately draught of the white cognac before him and turned a narrow leonine eye upon me. 'You observe me, Englishman?' he said with contemptuous rudeness. 'I observe you,' I replied cheerfully, sipping my drink. 'Do you understand what I say?' Somewhat to his surprise I said: 'Every word.' He leaned back and sighed deeply into his moustache, flexing his great arms and inflating his chest as prize-fighters do during a preliminary work-out. 'So he understands me,' he said in coarse triumph to the world in general. 'The Englishman, he actually understands.'

I could see from everyone's expression that this was regarded as having gone a bit too far—not only because I was English, but because impoliteness to any stranger is abhorred. The policemen stood up and braced themselves for the coming scuffle. Clito wagged his head sadly and uttered an apologetic *po-po-po*. This was obviously the point where our friend got himself edited like a strip of film. The policemen showed an understandable reluctance to act, however, and in the intervening silence Frangos had time to launch another derisive shaft at me. He threw up the great jut of his chin squarely and roared: 'And what do you reply to me, Englishman? What do you think sitting there in shame?'

'I think of my brother,' I said coolly.

'Your brother?' he said, caught slightly off his guard by this diversion which had just occurred to me.

'My brother. He died at Thermopylae, fighting beside the Greeks.'

This was a complete lie, of course, for my brother, to the best of my knowledge, was squatting in some African swamp collecting animals for the European zoos. I put on an air of dejection. The surprise was complete and a stunned silence fell on the wine-impregnated air of the tavern. Clito himself was so surprised that he forgot to turn off the spigot in the great cask of red wine and a stain began to spread across the dusty flea-bitten floor. Frangos looked as though someone had emptied a slop-pail over him, and I was rather ashamed of taking this easy advantage of him. 'Your brother,' he mumbled slowly, swallowing, not quite knowing which way to turn, and yet at the same time being unwilling to be so easily discountenanced.

'The Cypriots forget many things,' I said reproachfully. 'But we don't forget. My brother's corpse does not forget, and many another English boy whose blood stains the battlefield. . . .' I gave them a fragment from a newspaper peroration which I had once had to construe during a Greek lesson and which I had memorized for just such occasions. Frangos looked like a cornered bull, sheepishly turning his great head this way and that. It was clear now that he wasn't even drunk, but merely mellow. He had been acting the part expected of him on a Name Day. A fleeting expression of shy reproach crossed his face. It was as if he had said aloud: 'How damned unfair of you to introduce your brother just when I was getting into my stride. Perfidious Englishman!' I must say I sympathized; but I was unwilling to lose my advantage. It was clear that if I harped on my imaginary brother it would not be long before Frangos could be wrung out like a wet dish-rag. 'Your brother,' he mumbled again, uncertain of the proper mood to wear. I saved him now by calling for more drink and he subsided into a smouldering silence at one end of the room, casting a wicked eye at me from time to time. He was obviously turning over something in his mind.

'Englishman,' he said at last, having worked the whole thing out to his satisfaction, 'come and stand beside me and drink to the *palikars* of all nations.' This was indeed a handsome toast and I lost no time in honouring it in brandy. It was not long before all of us, including Clito himself and the policemen, were splendidly tipsy. Frangos sat down in the traditional Cypriot fashion upon five chairs, one for the rump and one for each member, and taunted Clito into a few rather unsteady dance-steps. I obliged with a rendering of the 'Forty Palikars' which met with great approval. The policemen giggled.

Our evening was at last brought to an end by the appearance of an extremely smart Inspector of Police, a Greek, who in exquisite English, and with an intimidating politeness, asked me to break the evening up. 'We might,' he explained gently, 'have a breach of the peace.' It sounded a splendid thing to have but for Frangos' own sake it seemed wiser to defer it, so we issued still amiably arguing and cursing into the moonlight where Frangos, after almost falling into a shop window, finally found his way to the tiny public garden where he unhitched an improbably small horse from an acacia tree and wavered off into the night accompanying his journey with toots on the flute. I gathered that he did not live far away.

Clito, who had accompanied the party, wearing the air of a man concerned for our safety, but in fact because he hated to miss the least of Frangos' drunken witticisms, now took my arm with an air of loving commiseration. 'You must have one last drink with me,' he said. It seemed wiser to refuse as the hour was late, but he pleaded with me like a small boy who is afraid to be left alone in the dark. 'For your brother's sake,' he said at last, convinced that this at least could not be shrugged off, and led my lagging steps back to his cavern. Several of the spigots had been left on or half on and the worm-eaten floor of the cavern was liberally bepuddled with country wine. He lit a candle, cursing the failure of the electric light which had reduced Kyrenia to darkness that evening. By its dim light I studied the place. The confusion was indescribable; piles of empty cases, bottles and barrels were piled up in every corner, climbed every wall. But his was not really a tavern so much as a wholesale wine-shop with a few chairs for customers who became too argumentative or bibulous to leave: it was understood that before buying a litre of wine one had the right to sample the contents of each and every butt which lined the back wall of the cave. Insensibly samplers turned into tavern-clients, for it is always difficult to make up one's mind in a hurry, and sometimes it might be necessary to have as many as three or four whacks at a cask before one was sure about it. Hence a few chairs and tables set about for the use of the undecided. Clito turned off all the spigots he could see, administered a well-aimed kick at some which were out of immediate reach, set up a bottle of cognac and two glasses, and sat himself down with a sigh of relief.

'Thank God Frangos has gone,' he said. 'Now we can drink to your brother. Long live your brother!'

He did not seem aware that a certain incongruity lay in such a toast. I echoed him solemnly, however, and raised a glass.

The front door of the wine-shop had been firmly locked behind us when we returned and it was some time before there came a knocking at the wooden panels. We were by this time deep in an argument about the growing of mushrooms—I cannot for the life of me think why, there are so few in Cyprus. Clito was laying down the law, and had actually banged the table to emphasize a point, when he heard his wife's voice in the street outside. He froze. 'What is it, dear?' he said in a small voice—the voice of a gnat attacked by the vapours. His wife replied in a clear voice. 'What are you doing in there? I want to come in.'

Clito put his fingers to his lips and said: 'Just stock-taking, my love.' There was an ominous pause during which we both emptied our glasses and winked at each other. It was an unconvincing statement on the face of it—for the whole tavern, and indeed its owner, bore the unmistakable signs of belonging to that ideal world where income tax and stock-taking have never been heard of. To my surprise his wife gave a cackle of good-natured laughter. 'You have become a great man of business, have you?' she said, and Clito answered, 'Yes, dear,' with a mixture of meekness and injured dignity. 'Why can't I come in?' asked his wife in a friendly voice full of indulgence to the great wine merchant. 'Because,' said Clito with a touch of asperity (he was on stronger ground here), 'there is a little disorder in our shop.' It was putting it mildly.

Over the bar hung a Victorian print. It was divided into two panels in the manner of a Byzantine icon. On one side sat an old gentleman in the prime of life, with elegant nankeen trousers and an opulent spread of gold watch-chain. A curled head of hair, neat whiskers of the mutton-chop variety, and spotlessly laundered cuffs, set off his appearance. He was seated jauntily before a roll-topped desk out of whose every drawer poured a cascade of

five-pound notes which drifted about his ankles. He was smiling
and held one thumb inside the flap of his tweed waistcoat. Under
him was written in Gothic script the legend: 'I sold for Cash
only.'

In the opposite corner sat another man, so yellow and cada-
verous as to appear to be in the last stages of consumption; his
rusty, moth-bedevilled business suiting and wrinkled dicky suggested extremes of dreadful indigence. His frayed cuffs and
yellow teeth, his bald head and purple eye, showed to what
lengths he had been driven by his refusal to adopt simple business maxims within the grasp of all. He too sat at a roll-topped
desk—but out of every drawer poured frightful IOU's which had
never been honoured. Under him was written in letters of fire
'I sold for Credit.'

I examined these two monitors while Clito engaged his good-
natured wife in further explanations, none of which sounded very
subtle to me. But she was obviously a good-tempered woman and
after a while she left us to ourselves, after extracting from him a
promise that he would not be late home.

'She is really a very *good* woman,' said my host grudgingly.
'But *much* trouble, *much* fuss, and brain—*finish*.' From time to
time, as a compliment to me, he dropped into a telegraphic
English. He added in Greek: 'We nearly starved, you know. Our
shop is still not a going concern. And a lot of work, too.'

The bottle of cognac was low and I now recognized in it,
despite its colourless innocence, a formidable adversary which, if
taken too lightly, would unhorse me completely; another bottle
I thought would have seen us both comfortably to hospital, so
I seized my host's arm as he was about to wring the neck of one,
and suggested a change to wine.

'Wine,' he said, and his voice was charged with a professional
tenderness. 'Such wine as Clito has you will not see in Cyprus.
Such wine.' He leaped up like a faun and smacked a cask with the
flat of his hand until it gave off a resonant boom like a distant
eructation of Frangos among the olive-glades. 'Wine from
Paphos' (bang), 'Wine from Lefka' (bang), 'Wine from Limassol'
(bang). He walked up and down the row of casks like someone

playing an arpeggio on a xylophone. 'And all fresh country wine, sent to me by my family, unbottled, free from chemicals.' He sat down and added in a small deflated voice: 'So cheap too, but nobody buys it.'

My curiosity aroused, I had him lay me out a dozen sample glasses which were filled, albeit somewhat unsteadily, from the line of spigots. There were, in all, about eight varieties of wine and cognac and we took our time, quietly going over the properties of each one as we drank it; Clito dwelt long and lovingly on the pedigree, the soil, the landscape and the character of its makers. His disquisition was so full of poetry that in some cases he made a sample taste a good deal better than it in fact was; but I was in no mood to cavil.

He also produced some pickled *beccafico* which I had read about but never before tasted, and together we crunched the small birds to bits as we tasted the wines of Cyprus and sagely assessed them. There is no knowing how long this expressive and rambling conversation would have gone on had we not been interrupted—this time by one of Clito's daughters who put her lips to the crack in the front door and shouted: 'Mother says unless you come at once she will call her mother.'

This threat had an electrifying effect on my friend. He made a swift tour of the spigots, blew out the candles and produced a bunch of keys. 'We must go,' he said regretfully. I made some attempt to settle the reckoning but he brushed aside my money with the remark I was to come to know so well: 'A stranger does not pay in Cyprus.' I thought I saw a reproachful flicker in the eyes of the two Victorians in the cartoon. 'Besides,' said Clito, 'none of my friends ever pays, and I consider you a friend after all we have passed through together tonight.' He seemed on the point of tears. I was afraid that he was thinking about my brother. 'Tell me,' I said to divert him, 'how would you set about buying a house here?' He thought. 'I should go to the biggest rogue in Kyrenia—of course everyone is a rogue in Kyrenia except me— but I should go to Sabri the Turk. He is a *terrestrial* rogue of business and has many houses.' He spread his arms to try to indicate the full extent of Sabri's roguery. I thought it odd that a Greek should recommend a Turk until I remembered how little he trusts his own compatriots. 'Sabri,' said Clito firmly. 'He's the one I would go to. But *beware*!'

His expiring hiss of warning died quietly on the moonlight. I saw his daughter take his unsteady arm and pilot him in the direction of home.

How to Buy a House

'Last of all came the Greeks and inquired of the Lord for their gift.
'"What gift would you like?" said the Lord.
'"We would like the gift of Power," said the Greeks.
'The Lord replied: "Ah, my poor Greeks, you have come too late.
All the gifts have been distributed. There is practically nothing left.
The gift of Power has been given to the Turks, the Bulgarians the gift
of Labour; the Jews of Calculation, the French of Trickery and the
English of Foolishness."
'The Greeks waxed very angry at this and shouted "By what intrigue
have we been overlooked?"
'"Very well," said the Lord. "Since you insist, you too shall have a
present and not remain empty-handed—may Intrigue be your lot,"
said the Lord.'

(Bulgarian Folk-tale)

———◆———

Sabri Tahir's office in the Turkish quarter of Kyrenia bore
a sun-blistered legend describing him as a valuer and estate
agent, but his activities had proliferated since the board was
painted and he was clearly many things besides. The centre of the
cobweb was a dark cool godown perched strategically upon a
junction of streets, facing the little Turkish shrine of some saint
or warrior whose identity had vanished from the record, but
whose stone tomb was still an object of veneration and pilgrimage
for the faithful. It stood under a dusty and desiccated pepper
tree, and one could always find an *ex voto* or two hanging beside
it.

Beyond was a featureless empty field of nettles in which stood
a couple of shacks full of disembodied pieces of machinery and
huge heaps of uncut carob and olive, mingled with old railway
sleepers and the carcasses of buses which always turned up here
at the end of the trail, as if to some Elephants' Graveyard, to be
turned into fuel. Sabri's Empire was still in an embryonic stage,
though it was quite clear that he was speculating wisely. A circular
saw moaned and gnashed all day in one of the shacks under the

ministrations of two handsome Turkish youths with green head-bands and dilapidated clothes; a machine for making cement blocks performed its slow but punctual evacuations, accompanied by a seductive crunch.

Sabri could watch all these diverse activities from the darkness of his shop where he sat for the greater part of the day before a Turkish coffee, unmoved, unmoving, but watchful. His desk was in the far corner against the wall, and to reach it one traversed a *terrain vague* which resembled the basement of Maple's, so crowded was it with armchairs, desks, prams, cooking-stoves, heaters, and all the impedimenta of gracious living.

The man himself was perhaps forty years of age, sturdily built, and with a fine head on his shoulders. He had the sleepy good looks—a rare smile with perfect teeth, thoughtful brown eyes—which one sees sometimes in Turkish travel posters. But what was truly Turkish about him was the physical repose with which he confronted the world. No Greek can sit still without fidgeting, tapping a foot or a pencil, jerking a knee, or making popping noises with his tongue. The Turk has a monolithic poise, an air of reptilian concentration and silence. It is with just such an air that a chameleon can sit, hour after hour, upon a shrub, staring unwinkingly at the world, living apparently in that state of suspended judgement which is summed up by the Arabic word *kayf*. I have seen Sabri loading logs, shouting at peasants, even running down a street; but never has he conveyed the slightest feeling of energy being expended. His actions and words had the smoothness of inevitability; they flowed from him like honey from a spoon.

On that first morning when I stepped into the shadows of his shop, the headquarters of the empire, he was sitting dreamily at his desk mending a faulty cigarette-lighter. His good-morning was civil, though preoccupied and indifferent; but as I approached he paused for one instant to snap finger and thumb and a chair materialized from the shadows behind him. I sat down. He abandoned his task and sat silent and unwinking before me. 'Mr. Sabri,' I said, 'I need your help. I have been making inquiries in Kyrenia and on all sides I am told that you are the most untrustworthy man of business in the place—in fact, the biggest rogue.'

He did not find the idea offensive so much as merely interesting. His shrewd eye sharpened a trifle, however, and he lowered his head to scan me more gravely. I went on. 'Now knowing the Levant as I do, I know that a reputation for being a rogue means one thing and one thing only. It means that one is *cleverer* than other people.' I accompanied this with the appropriate gesture—for cleverness in the hand-language is indicated by placing the forefinger of the right hand slowly and portentously upon the temple: tapping slightly, as one might tap a breakfast-egg. (Incidentally, one has to be careful, as if one turns the finger in the manner of turning a bolt in a thread, the significance is quite different: it means to be 'soft in the head' or to 'have a screw loose'.) I tapped my skull softly. '*Cleverer* than other people,' I repeated. 'So clever that the stupid are envious of one.'

He did not assent or dissent from the proposition. He simply sat and considered me as one might a piece of machinery if one were uncertain of its use. But the expression in his eyes shifted slightly in a manner suggesting the faintest, most tenuous admiration. 'I am here,' I went on, convinced by this time that his English was good, for he had followed me unerringly so far, to judge by his face, 'I am here as a comparatively poor man to ask you a favour, not to make you a business proposition. There is no money to be made out of me. But I want you to let me use your brains and experience. I'm trying to find a cheap village house in which to settle for a year or two—perhaps forever if I like it enough here. I can see now that I was not wrong; far from being a rogue you are obviously a Turkish gentleman, and I feel I can confide myself entirely to your care—if you will accept such a thing. I have nothing to offer except gratitude and friendship. I ask you as a Turkish gentleman to assist me.'

Sabri's colour had changed slowly throughout this harangue and when I ended he was blushing warmly. I could see that I had scored a diplomatic stroke in throwing myself completely upon the iron law of hospitality which underpins all relations in the Levant. More than this, I think the magic word 'gentleman' turned the trick in my favour for it accorded him an unaccustomed place in the consideration of strangers which he certainly merited, and which he thenceforward lived up to in his dealings with me. By a single tactful speech I had made a true friend.

He leaned forward at his desk, smiling now, and patted my hand gently, confidingly: 'But of course, my dear,' he said, 'of course.'

Then he suddenly threw up his chin and barked an order. A barefoot youth materialized from the shadows bearing Coca Cola on a tray, apparently ordered by some invisible gesture a while before. 'Drink,' he said quietly, 'and tell me what house you want.'

'A village house, not a modern villa.'

'How far away?'

'Not far. Among these hills.'

'Old houses need doing up.'

'If I can buy one cheaply I shall do it up.'

'How much can you spend?'

'Four hundred pounds.'

He looked grave at this and this was understandable, for the price of land had been soaring since the war, and indeed continued to soar until the time of my departure from the island when building plots in the centre of Nicosia cost roughly the same as those in Washington. 'My dear,' he said thoughtfully, and stroked his moustache. 'My dear.' Outside the darkness of his shop the spring sunshine glistened on trees loaded with cold tangerines; a cold wind touched the fronds of the palm-trees, quick with the taste of snow from the Taurus mountains across the water. 'My dear,' repeated Sabri thoughtfully. 'Of course if you lived very far away it would be quite easy, but do you wish to be within reach of the capital?' I nodded. 'If I run out of money then I shall have to work, and there is nothing to be found out of Nicosia.' He nodded. 'Somewhere not too far from Kyrenia you want an arty old house.' That summed it up perfectly. Sabri took a thoughtful turn or two among the shadows and stubbed out his cigarette on the box. 'Honestly, my dear,' he said, 'it will be a matter of luck. I do hear of things, but it is a matter of luck. And it is very difficult to find one person to deal with. You are at once in a bloody family, my dear.' I did not then know what he meant. I was soon to learn.

'Do not be disappointed if you hear nothing from me for a while. What you ask is not easy, but I think I can do it. I will be working on it even if I am silent. Do you understand, my dear?' His handshake was warm.

I had hardly reached the main street on my way back to Panos' house when Renos the boot-black came out of a side street and took my arm. He was a tiny little wisp of a man with the sort of eyes one finds sewn on to rag dolls. 'My friend,' he said, 'you have been to see Sabri.' This is the favourite Mediterranean game, a tireless spying upon the movements of friends and acquaintances, and is common to all communities which do not read, whose whole life is built up by oral tradition and common gossip. 'Yes,' I said.

'Phew.' He went through a pantomime in the hand language, burning his fingers on hot coals and blowing upon them. This meant 'You will be stung.' I shrugged my shoulders. 'What to do?' I said cheerfully. 'Aie aie,' said Renos, laying one hand to his cheek and rocking his head commiseratingly as if he had toothache. But he said no more.

By the time I got home Panos himself had been informed of my visit—doubtless by bush telegraph. 'You have been to see Sabri,' he said as I crossed the brilliant courtyard of the church and joined him on his balcony over the bewitching blueness of the spring sea. 'About a house?' I nodded. 'You have done well,' he said. 'Indeed I was going to suggest it.'

'Clito says he is a rogue.'

'Nonsense. His dealings with me have been perfectly honourable. He is a pretty sharp business man, of course, which is not usual among Turks who are always half asleep. But he is no more of a rogue than anyone else. In fact, Clito himself is a rogue, if it comes to that. He overcharged me for this bottle of Commanderia. Incidentally did you tell Sabri how much money you have?'

'No, I told him less than I actually had.'

Panos chuckled admiringly. 'I see you understand business in these parts. Everything gets gossiped about, so that whatever price you would be prepared to pay would soon be known to everyone. You did right to put it low.'

I accepted a glass of sweet Commanderia and a pickled pimento from the coloured china plate; the two children were doing a puzzle in the sunshine. The beadle crashed at the church bell in a sudden desultory burst of mania and then left the silence to echo round us in wing-beats of aftersound.

'I hear,' said Panos when the vibrations had died away, 'that your brother was killed at Thermopylae during the war.'

'To be absolutely honest with you,' I said, 'I made the whole thing up in order to . . .'

'Tease Frangos!'

'Yes. I was afraid there would be a fight.'

'Excellent. Capital.' Panos was delighted by the subtlety of my imagination. He struck his knee delightedly as he laughed. 'Capital,' he repeated. 'It is clear that as rogues go you are as bad as any of us.' It was a compliment to be thus included in the rogues' gallery of Kyrenia.

That evening it was I who recited the geography lesson while Panos stood behind me, nodding approvingly as I picked out the salient points of the Kyrenia range with a forefinger, travelling gently over the blue spines of the hills from the point where Myrtou lay invisible among its hazy farms and vineyards to where Akanthou (equally invisible) drowsed among its fields of yellow-green barley. In truth, by now I had memorized the lesson so well that the very names of the places I had yet to visit communicated a sharp visual image of them. I could see the lemon-groves of Lapithos and feel the dense cool air of its orchards: hear the sullen thunder of the headspring as it gushed into the valley from the mountain's summit. The great double-combed crown of Hilarion stood almost directly behind us with its castle taking the last lion-gold rays of the evening upon its tawny flanks. Over the saddle below it ran the main road to Nicosia, piercing the range at its lowest point. East of us loomed other peaks whose sulky magnificence echoed each other, mingling like the notes of a musical chord: Buffavento, seat of the winds, with the silent and graceful Gothic abbey of Bellapaix below it in the foothills; Pendedactyl whose five-fingered peak recalled the fingerprints of the hero Dighenis; fading all of them, and inclining slowly eastward into the mist like the proud sails of some Venetian argosy, to where Cape Andreas drowsed in spindrift at the end of the long stone handle of the Karpass. The place names chimed as one spoke them like a carillon, Greek Babylas and Myrtou, Turkish Kasaphani, Crusader Templos. . . . The mixture was a heady one.

'Very good,' said Panos at last, with a sigh of real pleasure. 'You really do know it. But now you must visit it.' I had intended to ere this, but my preoccupations about a house had quite consumed me, while problems of correspondence and the transport of luggage, money, etc. had made my mind too turbid for use. I had left it all lying there, so to speak, multiplying itself in my imagination, until I should be ready to go out and meet it. Apart from a few short excursions around Kyrenia in search of spring flowers and mushrooms I had been nowhere; indeed had done nothing except bathe and write letters. Life in an island, however rich, is circumscribed, and one does well to portion out one's experiences, for sooner or later one arrives at a point where all is known and staled by repetition. Taken leisurely, with all one's time at one's disposal Cyprus could, I calculate, afford one a minimum of two years reckoned in terms of novelty; hoarded as I intended to hoard it, it might last anything up to a decade.

That is why I wished to experience it through its people rather than its landscape, to enjoy the sensation of sharing a common life with the humble villagers of the place; and later to expand my field of investigation to its history—the lamp which illumines national character—in order to offer my live subjects a frame against which to set themselves. Alas! I was not to have time.

The month or so of spring weather with its promise of summer to follow proved fraudulent. One day we woke to a sky covered in ugly festoons of black cloud and saw drift upon drift of silver needles like arrows falling upon the ramparts of Kyrenia castle.

Thunder clamoured and rolled, and the grape-blue semi-darkness of the sea was bitten out in magnesium flashes as the lightning clawed at us from Turkey like a family of dragons. The stone floors turned damp and cold, the gutters brimmed and mumbled all day as they poured a cascade of rain into the street. Below us the sea dashed huge waves across the front where not a week ago we had been sitting in shorts and sandals, drinking coffee and *ouzo*, and making plans for the summer. It was a thrilling change, for one could feel the luxuriant grass fattening under the olives, and the spring flowers unwrapping their delicate petals on the anemone-starred slopes below Clepini.

It was hardly a propitious moment for Sabri to arrive, but arrive he did one black afternoon, wearing as his only protection a spotted handkerchief over his head against the elements. He burst through Panos' front door between thunder-flashes like an apparition from the underworld, gasping: 'My dear.' His suit was liberally streaked with rain. 'I have something for you to see —but *please*' (in anguish almost) 'don't blame me if it is not suitable. I haven't seen it myself yet. But it *may* be . . . ' He accepted a glass of wine in chilled fingers. 'It is in the village of Bellapaix, but too far from the road. Anyway, will you come? I have a taxi. The owner is a rogue of course. I can guarantee *nothing*.'

I could see that he was most anxious that I should not judge his professional skill by what might turn out to be a mistake. Together we galloped across the rain-echoing courtyard and down the long flight of stairs by the church to where Jamal and his ancient taxi waited. The handles were off all the doors and there ensued a brief knockabout scene from a Turkish shadow-play among the three of us which finally resulted in our breaking into the vehicle at a weak point in its defences. (Jamal had to crawl through the boot, and half-way through the back seat, in order to unlatch for us.) Then we were off through a landscape blurred with rain and the total absence of windscreen wipers. Jamal drove with his head out of the window for the sake of safety. Outside, the rain-blackened span of mountains glittered fitfully in the lightning-flashes.

Just outside Kyrenia a road turned to the right and led away across a verdant strip of olive and carob land towards the foot-hills where Bellapaix stood in rain and mist. 'Nevertheless,' said Sabri thoughtfully, 'it is a good day, for nobody will be out of doors. The café will be empty. We won't cause the gossips, my dear.' He meant, I suppose, that in any argument over prices the influence of the village wiseacres would seriously affect the owner's views. A sale needed privacy; if the village coffee shop undertook a general debate on a transaction there was no knowing what might happen.

I was prepared for something beautiful, and I already knew that the ruined monastery of Bellapaix was one of the loveliest Gothic survivals in the Levant, but I was not prepared for the breath-taking congruence of the little village which surrounded and cradled it against the side of the mountain. Fronting the last rise, the road begins to wind through a landscape dense with orange and lemon trees, and noisy with running water. Almond and peach-blossom graze the road, as improbably precise as the décor to a Japanese play. The village comes down to the road for the last hundred yards or so with its grey old-fashioned houses with arched vaults and carved doors set in old-fashioned mould-ings. Then abruptly one turns through an arc of 150 degrees under the Tree of Idleness and comes to a stop in the main square under the shadow of the Abbey itself. Young cypresses bent back against the sky as they took the wind; the broad flower beds were full of magnificent roses among the almond trees. Yet it all lay deserted in the rain.

The owner of the house was waiting for us in a doorway with a sack over his head. He was a rather dejected-looking man whom I had already noticed maundering about the streets of Kyrenia. He was a cobbler by trade. He did not seem very exuberant— perhaps it was the weather—but almost without a word spoken led us up the boulder-strewn main street, slipping and stumbling amongst the wet stones. Irrigation channels everywhere had burst their banks and Sabri, still clad in his handkerchief, gazed gloomily about him as he picked his way among the compost heaps where the chickens browsed. 'It's no good, my dear,' he said after we had covered about a hundred yards without arriving at the house. 'You could never get up here.' But still the guide led on, and curiosity made us follow him. The road had now become very steep indeed and resembled the bed of a torrent; down the centre poured a cascade of water. 'My God,' groaned Sabri, 'it is a trout-stream, my dear.' It certainly seemed like one. The three of us crept upwards, walking wherever possible on the facing-stones of the irrigation channel. 'I am terribly sorry,' said Sabri. 'You will have a cold and blame me.'

The atmosphere of the village was quite enthralling; its architecture was in the purest peasant tradition—domed Turkish privies in courtyards fanning out from great arched doors with peasant mouldings still bearing the faint traces of a Venetian influence; old Turkish screen-windows for ventilation. It had the purity and authenticity of a Cretan hamlet. And everywhere grew roses, and the pale clouds of almond and peach blossom; on the balconies grew herbs in window-boxes made from old petrol tins; and crowning every courtyard like a messenger from my Indian childhood spread the luxuriant green fan of banana-leaves, rattling like parchment in the wind. From behind the closed door of the tavern came the mournful whining of a mandolin.

At the top of the slope where the village vanished and gave place to the scrubby outworks of the mountain behind, stood an old irrigation tank, and here our guide disappeared round a corner, drawing from his breast an iron key the size of a man's forearm. We scrambled after him and came upon the house, a large box-like house in the Turkish-Cypriot mode, with huge carved doors made for some forgotten race of giants and their oxen. 'Very arty, my dear,' said Sabri, noting the fine old windows with their carved screens, 'but what a place'; and then he kicked the wall in an expert way so that the plaster fell off and revealed the mysteries of its construction to his practised eye. 'Mud brick with straw.' It was obviously most unsatisfactory. 'Never mind,' I said, stirred by a vague interior premonition which I could not put exactly into words. 'Never mind. Let's look now we're here.'

The owner swung himself almost off the ground in an effort to turn the great key in the lock which was one of the old pistol-spring type such as one sees sometimes in medieval English houses. We hung on to his shoulders and added our strength to his until it turned screeching in the lock and the great door fell open. We entered, while the owner shot the great bolts which held the other half of the door in position and propped both open with a faggot. Here his interest died, for he stayed religiously by the door, still shrouded in his sack, showing no apparent interest in our reactions. The hall was gloomy and silent—but remarkably dry considering the day. I stood for a while listening to my own heart beating and gazing about me. The four tall double doors were splendid with their old-fashioned panels and the two windows which gave internally on to the hall were fretted with wooden slats of a faintly Turkish design. The whole proportion and disposition of things here was of a thrilling promise; even Sabri glowed at the woodwork which was indeed of splendid make and in good condition.

The floor, which was of earth, was as dry as if tiled. Obviously the walls of the house offered good insulation—but then earth brick usually does if it is laid thickly enough. The wind moaned in the clump of banana trees, and at intervals I could still hear the whimper of the mandolin.

Sabri, who had by now recovered his breath, began to take a more detailed view of things, while I, still obscured by premonitions of a familiarity which I could not articulate, walked to the end of the hall to watch the rain rattling among the pomegranates. The garden was hardly larger than twenty square yards, but crammed with trees standing shoulder to shoulder at such close quarters that their greenery formed an almost unbroken roof. There were too many—some would have to go: I caught myself up with a start. It was early for me to begin behaving like the house's owner. Abstractedly I counted them again: six tangerines, four bitter lemons, two pomegranates, two mulberry trees and a tall leaning walnut. Though there were houses on both sides they were completely hidden by greenery. This part of the village with its steep slope was built up in tiers, balcony upon balcony, with the trees climbing up between. Here and there through the green one caught a glint of the sea, or a corner of the Abbey silhouetted against it.

My reverie was interrupted by a moan and I feared for a moment that Sabri had immolated himself in one of the rooms upon the discovery of some dreadful fact about the woodwork. But no. A heifer was the cause of the noise. It stood, plaintively chewing something in the front room, tethered to a ring in the wall. Sabri clicked his tongue disapprovingly and shut the door. 'A bloody cow, my dear,' he smiled with all the townsman's indulgence towards the peasant's quirks. 'Inside of the house.' There were two other rather fine rooms with a connecting door of old workmanship, and a couple of carved cupboards. Then came a landslide. 'Don't open it!' shouted the owner and flew to the help of the gallant Sabri who was wrestling with a door behind which apparently struggled some huge animal—a camel perhaps or an elephant? 'I forgot to tell you,' panted the owner as we all three set our shoulders to the panels. The room was stacked breast-high with grain which had poured out upon Sabri as he opened the door. Together we got it shut but not before the observant Sabri had noticed how dry the grain was in its store. 'This place is dry,' he panted grudgingly. 'So much I can say.'

But this was not all; we were about to leave when the owner suddenly recollected that there was more to see and pointed a quavering finger at the ceiling in the manner of Saint John in the icons. 'One more room,' he said, and we now took a narrow outside staircase where the rain still drizzled, and climbed out upon a balcony where we both stood speechless. The view was indescribable. Below us, the village curved away in diminishing perspective to the green headland upon which the Abbey stood, its fretted head silhouetted against the Taurus range. Through the great arches gleamed the grey-gold fields of cherries and oranges and the delicate spine of Kasaphani's mosque. From this high point we were actually looking down upon Bellapaix, and beyond it, five miles away, upon Kyrenia whose castle looked absurdly like a toy. Even Sabri was somewhat awed by the view. Immediately behind, the mountain climbed into blue space, topped by the ragged outcrop and mouldering turrets of Buffavento. 'My God,' I said feebly. 'What a position.'

The balcony itself was simply a flat platform of earth with no balustrade. Up here in one corner of it was a rather lofty and elegant room, built on a bias, and empty of everything save a pair of shoes and a pile of tangerines. We returned to the balcony with its terrific panorama. The storm had begun to lift now and sun was struggling feebly to get out; the whole eastern prospect was suffused with the light which hovers over El Greco's Toledo.

'But the balcony itself,' said Sabri with genuine regret, 'my dear, it will need concrete.' 'Why?' He smiled at me. 'I must tell you how the peasant house is built—the roof. Come down.' We descended the narrow outside stair together, while he produced a notebook and pencil. 'First the beams are laid,' he said indicating the long series of magnificent beams, and at the same time scribbling in his book. 'Then some reed mats. Then packets of osiers to fill the airspace, or perhaps dried seaweed. Then Carmi earth, then gravel. Finally it all leaks and you spend the whole winter trying to stop the leaks.'

'But this house doesn't,' I said.

'Some do sooner than others.'

I pointed to the mason's signature upon the graven iron plaque which adorned the main door. It bore the conventional Orthodox cross embossed on it with the letters IE XR N (Jesus Christ Conquers) and the date 1897. Underneath, on the lower half of the plate, in the space reserved to record subsequent building or alteration was written only one date (9th September 1940), when presumably some restoration work had been undertaken. 'Yes, I know, my dear,' said Sabri patiently. 'But if you buy this house you will have to rebuild the balcony. You are my friend, and so I shall insist for your own good.'

We debated this in low tones on the way down the hill. Though the rain had slackened the village street was empty save for the little corner shop, a grocery store, where a thickset young man sat alone, amid sacks of potatoes and dry packets of spaghetti, playing patience on a table. He shouted good afternoon.

In the main square Jamal sat uneasily under the Tree of Idleness beneath an open umbrella, drinking coffee. I was about to engage the owner of the house in discussion as to the sort of price he had in mind for such a fine old relic when Sabri motioned me to silence. The coffee-house was gradually filling up with people and faces were turning curiously towards us. 'You will need time to think,' he said. 'And I have told him you don't want to buy it at all, at any price. This will make the necessary despondence, my dear.'

'But I'd like to have an idea of the price.'

'My dear, he has no idea *himself*. Perhaps five hundred pounds, perhaps twenty pounds, perhaps ten shillings. He is completely vacant of ideas. In the bargaining everything will get cleared. But we must take time. In Cyprus time is everything.'

I rode regretfully down the green winding ways to Kyrenia thinking deeply about the house which seemed more desirable in retrospect than it had in actual fact. Meanwhile Sabri talked to me in knowledgeable fashion about the drawbacks to buying out there. 'You simply have not considered such problems,' he said, 'as water, for example. Have you?'

I had not, and I felt deeply ashamed of the fact. 'Give me two days,' said Sabri, 'and I will find out about the land and water-rights of the property. Then we will ask the man and his wife for the big price-conversation at my office. By God, you will see how tricky we are in Cyprus. And if you buy the house I will send you to a friend of mine to do the rebuilding. He is a rogue, of course, but just the man. I only ask, give me time.'

That night when I told Panos that I had seen what might prove to be a suitable house for me at Bellapaix he was delighted, for he had lived there for several years, teaching at the local school. 'They are the laziest people in the world,' he said, 'and the best-natured in Cyprus. And you have honey, and also in the valley behind the house nightingales, my friend.'

He did not mention silk, almonds and apricots: oranges, pome-granates, quince. . . . Perhaps he did not wish to influence me too deeply.

Sabri meanwhile retired into silence and contemplation for nearly a week after this; I imagined him sharpening himself for the coming contest of wills by long silent fasts—broken perhaps by a glass of sherbet—or perhaps even prayer for long stretches. The skies turned blue and hard again, and the orange-trees in the Bishopric put out their gleaming suns. The season was lengthening once more into summer, one felt; was stretching itself, the days beginning to unfold more slowly, the twilights to linger. Once more the little harbour filled up with its crowds of chaffering fishermen darning their nets, and of yachtsmen dawdling over caulked seams and a final coat of paint.

Then at last the summons came; I was to present myself at Sabri's office the next morning at eight. Panos brought me the message, smiling at my obvious anxiety, and telling me that Sabri was rather despondent because it now appeared that the house was owned not by the cobbler but by his wife. It had been her dowry, and she herself was going to conduct the sale. 'With women,' said my friend, 'it is always a Calvary to argue. A Golgotha.' Nevertheless Sabri had decided to go forward with the business. The intervening space of time had been valuable, however, because he had come into possession of a piece of vital information about the water supply. Water is so scarce in Cyprus that it is sold in parcels. You buy an hour here and an hour there from the owner of a spring—needless to say no quantity measure exists. The trouble lies here: that water-rights form part of property-titles of citizens and are divided up on the death of the owner among his dependants. This is true also of land and indeed of trees. Families being what they are, it is common for a single spring to be owned by upwards of thirty people, or a single tree to be shared out among a dozen members of a family. The whole problem, then, is one of obtaining common consent—usually one has to pay for the signatures of thirty people in order to achieve any agreement which is binding. Otherwise one dissident nephew and niece can veto the whole transaction. In the case of some trees, for example, one man may own the produce of the tree, another the ground on which it stands, a third the actual timber. As may be imagined the most elementary litigation assumes gigantic proportions—which explains why there are so many lawyers in Cyprus.

Now Sabri had got wind of the fact that the Government was planning to install the piped water supply to the village which had been promised for so long; moreover that the plans were already being drawn up. The architect of the Public Works happened to be a friend of his so he casually dropped into his office and asked to see where the various water-points were to be placed. It was a stroke of genius, for he saw with delight that there was to be a public water-point outside the very front door of the old house. This more than offset the gloomy intelligence that the only water the cobbler owned was about an hour a month from the main spring—perhaps sixty gallons: whereas the average water consumption of an ordinary family is about forty gallons a *day*. This was a trump card, for the cobbler's water belonged in equal part to the rest of his wife's family—all eighteen of them, including the idiot boy Pipi whose signature was always difficult to obtain on a legal document. . . .

I found my friend, freshly shaven and spruce, seated in the gloom of his office, surrounded by prams, and absolutely motionless. Before him on the blotter lay the great key of the house, which he poked from time to time in a reproachful way. He put his finger to his lips with a conspiratorial air and motioned me to a chair. 'They are all here, my dear,' he hissed, 'getting ready.' He pointed to the café across the road where the cobbler had gathered his family. They looked more like seconds. They sat on a semicircle of chairs, sipping coffee and arguing in low voices; a number of beards waggled, a number of heads nodded. They looked like a rugger scrum in an American film receiving last-minute instructions from their captain. Soon they would fall upon us like a ton of bricks and gouge us. I began to feel rather alarmed. 'Now, whatever happens,' said Sabri in a low voice, tremulous with emotion, 'do not surprise. You must never surprise. And you don't want the house at all, see?'

I repeated the words like a catechism. 'I don't want the house. I absolutely don't want the house.' Yet in my mind's eye I could see those great doors ('God,' Sabri had said, 'this is fine wood. From Anatolia. In the old days they floated the great timbers over the water behind boats. This is Anatolian timber, it will last for ever'). Yes, I could see those doors under a glossy coat of blue paint. . . . 'I don't want the house,' I repeated under my breath, feverishly trying to put myself into the appropriate frame of mind.

'Tell them we are ready,' said Sabri to the shadows and a bare-footed youth flitted across the road to where our adversaries had gathered. They hummed like bees, and the cobbler's wife detached herself from the circle—or tried to, for many a hand clutched at her frock, detaining her for a last-minute considera-tion which was hissed at her secretively by the family elders. At last she wrenched herself free and walked boldly across the road, entering Sabri's shrine with a loud 'Good morning' spoken very confidently.

She was a formidable old faggot, with a handsome self-indul-gent face, and a big erratic body. She wore the white headdress and dark skirt of the village woman, and her breasts were gathered into the traditional baggy bodice with a drawstring at the waist, which made it look like a loosely furled sail. She stood before us looking very composed as she gave us good morning. Sabri cleared his throat, and picking up the great key very deli-cately between finger and thumb—as if it were of the utmost fragility—put it down again on the edge of the desk nearest her with the air of a conjurer making his opening dispositions. 'We are speaking about your house,' he said softly, in a voice ever so faintly curdled with menace. 'Do you know that all the wood is . . .' he suddenly shouted the last word with such force that I nearly fell off my chair, 'rotten!' And picking up the key he banged it down to emphasize the point.

The woman threw up her head with contempt and taking up the key also banged it down in her turn exclaiming: 'It is not.'

'It *is*.' Sabri banged the key.

'It is *not*.' She banged it back.

'It *is*.' A bang.

'It is *not*.' A counter-bang.

All this was not on a very high intellectual level, and made me rather ill at ease. I also feared that the key itself would be banged

63

out of shape so that finally none of us would be able to get into the house. But these were the opening chords, so to speak, the preliminary statement of theme.

The woman now took the key and held it up as if she were swearing by it. 'The house is a good house,' she cried. Then she put it back on the desk. Sabri took it up thoughtfully, blew into the end of it as if it were a six-shooter, aimed it and peered along it as if along a barrel. Then he put it down and fell into an abstraction. 'And suppose we wanted the house,' he said, 'which we don't, what would you ask for it?'

'Eight hundred pounds.'

Sabri gave a long and stagy laugh, wiping away imaginary tears and repeating 'Eight hundred pounds' as if it were the best joke in the world. He laughed at me and I laughed at him, a dreadful false laugh. He slapped his knee. I rolled about in my chair as if on the verge of acute gastritis. We laughed until we were exhausted. Then we grew serious again. Sabri was still fresh as a daisy, I could see that. He had put himself into the patient contemplative state of mind of a chess player.

'Take the key and go,' he snapped suddenly, and handing it to her, swirled round in his swivel chair to present her with his back; then as suddenly he completed the circuit and swivelled round again. 'What!' he said with surprise. 'You haven't gone.' In truth there had hardly been time for the woman to go. But she was somewhat slow-witted, though obstinate as a mule: that was clear. 'Right,' she now said in a ringing tone, and picking up the key put it into her bosom and turned about. She walked off stage in a somewhat lingering fashion. 'Take no notice,' whispered Sabri and busied himself with his papers.

The woman stopped irresolutely outside the shop, and was here joined by her husband who began to talk to her in a low cringing voice, pleading with her. He took her by the sleeve and led her unwillingly back into the shop where we sat pointedly reading letters. 'Ah! It's you,' said Sabri with well-simulated surprise. 'She wishes to discuss some more,' explained the cobbler in a weak conciliatory voice. Sabri sighed.

'What is there to speak of? She takes me for a fool.' Then he

64

suddenly turned to her and bellowed, 'Two hundred pounds and not a piastre more.'

It was her turn to have a paroxysm of false laughter, but this was rather spoiled by her husband who started plucking at her sleeve as if he were persuading her to be sensible. Sabri was not slow to notice this. 'You tell her,' he said to the man. 'You are a man and these things are clear to you. She is only a woman and does not see the truth. Tell her what it is worth.'

The cobbler, who quite clearly lacked spirit, turned once more to his wife and was about to say something to her, but in a sudden swoop she produced the key and raised it above her head as if she intended to bring it down on his hairless dome. He backed away rapidly. 'Fool,' she growled. 'Can't you see they are making a fool of you? Let me handle this.' She made another pass at him with the key and he tiptoed off to join the rest of her relations in the coffee-shop opposite, completely crushed. She now turned to me and extended a wheedling hand, saying in Greek, 'Ah come along there, you an Englishman, striking a hard bargain with a woman. . . .' But I had given no indication of speaking Greek so that it was easy to pretend not to understand her. She turned back to Sabri, staring balefully, and banging the key down once more shouted 'Six hundred,' while Sabri in the same breath bellowed 'Two hundred.' The noise was deafening.

They panted and glared at each other for a long moment of silence like boxers in a clinch waiting for the referee to part them. It was the perfect moment for Sabri to get in a quick one below the belt. 'Anyway, your house is mortgaged,' he hissed, and she reeled under the punch. 'Sixty pounds and three piastres,' he added, screwing the glove a little to try to draw blood. She held her groin as if in very truth he had landed her a blow in it. Sabri followed up swiftly: 'I offer you two hundred pounds plus the mortgage.'

She let out a yell. 'No. Never,' and banged the key. 'Yes, I say,' bellowed Sabri giving a counter-bang. She grabbed the key (by now it had become, as it were, the very symbol of our contention. The house was forgotten. We were trying to buy this old rusty key which looked like something fitter for Saint Peter's key-ring than my own). She grabbed the key, I say, and put it to her breast like a child as she said: 'Never in this life.' She rocked it back and forth, suckled it, and put it down again.

Sabri now became masterful and put it in his pocket. At this she let out a yell and advanced on him shouting: 'You give me back my key and I shall leave you with the curses of all the saints upon you.' Sabri stood up like a showman and held the key high above his head, out of her reach, repeating inexorably: 'Two hundred. Two hundred. Two hundred.' She snapped and strained like a hooked fish, exclaiming all the time: 'Saint Catherine defend me. No. No.' Then quite suddenly they both stopped, he replaced the key on the desk and sat down, while she subsided like a pan of boiling milk when it is lifted off the fire. 'I shall consult,' she said briefly in another voice and leaving the key where it was she took herself off across the road to where her seconds waited with towels and sponges. The first round was a draw, though Sabri had made one or two good points.

'What happens now?' I said, and he chuckled. 'Just time for a coffee. I think, you know, my dear,' he added, 'that we will have to pay another hundred. I feel it.' He was like a countryman who can tell what the weather will be like from small signs invisible to the ordinary townsman. It was an enthralling spectacle, this long-drawn-out pantomime, and I was now prepared for the negotiations to go on for a week. 'They don't know about the water,' said Sabri. 'They will let us have the house cheap and then try and sting us for the water-rights. We must pretend to forget about the water and buy the house cheaper. Do you see?' I saw the full splendour of his plan as it unfolded before us. 'But,' he said, 'everything must be done today, now, for if she goes back to the village and makes the gossips nothing will be consummated.' It seemed to me that she was already making the gossips in the café opposite, for a furious altercation had broken out. She was accusing her husband of something and he was replying waspishly and waving his arms.

After a while Sabri whispered: 'Here she comes again,' and here she came, rolling along with sails spread and full of the cargo of her misfortunes. She had changed her course. She now gave us a long list of her family troubles, hoping to soften us up; but by now I felt as if my teeth had been sharpened into points. It was clear that she was weakening. It was a matter of time before we could start winding her in. It was, in fact, the psychological moment to let out the line, and this Sabri Tahir now did by offering her another hundred ('a whole hundred,' he repeated juicily in a honeyed voice) if she would clinch the deal there and then. 'Your husband is a fool,' he added, 'and your family ignorant. You will never find a buyer if you do not take this gentleman. Look at him. Already he is weakening. He will go elsewhere. Just look at his face.' I tried to compose my face in a suitable manner to play my full part in the pantomime. She stared at me in the manner of a hungry peasant assessing a turnip and suddenly sat herself down for the first time, bursting as she did so into heartrending sobs. Sabri was delighted and gave me a wink.

She drew her wimple round her face and went into convulsions, repeating audibly: 'O Jesus, what are they doing to me? Destruction has overtaken my house and my line. My issue has been murdered, my good name dragged in the dust.' Sabri was in a high good humour by this time. He leaned forward and began to talk to her in the voice of Mephistopheles himself, filling the interstices between her sentences with his insinuations. I could hear him droning on 'Mortgage . . . two hundred . . . husband a fool . . . never get such an opportunity.' Meanwhile she rocked and moaned like an Arab, thoroughly enjoying herself. From time to time she cast a furtive glance at our faces to see how we were taking it; she could not have drawn much consolation from Sabri's for he was full of a triumphant concentration now; in the looming shadows he reminded me of some great killer shark—the flash of a white belly as it turned over on its back to take her. 'We have not spoken of the water as yet,' he said, and among her diminishing sobs she was still able to gasp out, 'That will be another hundred.'

'We are speaking only of the house,' insisted Sabri, and at this a look of cunning came over her face. 'Afterwards we will speak of the water.' The tone in which he said this indicated subtly that he had now moved over on to her side. The foreigner, who spoke no Greek, could not possibly understand that without water-rights the house itself was useless. She shot a glance at me and then looked back at him, the look of cunning being replaced by a look almost of triumph. Had Sabri, in fact, changed sides? Was he perhaps also planning to make a killing, and once the house was bought. . . . She smiled now and stopped sobbing.

'All this can only be done immediately,' said Sabri quietly. 'Look. We will go to the widow and get the mortgage paper. We will pay her mortgage before you at the Land Registry. Then we will pay you before witnesses for the house.' Then he added in a low voice: 'After that the gentleman will discuss the water. Have you the papers?'

We were moving rather too swiftly for her. Conflicting feelings beset her; ignorance and doubt flitted across her face. An occasional involuntary sob shook her—like pre-ignition in an overheated engine which has already been switched off. 'My grandfather has the title-deeds.'

'Get them,' said Sabri curtly.

She rose, still deeply preoccupied, and went back across the street where a furious argument broke out among her seconds. The white-bearded old man waved a stick and perorated. Her husband spread his hands and waggled them. Sabri watched all this with a critical eye. 'There is only one danger—she must not get back to the village.' How right he was; for if her relations could make all this noise about the deed of sale, what could the village coffee-shop not do? Such little concentration as she could muster would be totally scattered by conflicting counsels. The whole thing would probably end in a riot followed by an island-wide strike. . . .

I gazed admiringly at my friend. What a diplomat he would make! 'Here she comes again,' he said in a low voice, and here she came to place the roll of title-deeds on the table beside the key. Sabri did not look at them. 'Have you discussed?' he said sternly. She groaned. 'My grandfather will not let me do it. He says you are making a fool of me.' Sabri snorted wildly.

'Is the house yours?'

'Yes, sir.'

'Do you want the money?'

'Yes.'

'Do you want it today?'

'Yes.'

My friend leaned back in his chair and gazed up at the cobwebs in the roof. 'Think of it,' he said, his voice full of the poetry of commerce. 'This gentleman will cut you a chekky. You will go to the Bank. There they will look with respect at it, for it will bear his name. They will open the safe. . . .' His voice trembled and she gazed thirstily at him, entranced by the story-book voice he had put on. 'They will take from it notes, thick notes, as thick as a honeycomb, as thick as salami' (here they both involuntarily licked their lips and I myself began to feel hungry at the thought of so much edible money). 'One . . . two . . . three,' counted Sabri in his mesmeric voice full of animal magnetism. 'Twenty . . . sixty . . . a hundred' gradually getting louder and louder until he ended at 'three hundred.' Throughout this recital she behaved like a chicken with her beak upon a chalk line. As he ended she gave a sigh of rapture and shook herself, as if to throw off the spell. 'The mortgage will have been paid. The widow Anthi will be full of joy and respect for you. You and your husband will have *three hundred pounds.*' He blew out his breath and mopped his head with a red handkerchief. 'All you have to do is to agree. Or take your key.'

He handed her the key and once more swivelled round, to remain facing the wall for a full ten seconds before completing the circle.

'Well?' he said. She was hovering on the edge of tears again. 'And my grandfather?' she asked tremulously. Sabri spread his hands. 'What can I do about your grandfather? Bury him?' he asked indignantly. 'But act quickly, for the gentleman is going.' At a signal from him I rose and stretched and said, 'Well I think I . . .' like the curate in the Leacock story.

'Quick. Quick. Speak or he will be gone,' said Sabri. A look of intense agony came over her face. 'O Saint Matthew and Saint Luke,' she exclaimed aloud, tortured beyond endurance by her doubts. It seemed a queer moment to take refuge in her religion,

but obviously the decision weighed heavily upon her. 'O Luke,
O Mark,' she rasped, with one hand extended towards me to prevent me from leaving.

Sabri was now like a great psychologist who divines that a
difficult transference is at hand. 'She will come,' he whispered to
me, and putting his fingers to his mouth blew a shrill blast which
alerted everybody. At once with a rumble Jamal, who had apparently been lurking down a side street in his car, grated to the door
in a cloud of dust. 'Lay hold of her,' Sabri said and grabbed the
woman by the left elbow. Following instructions I grabbed the
other arm. She did not actually resist but she definitely rested on
her oars and it was something of an effort to roll her across the
floor to the taxi. Apparently speed was necessary in this *coup de
main* for he shouted: 'Get her inside' and put his shoulder to her
back as we propelled her into the back of the car and climbed in
on top of her.

She now began to moan and scream as if she were being
abducted—doubtless for the benefit of the grandfather—and to
make dumb appeals for help through the windows. Her sup-
porters poured out into the road, headed by a nonagenarian
waving a plate and her husband who also seemed in tears. 'Stop.'
'You can't do that,' they cried, alerting the whole street. Two
children screamed: 'They are taking Mummy away,' and burst
into tears.

'Don't pay any attention,' said Sabri now, looking like Napoleon on the eve of Wagram. 'Drive, Jamal, drive.' We set off with
a roar, scattering pedestrians who were making their way to the
scene of the drama, convinced perhaps that a shot-gun wedding
was in progress. 'Where are we going?' I said.

'Lapithos—the widow Anthi,' said Sabri curtly. 'Drive, Jamal,
drive.'

As we turned the corner I noticed with horror that the cobbler
and his family had stopped another taxi and were piling into it
with every intention of following us. The whole thing was turning
into a film sequence. 'Don't worry,' said Sabri, 'the second taxi
is Jamal's brother and he will have a puncture. I have thought of
everything.'

How to Buy a House

In the brilliant sunshine we rumbled down the Lapithos road. The woman looked about her with interest, pointing out familiar landmarks with great good-humour. She had completely recovered her composure now and smiled upon us both. It was obviously some time since she had had a car-ride and she enjoyed every moment of it.

We burst into the house of the widow Anthi like a bomb and demanded the mortgage papers; but the widow herself was out and they were locked in a cupboard. More drama. Finally Sabri and the cobbler's wife forced the door of the cupboard with a flat-iron and we straggled back into the sunshine and climbed aboard again. There was no sign of the second taxi as we set off among the fragrant lemon-groves towards Kyrenia, but we soon came upon them all clustered about a derelict taxi with a puncture. A huge shout went up as they saw us, and some attempt was made to block the road but Jamal, who had entered into the spirit of the thing, now increased speed and we bore down upon them. I was alarmed about the safety of the grandfather, for he stood in the middle of the road waving his stick until the very last moment, and I feared he would not jump out of the way in time. I closed my eyes and breathed deeply through my nose: so did Sabri, for Jamal had only one eye and was unused to speeds greater than twenty miles an hour. But all was well. The old man must have been fairly spry for when I turned round to look out of the back window of the car I saw him spread-eagled in the ditch, but quite all right if one could judge by the language he was using.

The clerks in the Registry Office were a bit shaken by our appearance for by this time the cobbler's wife had decided to start crying again. I cannot for the life of me imagine why—there was nobody left to impress; perhaps she wanted to extract every ounce of drama from the situation. Then we found she could not write—Grandfather was the only one who could write, and she must wait for him. 'My God, if he comes, all is lost again, my dear,' said Sabri. We had to forcibly secure her thumbprint to the article of sale, which sounds easy, but in fact ended by us all being liberally coated with fingerprint ink.

How to Buy a House

She only subsided into normality when the ratified papers were handed to Sabri; and when I made out her cheque she positively beamed and somewhat to my surprise insisted on shaking hands with me, saying as she did so, 'You are a good man, may you be blessed in the house.'

It was in the most amiable manner that the three of us now sauntered out into the sunlight under the pepper trees. On the main road a dusty taxi had drawn up and was steadily disgorging the disgruntled remains of the defeated army. Catching sight of her they shouted vociferously and advanced in open order, waving sticks and gesticulating. The cobbler's wife gave a shriek and fell into her grandfather's arms, sobbing as if overtaken by irremediable tragedy. The old man, somewhat tousled by his expedition, and with grass in his eyebrows, growled protectively at her and thundered: 'Have you done it?' She sobbed louder and nodded, as if overcome. The air was rent with execrations, but Sabri was quite unmoved. All this was purely gratuitous drama and could be taken lightly. With an expressive gesture he ordered Coca-Cola all round which a small boy brought from a barrow. This had the double effect of soothing them and at the same time standing as a symbolic drink upon the closing of a bargain—shrewdly calculated as were all his strokes. They cursed us weakly as they seized the bottles but they drank thirstily. Indeed the drive to Lapithos is a somewhat dusty one.

'Anyway,' said the cobbler at last when they had all simmered down a bit, 'we still have the water-rights. We have not yet discussed those with the gentleman.' But the gentleman was feeling somewhat exhausted by now, and replete with all the new sensations of ownership. I possessed a house! Sabri nodded quietly. 'Later on,' he said, waving an expressive hand to Jamal, who was also drinking a well-earned Coca-Cola under a pepper tree. 'Now we will rest.' The family now saw us off with the greatest good humour, as if I were a bridegroom, leaning into the taxi to shake my hand and mutter blessings. 'It was a canonical price,' said the old greybeard, as a parting blessing. One could not say fairer than that.

How to Buy a House

'And now,' said Sabri, 'I will take you to a special place of mine to taste the *meltemi* wind—what is the time? Yes, in half an hour.'

High upon the bastions of Kyrenia castle was a narrow balcony which served the police officers as a mess. Sabri, I discovered later, was a sergeant in the specials. Here, gazing across the radiant harbour-bar towards the Caramanian mountains, we sat ourselves down in solitude and space like a couple of emperors while a bewildering succession of cold beers found their way out on to the table-cloth, backed up by various saucers full of delicious Cypriot comestibles. And here Sabri's wind punctually arrived—the faintest breath of coolness, stirring across the waters of the harbour, ruffling them. 'You see?' he said quietly, raising his cheek to it like a sail. He was obviously endowed with that wonderful Moslem quality which is called *kayf*—the contemplation which comes of silence and ease. It is not meditation or reverie, which presupposes a conscious mind relaxing: it is something deeper, a fathomless repose of the will which does not even pose to itself the question: 'Am I happy or unhappy?'

He had been jotting on a slip of paper and now he handed it to me, saying: 'Now your troubles begin, for you will have to alter the house. Here, I have costed it for you. A bathroom will cost you so much. The balcony, at so much a cubic foot, should cost you so much. If you sell the beams—they fetch three pounds each, and there are eighty—you should have so much in hand. This is only for your private information, as a check, my dear.' He lit a cigarette and smiled gently. 'Now the man you want to build for you is Andreas Kallergis. He is good and honest—though of course he is a rogue like me! But he will do you a solid job—for much can go wrong, you know. You will find the cost of cement brick there, and rendering per cubic metre.'

I tried to express my gratitude but he waved his hand. 'My dear Durrell,' he said, 'when one is warm to me I am warm to him back. You are my friend now and I shall never change even if you do.'

We drank deeply and in silence. 'I was sent to you by a Greek,' I said, 'and now the Turk sends me back to a Greek.'

He laughed aloud. 'Cyprus is small,' he said, 'and we are all friends, though very different. This is Cyprus, my dear.'

It seemed in that warm honey-gold afternoon a delectable island in which to spend some years of one's life.

The Tree of Idleness

'Perched on a mountain-side, her terraces looking down into the gardens of Cerinia, and across the waters of Adana towards the glens and pastures of the Bulghar Dagh, her situation is no less lovely and secluded than herself. Her name is Peace. Nestling in woods, high above the port, her Anglo-Norman builders called her Peace—convent of Peace—Cloîture de la Paix; a beautiful and soothing name, which the intruding Cypriotes corrupted into Delapays, and their Venetian masters into Bellapaese. Here during many ages, gallant Western men and pious Western women found their rest.'

(*British Cyprus* by W. HEPWORTH DIXON, 1887)

———◦◦———

Andreas Kallergis proved to be a sort of Shock-headed Peter from a story-book. He lived with his pretty wife in a tumble-down little house among the orange groves below the Bishopric. Though he spoke very fair English he was delighted by my evident desire to speak Greek, and it was in his little car that I made my next visit to what was to become 'my' village, sweeping up through the bland green foothills in true spring sunshine towards where the grave hulk of the Abbey lay, like some great ship at anchor. He too was something of a diplomat and coached me in those little points of protocol which are essential if one intends to make the right sort of impression.

Together we called upon the Bellapaix *muktar* whose house actually formed part of the Abbey and who waited for us on a balcony hung high above the smiling groves which stretch toward Kasaphani. He was a thick-set, handsome man in his late forties, slow in manner, with a deep true voice and a magnificent smile. He stood, impressively booted and belted for the shoot upon which he was about to embark (he was a passionate hunter), lovingly handling a gun while his handsome dark wife dispensed the traditional sweet jam and spring water which welcomes the stranger to every Greek house. He noticed my admiring glance and handed the weapon to me saying: 'A twelve-bore by Purdy.

75

I bought it from an Englishman. I waited a year for it.' We turned it upon the kestrels and turtle-doves which flickered down below us over the plain, trying it for balance and admiring it, as he questioned me quietly and discreetly about my intentions. He had already heard of the sale of the house. ('Two things spread quickly: gossip and a forest fire'—Cypriot proverb.) I told him what was in my mind and he smiled approvingly with calm self-possession. 'You'll find the people very quiet and kindly,' he said in his deep voice, 'And since you speak Greek you know that a little politeness goes a long way; but I must warn you, if you intend to try and work, not to sit under the Tree of Idleness. You have heard of it? Its shadow incapacitates one for serious work. By tradition the inhabitants of Bellapaix are regarded as the laziest in the island. They are all landed men, coffee-drinkers and card-players. That is why they live to such ages. Nobody ever seems to die here. Ask Mr Honey the grave-digger. Lack of clients has almost driven him into a decline. . . .'

Still talking in this humorous, sardonic vein he led us through the thick grove of orange-trees to Dmitri's café, which stands outside the great barbican, and here in the sunlight I had a first glimpse of my villagers. Most of the young men and women were in the fields and Dmitri's clients were mostly grandfathers wearing the traditional baggy trousers and white cotton shirts. Gnarled as oak-trees, bent almost double by age and—who knows?—professional idleness, they were a splendid group, grey-bearded, shaggy-haired, gentle of voice and manner.

They gave us a polite good day in voices of varying gruffness, and it seemed to me from the number of crooks and sticks which had collected like a snowdrift in the corner of the tavern that many of them must have deserted their flocks for a mid-morning coffee. We did not sit under the Tree of Idleness, though the temptation was strong, but gathered about a table set for us under the fine plane-tree which spans the terrace of the café, and here (as if to introduce me fittingly to Cypriot life) the *muktar* ordered a small bottle of amber-coloured brandy and some black olives of a size which betokened comestibles specially prepared against a feast-day. I had already noticed with disappointment that the

Cypriot olive is a small and flavourless cousin of the Italian and Greek olive, and I was surprised at the size and richness of the plateful which the good Dmitri set for us. There is only one place in Greece which produces such an olive—and I scored a triumph in pronouncing its name, Kalamata. I earned a respectful glance from the *muktar* for this observation which showed me to be a person of experience and discrimination, and Andreas smiled warmly upon me, making it clear that I had won my spurs by it.

I had been casting covetous eyes upon the Abbey, which I was dying to explore—indeed I was already beginning to feel somehow a part-owner in it—when a short sturdy man clad in the uniform of an antiquity-warden emerged from among the flowering roses and joined us with a smile of welcome. He had the round good-natured face of a Friar Tuck and a brightly quizzical eye, and he addressed me in excellent pointed English. 'Your brother', he told me briefly, 'died at Thermopylae. You must have a drink with me, and see *my* private property.' This was a shaft aimed at the *muktar*. 'It is a good deal more impressive than *his* house. Look at it!'

Indeed the Abbey cloisters with their heavily loaded orange-trees and brilliant flower-gardens were a study in contrasts—the grave contemplative calm of Gothic pricked everywhere, as silence is by music, by the Mediterranean luxuriance of yellow fruit and glittering green leaves. 'Somewhere to walk,' said Kollis, for that was the newcomer's name, 'to think, whenever you please, to be quiet among the lemon-trees.'

The *muktar* must have read my mind for he suddenly said: 'Wouldn't you like to visit it? Go along with Kollis, it won't take long. Andreas and I will wait here and talk.'

We entered the broad gate of the outer barbican in sympathetic silence, Kollis smiling to himself as if he surmised my own surprise and pleasure. Indeed Bellapaix on that radiant spring morning looked like a back-drop for *Comus*. The great church-doors stood open upon the rich shadowy interior with its one coloured window which stained the flags with a splash as of spilt wine. Footsteps and voices echoing in the musty interior. We paused to buy a farthing dip before examining the icons in the little chancel.

'The church is still in use,' explained my guide, 'and that gives the whole ruin life. It's something more than just an antiquity. It is the village church, *my* church—and indeed your own since you are coming to live here.' Outside in the courtyard lay the familiar branches of green laurel which would later make incense for the villagers. On the breathless silence of the cool air came the small sounds of the village which later I could identify exactly, attaching to each the name of a friend: Michaelis' bees burring among the blossoms, Andreas' pigeons murmuring; the sharp knocking and planing from Loizus' little carpentry shop; the rumble of an olive-drum being rolled along the street by Anthemos to where a bus waited; the high clear voice of Lalou singing to the dirge of the spindle. . . . They existed for me as sounds without orchestration or meaning, not more human than the whistle of swifts below the Abbey, or the distant whirr of a motor-car spinning.down the white ribbon of road below.

The full magnificence of the Abbey's position is not clear until one enters the inner cloister, through a superb gate decorated with marble coats of arms, and walks to the very edge of the high bluff on which it stands, the refectory windows framing the plain below with its flowering groves and curling palm-trees. We looked at each other, smiling. Kollis was too wise to waste words on it, realizing perhaps how impossible it would be to do justice to the whole prospect. He told me nothing about it, and I wished to know nothing; we simply walked in quiet, bemused friendship among those slender chipped traceries and tall-shanked columns, among the armorial shields of forgotten knights and the blazing orange-trees, until we came into the shadow of the great refectory with its high roofs where the swallows were building, their soft agitations echoing in the silence like breathing, our own breathing, captured and magnified in the trembling silence with an unearthly fidelity. I found myself repeating in my mind, without conscious thought, but irresistibly—echoes in a sea-shell—some lines from *Comus*, built as this place had been built, as a testimony to the powers of contemplation which rule our inner lives. Bellapaix, even in ruins, was a testimony to those who had tried, however imperfectly, to grasp and retain their grip on the inner substance of the imagination, which resides in thought, in contemplation, in the Peace which had formed part of its original name, and which in my spelling I have always tried to retain. The Abbey de la Paix, corrupted by the Venetians into Bella Paise. . . . It was to take me nearly a year to gain currency for the spelling Bellapaix, which is as near as one can get today to its original.

But no such thought was in my mind that first spring morning as I walked in those deserted cloisters, touching the rosy stones of the old Abbey with an idle hand, noticing the blaze of flowers from the beds which Kollis tended so lovingly—and here and there, bursting from a clump of fallen masonry, cracking the rock triumphantly, the very plumes of yellow fennel which the good Mrs Lewis had observantly noticed, adding with all the delight of the amateur botanist: 'It is the Narthex of Prometheus. It likes old ruins best, growing there more freely than on the natural rock. In the hollow tube of its long dry cane, which remains stiffly standing when the flowers and leaves have perished, Aeschylus says Prometheus brought down the fire from heaven, and thus speaks Prometheus bound:

> *I bear the yoke who stole*
> *The fount of fire and in a reed* (narthex) *enclosed*
> *Transferred to men the precious gift which hath*
> *Become the mistress of all arts and crafts.*'

In that silence the light airs of the plain climbed up to us, full of the small sound of birds as they stooped and dived in the blue gulf below. Somewhere near at hand came the rustle and dribble of spring-water feeding the flowers.

'If this were all, it would be enough,' said Kollis, 'but let us go up.' He led the way up a crumbling staircase to where the roofs fanned away in galleries, and from which new panoramas opened to the east and west. As we ascended, Kyrenia came into view again and the whole fretted coast like lacework. I had begun to feel guilty of an act of fearful temerity in trying to settle in so fantastic a place. Could one ever do any work with such scenery to wonder at? And this fantastic mixture of the Gothic north and the gentle alluring Levantine plains spreading out from the Kyrenia range soft as a lion's paw. . . . How did Lady Hester come to miss this Abbey?

We walked out of the great arch once more into the little square where the others sat waiting for us. The group had now been swelled by one or two fine-looking old gentlemen who were quite obviously consumed with curiosity about the new foreigner. They were massive and booted mountaineers with craggy faces and splendid sweeping moustaches. One of them, Morais, owned the house directly above mine, where he lived alone with his young daughter. He addressed a few rough questions to the *muktar*, accompanied by a keen and by no means friendly glance or two at me, before stumping off up the street leading a pony laden with sacks. 'You may have words with him,' said the *muktar* quietly. 'He's not a bad chap—but, well—many of them feel strongly about Enosis these days. But take it calmly.'

Of the friendliness of the other two men there could be no doubt. Andreas Menas was as brown as a nut, with the liveliest and kindest eyes one could hope to see; he was in his late fifties but in every movement betrayed an agility and ease of movement which suggested a body kept young by unremitting physical work. His handshake was warm and innocent. He was my next-door neighbour but one. He at least belied the indolence attributed to the villagers by popular superstition, for when he came to work on the house he never left his job before dusk had fallen, and he was always there on the dot in the morning. And this, despite the fact that every Sunday he took his morning coffee under the fatal tree! Michaelis was big and moustached like a pirate or a Keystone cop; his massive strength, like that of a rooted tree, showed in every movement which threw out the line of a bicep against his rough sailor's jersey. But it was strength without guile—his shy slow smile spoke of good fellowship and spontaneity. He came of a long line of gentle topers who had filled the air of village taverns with the noise of singing and laughter, and as a story-teller he was incomparable. During the lunch hour, while we worked on the house, he would take his food and can of wine to the shade of a lemon-tree and tell stories which held the other workmen enthralled. Indeed so successful was he that work itself began to fall off until I put a veto on his gift. Thereafter he would sit with a somewhat reproachful air under the tree and tease the workmen who always besought him for stories: 'Ah, Michaelis, tell us a story, do. Just a short one.'

'And the boss?' he would say, his eyes glittering with mischief, as he looked across at me. 'The boss hears,' I would say. 'In half an hour we work.'

'Tell us a short one,' they would plead.

'Ask the boss,' he would say, 'and I'll tell you of the comedy of the Englishman who came to our village to buy a house and of the wicked widow who cast eyes upon him. . . .'

Laughter. 'Tell us. Tell us,' they pleaded; and indeed my own pleasure and instruction demanded that we should hear him out, so that sometimes I found myself pleading too. 'That's a fine state of affairs,' he would rumble. 'First the boss stops me telling stories. Then he himself wants a story. And he a writer of stories!'

It was Michaelis who now stood massively smiling, with one arm resting on the shoulder of Anthemos, the grocer, whose little shop stood at the foot of the hill and from whom I would have to obtain food and fuel. He was a portly youth full of quaint humours. 'Sir, I am hoping to grow fat on you. My shop needs a Noble Buyer like yourself. Otherwise how shall I marry next year?'

'What of your wife's dowry?' I said, and got my laugh. 'His wife's dowry is already consumed,' said Andreas. They were all still entranced by the novelty of my Greek—a fact which never ceased to puzzle me. Indeed, throughout my stay in Cyprus, wherever I went, the fact that I spoke Greek was regarded as a phenomenon. It thrilled people. Why, I don't know. There were a number of Government officials who knew the language better than I. But always a conversation in Greek created a stir, until I felt like a Talking Mongoose.

When formal introductions had been completed the whole company drifted with me up the hill, talking and laughing, to visit the house. I was pleased to learn from them that the price I had paid for it was a reasonable one. The cobbler was regarded as rather a fool, however, for not asking twice the sum and sticking to it. News of the water supply had gone round now, and the *muktar* agreed that a water-point outside my door would enable me to pipe off as much as I needed for domestic use. That would certainly increase the value of the house. And later when the electric light came, as it had already come to Lapithos . . . another increase.

All this was warming news, as warming as the cries of 'Welcome' which came to me from the old carved porches and windows fronting the stony path up to the house. There was a spontaneous guileless joy about them—so that all my doubts vanished at once, and I was only afraid that the old house itself would not come up to expectations. I had put the huge key in the breast-pocket of my coat and now I produced it amidst acclamations. Andreas seized it from me and, agile as a monkey, vanished ahead of us to open the doors and set everything to rights for the contractor's examination. My rucksack was grabbed from me and heaved on to Michaelis' great shoulder. Andreas Kallergis took my book and bottle of wine. I had the feeling that if I wasn't careful they would pick me up and carry me up the steep and stony incline, so that I might be spared the breathless scramble of the last hundred yards.

Everything confirmed itself, like the quivering of a magnetic needle as it settles on the Pole Star, when I saw the house again in full sunlight. The great high hallway was cool and shadowy. The heifer and the barley alike had vanished. We climbed upon the balcony as if upon a cloud to watch a flock of white pigeons take off from the roof below and fan out in perfect formation on the blue, the flicker of their wings twinkling frostily like the early Pleiades. We drank a glass of wine up there in the crisp air while Andreas Menas told the trees, with the sort of loving comprehension that comes to those who have planted them and watched them bear. 'A vine here and a vine there,' he said stroking his moustache with a brown hand, 'and in a year you could give this whole balcony shade. Why bother with concrete?' He pronounced the word after the village fashion, 'gon-gree'. Meanwhile Michaelis explored the two fine cellars and pronounced them large enough to house anything up to two camels. Andreas Kallergis sat draw-

ing in the dust with his finger, waiting to see what ideas I had
for the place.

Outside in the stony street a crowd of small children and
several old men had gathered. Quite a conversation was going on
—in such pure *patois* that I couldn't follow it, but Michaelis
clicked his tongue disapprovingly and glared down upon them
from the high balcony, asking whether he might be permitted to
throw a little water on them. 'Why?' I asked. He looked very dis-
tressed. 'It's that fellow Morais, saying things again.'

Morais was carrying on a grumbling monologue in a harsh
voice which went something like this: 'And now if we are going
to have the swine actually living in our villages. . . . It's bad
enough to have them as masters. . . .' He was not receiving any
moral support from his audience I noticed, even though they
must all sympathize with his views. Indeed, I could see from their
expressions that this outburst was regarded as in very poor taste
—for it infringed the iron law of hospitality. 'You go down,' said
Andreas to Michaelis, 'and tell him off.'

But I thought that here I saw an opening for my talent. Long
residence in remote Greek islands had made me not unskilful in
dealing with ruffled feelings—and, after all, Morais was only
behaving like a Scotsman or a Welshman when faced with the
foul invader. Indeed Cypriot manners at their worst never came
near the stupidities and impertinences I endured from the Scots
on my only visit to the Rump. Besides, being of a somewhat
scientific turn of mind I wished to see whether Morais would
prove an exception to the law I had formulated about Greek
character, namely: 'To disarm a Greek you have only to embrace
him.'

Accordingly I said: 'Let me go. After all, we are to be neighbours.'

They looked most anxious as I went down the staircase into
the hall and out through the front door. Morais stood there in
the street with a troubled aggressive expression on his face, holding a willow crook. Knife and water-bottle were at his waist. He
was leaning against the wall of the old water-tank. I walked up to
him and embraced him saying: 'Neighbour, I have come to live

with you. I know what Greek hospitality is. I want you to know that I am always ready to be of service to my neighbour. I have heard praise of you everywhere in the village as a fine honest farmer.'

Inexorable chain of scientific reasoning! He looked absolutely amazed and put out of countenance. He began to stammer out something, but I ducked back into the door and left him to the mercy of his friends who had shown an evident delight and appreciation of this little performance. 'Well said,' cried an old man, who looked as if he wanted to snatch a kiss while they were flying about; and from the balcony above Andreas and Michaelis growled approvingly. Poor Morais! He made one or two ineffectual attempts to speak but was drowned by the voices chiding him. 'There!' they cried. 'Is that any way to behave to a neighbour? You see what you've done with your boorishness? Given us all a bad reputation.'

He stamped up the hill to his house looking extremely thoughtful. My friends on the balcony greeted me with chuckles and acclamations, as if I had pulled off a splendid diplomatic *coup*—which perhaps I had. At any rate it was a valuable test of the public temper for it showed that, despite the political tide, I could count on sympathies based in common neighbourliness. Indeed never once in the dark days to come did the affection of my village neighbours falter.

And now the patient and laborious task of costing began and Andreas moved from point to point, from room to room, with his footrule poised like a stethoscope to sound every corner of the old house. He pronounced the whole of stout workmanship and provided I built lightly and skilfully over it, likely to last me 'half a dozen lifetimes'. As we walked and talked, too, ideas came to me. The hall could be enclosed by an arch which would take the stress of the balcony at the garden end; the bathroom could go beside the main staircase with a storage tank above it. If I threw a roof across the lower end of the balcony it would give me two extra rooms which would share the magnificent view of the Abbey. I was beginning to be seized by the most intoxicating of all manias—that of building for oneself. What made it doubly exciting was the fact that I had so little money with which to carry out the work—and even that little was dwindling day by day as I lived on it. Detail was going to be of the utmost importance here, and it was not long before I had a notebook full of relevant data about labourers' wages, costings for materials, and so on. . . .

It was nearly four o'clock before that first long session was complete and Andreas' tireless footrule had measured up every centimetre of wall length in the house. The wine had gone now, and one by one my new friends had sauntered off about their various tasks. We decided, after one more look round from the balcony, to go down to Dmitri for a glass of something cold. In the courtyard below me Lalou sat, tirelessly spinning, her blonde Frankish head of curls inclined towards the old carved uprights of the loom as if to a harp. Her father and mother unloaded the mule. In the little dome-shaped oven bread was baking; plates loaded with gleaming tangerines and almonds stood on a table under a vine. Chickens sauntered about their lawful occasions. The banana leaves crackled in the light breeze.

To the east of me, now deeply shadowed by the steep mountain behind, which had covered the sun, stood another old house covered by the luxuriance of a gigantic apricot-tree, where two fine-looking girls combed out their hair upon a balcony. Below them a tough young man polished a motor-cycle while two more sawed wood, and an old woman with a grave classical face stuffed pimento. The great gates of the courtyard stood open. I was soon to know why.

It all started with distant shouts and oaths and the noise of hooves—as if a company of ogres had set about one another in the olive glades above us. (The great earthquake which followed later that year made no such impression on me.) It bore down on us gradually increasing in volume, the human shouts mingled with the strangled lowing of cattle *in extremis*, and swelling to a roar as it entered the ravine to mingle with the rushing sound of the spring. It sounded like someone leading a desperate cavalry charge. 'What on earth is that?' I said. We went to the balcony's edge and peered up into the grained back-drop of mountain. A group of children spouted out of one of the narrow alleys screaming with laughter and shouting: 'He's coming now. Look out everyone.' And as the noise grew louder elderly gentlemen hopped spryly into doorways to take cover while the family under the apricot-tree cocked an ear and began to giggle. 'Here he comes, the fool,' said the old Homeric lady baring her toothless gums. I was a little reassured by their evident familiarity with the phenomenon, whatever it might prove to be. 'Here he comes,' shouted another excitable old gentleman waving a wand. The windows about us were now stocked with smiling faces, as if we were to be treated to some sort of spectacle, which indeed we were.

A dozen cattle came slipping and sliding down that stony brink at the pace of racehorses, bursting across the main street in a confused tangle of horns and udders, urged on by the inhuman yells of the man who, half dragged along, shouting with laughter, held the twisted tail of the hindmost in his knotted hand. He was screwing it as he shouted. In his free arm he was waving a water-gourd. His roars and screams were fearsome to hear, but they set the whole street in a roar of laughter. With his great sweeping moustache, sweat-beslobbered shirt and black trews set off by tall mountaineer's boots, he was a heroic figure belonging to the age of the Titans; he looked like some dispossessed character from the same Homeric cycle, who had yoked the oxen of the sun.

It was Frangos. His charges sped into their stalls like bullets, still pitifully lowing, while he, releasing the tail of the last cow, bestowed a last shriek and a kick on it. Then he stood in his own courtyard, arms akimbo, roaring for water like a lion and cursing everyone for being so slow. Bent double with laughter, his two tall daughters made their way to him bearing a jug and basin. Still growling he seized the jug and emptied it over the crown of his head, gasping and shouting in mock-anger at the coldness of the water, expelling his breath in a great swish like a steam boiler and calling everyone in the house a lazy cuckold.

'There. That will do,' shouted the old lady Helen, his wife. 'We don't want any more of your foul tongue about this house.' But the two spirited daughters rallied him unmercifully and he made a playful grab at the skirt of one, threatening to spank her.

He was like a celebrated actor playing a familiar role to an audience which has seen it many times, knows it almost word for word, and loves it. 'Eh, you, motor-bicycle polisher, cuckold, ape, door-post.'

'You leave me alone,' said his son-in-law to be, 'or I'll throw you to your cattle, compost-heap.' A series of violent pleasantries in this vein were thrown from balcony to courtyard and back again.

A small boy, passing outside the house, saw us leaning over the balcony and explained: 'Every day Frangos comes back with the cattle like that.'

'I see,' said Andreas.

'He calls it the defeat of the Bulgarians at Marathassa. It's the last charge. Usually we all cheer.'

I was glad to hear it, though Frangos' history seemed a bit weak. (I found later that he made up everything out of his own head, and reckoned books not worth a fig.)

Now he sat with a somewhat portentous air under his own fine tree and his wife brought him a long drink of wine and a clean handkerchief with which to mop his tousled head. His eldest daughter brought a comb and mirror with which he combed his fine moustache. Then he gave a sigh and betook himself to the little domed privy at the garden's end, where he squatted down and, between epic grunts, conducted a disjointed conversation with his wife. 'I hear a stranger has come to stay in the village. Some pest of an Englishman, eh?' She replied, 'He has bought Kakojannis' house. He is on the balcony watching you.' There was silence for a moment. 'Ho ho ha ha,' said Frangos at last and then, catching sight of me, gave another great whoop and put up his great paw. 'Yasu,' he cried formally, addressing me as if I were in the next valley; and then taking a step towards me he added: 'Ho there, Englishman, we drank together, did we not?'

'We did. To the *palikars* of all nations.'

'God be with them.'

'God be with them.'

There was a silence. He appeared to be struggling against his

87

innate friendliness. 'What have you come to Bellapaix for?' he asked me at last in a loud, provocative tone, but without any real sting in it. It was as if his self-possession were not quite complete: perhaps my brother's death at Thermopylae had holed him below the water-line.

'I have come to learn to drink,' I said drily, and he gave a great snort of laughter and banged his knee until the dust flew out of the folds of his baggy trousers. 'Do you hear that?' he said, turning to his family for approval. 'To drink! Good! Excellent!' Then turning back to me he boomed: 'I shall be your master.'

'Agreed.'

'And what will you give me in exchange?'

'Whatever you wish.'

'Even my freedom?'

I was about to extricate myself from this small predicament by a sophistry which would not have damaged friendly relations when a welcome interruption occurred. Andreas Kallergis put his face over the wall and said: 'Frangos, you rogue, you owe me money,' and a furious argument now broke out about the cost of a barn which Andreas had converted. 'I just gave it a kick and it fell down,' shrieked Frangos; 'what sort of building is that?' 'Anything you kicked would be bound to fall down,' said Andreas. 'Why don't you save your kicks for your good-for-nothing sons?' Frangos beetled. 'As for you, you're not man enough to be able to make a son.' All this in roaring good humour.

We parted in amity, shouting and screaming at one another, and set off down the hill. At the first corner stood a shy little girl of about fifteen, with very beautiful dark eyes and long hair in pigtails. She advanced on us as timorously as a squirrel, holding her hand behind her back. Her hesitation was touching as she sidled up. Behind her back she had a small wicker basket with a bundle of shallots in it and a blood orange; in her other hand a bunch of wild anemones wrapped in the broad leaf of an arum lily. These gifts she handed to me saying: 'My father Morais sends these to you and says welcome to your new house.'

I felt inordinately proud of having earned this gesture and

thought it worth cementing with a counter-gift, so I detached the
heavy pocket-knife which I had bought the day before from my
belt and gave it to her with an appropriate message.

When we got down to the little square by the Abbey we found
it crowded, for by now the village had come home from work.
Knots of coffee-drinkers lounged perilously under the Tree of
Idleness, gossiping. I scanned their faces closely for marks of the
spiritual ravages caused by idleness and it did seem to me that
several looked upon the point of sleep. The tavern was full now,
and Dmitri with his curious disjointed walk—like a sailor on a
heaving deck—was dispensing drink and coffee as fast as he was
able. The tower of the Church took the tawny golden light softly
upon its ancient face, so that the stonework now looked as if it
were made of the compressed petals of the rambler roses which
bordered the walks. Kollis and the *muktar* were taking their coffee
soberly at a corner table where we joined them with our sheaves
of calculations.

'I will get these people to build for you,' said Andreas quietly,
'your own villagers. There are one or two good masons here—
like Thalassinos over there—and Loizus for the woodwork. But
it will take me time to work out a detailed tender. When would
you like to start?'

'This week.'

'So soon?'

'Yes. I will tell you what money I have and you can work out
what can be done with it.'

I had already noticed that costing in Cyprus was an altogether
vague affair by European standards. Prices fluctuated hopelessly
according to shortages; if a consignment of European goods were
held up, and the shops empty of it—say paint—the price could
double in a matter of weeks. The trick was to make one's outlay
in raw materials all at once. Local contractors, through lack of
capital perhaps, tended to build wall by wall, thus putting themselves at the mercy of price fluctuations in material. This
accounted for the number of English people who claimed to have
been cheated by contractors. In fact, with costing so hopelessly
out of ratio, a contractor very often found himself woefully out in

his calculations—and during my reconstruction period on more than one occasion the masons could in fact have cheated themselves by several pounds. All this was the fruit of my conversations with the sapient Sabri. 'What we must do is to buy the brick, mortar and cement, for the whole job; get it up the hill; then see where we stand.'

I had divined that this method also suited the wage-structure of the workmen. It was not that wages fluctuated but that the other community needs drew off workmen from one project to another. There was no question of contracts. In the season of olive-pressing or carob-gathering the whole village turned out in a body—and at a blow one lost masons, carpenters, plumbers, everyone. Therefore, in order to build reasonably, one had to plan in short bursts, for such times as one could assemble a whole team. Otherwise work dragged—the absence of a foreman or a carpenter might keep a whole team of masons hanging about while a window-frame or door-jamb lacked, and while the carpenter who should have built it was out in the fields attending to a crop of apples, almonds or carobs. All these hold-ups cost money, and the art of building was to limit them.

All this had to be legislated for; but meanwhile the raw materials must be brought to the site. The good Sabri could provide the bricks and concrete, but as no lorry could reach the house, we would need donkeys and mules with panniers to get the stuff up the hill. It was here the *muktar* came in, for he was to mobilize the teams with which we could achieve the desired result at short notice.

We sat now like a jury and selected our men by eyes—Pambos, Kalopanis, Dmitri Rangis, Korais: gallery of whiskers and eyebrows such as one would never see outside Drury Lane. Andreas Menas undertook to supervise, and Michaelis to lend voice and colour to the unloading site at the house. I felt that the two ends of the rope, so to speak, were in good hands. There would be no hanging about with Andreas at the foot of the hill and Michaelis at the crown. One by one the gallery of ruffians was consulted and engaged. Soberly we assessed costs. It seemed to me that the transport problem would demand an intensive ten days' work;

after that we'd have our building materials to hand and we could then tackle the builders.

All this planning had been conducted with admirable despatch, thanks to the *muktar*, and now, abandoning Andreas' little car, I accepted the invitation of Kollis to walk down to Kyrenia with him, through the cyclamen-carpeted groves, among the cherry-trees, to where the good Panos would be sitting with his glass of Commanderia on a quiet terrace above the violet sea.

The Swallows Gather

'Very soon the atmosphere grew convivial, and the priest, swilling his wine, began to sing in a strong Greek baritone:

> "*The horizon opens,*
> *The sky is filled with light,*
> *Jerusalem rejoice,*
> *For Christ is risen.*"

'"Jesus, he gone up," the schoolmaster explained.

'The Mukhtar followed, wailing folk melodies in a high almost falsetto tenor voice:

> "*The world goes round and round like a wheel . . .*
> *Men come together and then they separate . . .*
> *And then . . .*"

'All knew what happened then, and joined in the refrain. . . .'

(The Orphaned Realm by Patrick Balfour)

It was not long before the mule-teams began to travel up the narrow streets of the village, each bearing its grunting burden of pierced concrete bricks or dusty sacks of cement; from the eyrie I had established in the lemon groves high above the Abbey I could watch them from an eagle's angle of vision as they slipped and staggered up the stony incline. From the cyclamen-bewitched patch of shadow where I spent my day now they looked like ants hastening back to the nest, each with a grain of wheat in its jaws.

Spring had lengthened into summer now and soon the wheat would be winnowed on the old threshing floors, freeing the specialists who would be responsible for relaying the balcony and putting in windows. I had already met some of them: first there was Thalassinos, 'the Seafarer', with his quiet dour manner and clipped moustache. He was in his early forties, and maintained throughout the work an earnest and prosaic air. I was all the more surprised to catch him in a fantasy of his own invention—for every Sunday he appeared in the coffee shop in clothes of his own design: tall top-boots made in soft suède, jodhpurs, and a check tweed coat set off by a hard collar and a tie of American design with a chorus girl in flames hand-painted on it. He strolled about with an air of distinction in these clothes which were much admired.

Little Loizus—'the Bear'—was a pillar of the Church and a very serious fellow altogether. His deportment betrayed the sidesman, and he spoke in a series of gentle hesitations, stops and starts, like an intermittently functioning Morse transmitter. He was afflicted by the tiresome village moralizing instinct of the 'rustic' novel; and worse still, bedevilled by his considerations for first principles. It you asked him to build a window he would lick his lips and begin in a faraway tone: 'Now windows for the ancient Greeks were holes in a wall. To them the question of light . . .' he would drone on; only when he had established the Platonic idea of a window and traced it up through the Phoenicians, Venetians, Hindus and Chinese, did he emerge once more on to the table-land of the present and add: 'I can't because I've broken my plane.' But he was gentle and industrious, and had an endearing way of putting out his tongue as he tried to get his spirit-level to show a true surface—which it almost never did.

Mr Honey was another new acquaintance with marked idiosyncrasies. He was tall and lean and very short-sighted; and he walked about the village swaying gracefully and manipulating his long graceful hands in gestures which reminded one of a lady of fashion in the period of Madame Récamier. His long dark face with its glazed eyes betrayed a fond vague happiness. He was the grave-digger; but as nobody died in the village he had a lot of time free for self-examination, and since a man must eat he had turned his talents to the digging of cess-pits at so much a cubic metre. He was the philosopher of main drainage. 'What is the meaning of life?' he asked me once in a tragic slurring voice. 'It all goes in here,' raising a bottle of wine to his lips for a long swig; 'and it all goes out *there*,' pointing to the pit he was digging.

'What does it all mean?' Poor Mr Honey! I have often pondered on the subject myself.

These, too, together with Andreas and Michaelis, were my first historians of Cyprus, and hardly a day passed without my learning something about the island's past; each added a piece of the common fund of knowledge about Cyprus which belongs to the large vague jig-saw which Panos had established for me. It is the best way to learn, for my informants told me these things in their own tongue, and acted them as they did so. I can never think of St Barnabas reproving the naked pagans at Paphos, or praying for God to blight the ancient shrine of Aphrodite, without seeing Michaelis' curling moustache as he dipped his shaggy head in an illustration of prayer, or with flashing eyes apostrophized the pagans in the very words of the saint: 'Hey, you, walking about like plucked chickens with your private parts open to heaven . . . have you no shame?' His illustration of the thunder-flash was dramatic, too; looking heavenward in terror from under his raised forearms with their clenched fists as the great radiance of the Light dawned in the sky. 'Bang! went the saint, and Bang! Bang!' Then spreading his fisted arms he gazed slowly at the ruins caused by Barnabas' prayers, pityingly, uncomprehendingly, raising here a head and there an arm of a pagan to see if they were dead. They were. The heads and arms fell listlessly back into position. It was all over! Later, on the road to Tammasos, Paul and Barnabas sat down to a frugal lunch consisting of olives. The trees which stand there today grew from the pips they spat out. Andreas himself had been a workman in Paphos when they discovered the cone-shaped black stone, idol of Aphrodite, in some abandoned byre. According to him the youths of Paphos still go out at night and anoint the stones of the temple with oil and almond-water on a certain night of the year, while women leave their rings and fragments of their petticoats as *ex votos* against barrenness.

Heaven knows how true all this was: but it was true for them. And the bibliography of Cyprus is so extensive and detailed that the truth must somewhere be on record. . . . That could come later, I felt. I preferred to learn what I could from the lips of these peasants with their curious mediaeval sense of light and shade, and their sharp sense of dramatic values. Oddly enough, too, their stories proved true sometimes when they sounded utterly improbable; Andreas, for example, in describing ancient Cyprus to me produced a home-made imitation of a hippopotamus walking around and browsing in my courtyard which was worthy of Chaplin. It was nearly a year before I caught up with the report of the dwarf hippopotamus which had been unearthed on the Kyrenia range: a prehistoric relic. It was only justice, I suppose, that I myself should be disbelieved by them when I claimed to have seen a brown seal floating lazily in the tepid summer water by the little mosque where later I used to bathe.

No, they were not often wrong; and their versions of historic events had the merit of giving me a picture-gallery of faces to interpret the events by: I still see the Governor Sergius being converted to Christianity by Michaelis—only he wears forever the gaping rustic face of Mark the concrete-mixer as he leans on a shovel to watch the storyteller.

It was a way of travelling, too, by standing still; or rather by sitting still, under an olive tree with a can of wine beside one. Michaelis had suffered from the stone, and his great pilgrimage in search of a cure was a saga in itself. He had stumped up the verdant crown of Olympus to try the wonder-working image at Kykko; had panted along the dusty road which is ruled across the green plain to the dry well where Barnabas' bones were found, near Salamis. He had consulted the withered head of the martyr St Heracleides in its glass case, touching the red velvet with his finger to take some dust from the relic which he sniffed up into his right nostril: without avail. Everyone told him he would have to submit to the knife. But somehow he couldn't believe that the island saints would let him down, even though the mineral springs might fail him. (I learned of their qualities, which he illustrated by a series of grimaces—so that each spring has an accompanying picture. Worst of all, Kalopanayotis provoked intestinal rumblings which suggested something even more powerful than the prayers of St Barnabas. Banging his fist on a lintel he imitated these tremors, and added: 'Days and nights of remorseless bombardment after only a pint of it.') But at last he found his cure; on the dramatic scarp where Stavrovouni rises he said his prayers to the holy relic which he said was part of the cross of the Penitent Thief, bequeathed by Helena, the great and good Empress. ('Empress of where?' 'I don't know.') In a dream he was told to live for two months only on the juice of the Prodromos apples and cherries, and this at last cured him.

But while these fellow villagers of mine brought me knowledge of saints and seasons, of icons and wine, the swallows were beginning to gather—the human swallows which make life endurable for those who elect to live on islands. Life in a small island would be unbearable for anyone with sensibility were it not enriched from time to time by visitants from other worlds, bringing with them the conversations of the great capitals, refreshing the quotidian life in small places by breaths of air which make one live once more, for a moment, in the airs of Paris or London.

So it was that for a whole day I was able to gossip with John Lehmann on the empty beach at Pachyammos, eagerly questioning him about new books and new writers; or talking of the writers who were to follow him out to Cyprus as we gathered anemones at Klepini or walked through the haunted moonlit streets of old Famagusta at midnight, listening to the ravens sleepily crowing. These are the lucky interludes one enjoys nowhere so much as on an island—to see the Lion Mount, as if for the first time, through the cool rare eyes of Rose Macaulay, herself bound for ruins stretching still further back into time than this Gothic castle in the shadow of which I lived. ('Have you ever wondered how it is that the utilitarian objects of one period become objects of aesthetic value to succeeding ones? This thing was constructed purely to keep armies at bay, to shatter men and horses, to guard a pass. How do we find it more beautiful than the Maginot Line? Does time itself confer something on relics and ruins which isn't inherent in the design of the builder? Will we ever visit the Maginot Line with such awe at its natural beauty?') The thoughts of a fellow-writer which tease the mind long after she has gone. . . .

But among the swallows were one or two who had built their

nests upon this fertile range. I had noticed, for instance, a fair-haired girl. She walked about the harbour at Kyrenia with a book and with the distracted air which betokened to my inexpert eye evidence of some terrible preoccupation—perhaps one of those love-affairs which mark one for life. I had seen her, too, in her little green car, driving about the hills with the same *princesse lointaine* expression. The mystery was only made plain to me when I met her and found that the subdued air of anguish on her face could be traced back to preoccupations which matched mine. She was trying to build a house on a spectacular deserted point opposite the little Tekke of Hazaret Omer—a remarkable site for the choice of a private house. You would think that such a choice betokened an inordinate world-weariness, yet Marie was anything but world-weary. She flashed in and out of Cyprus half a dozen times a year bringing with her the best conversation of three capitals as a staple; and until the house should be ready she had constructed a small hut of bamboos of a strongly Indonesian flavour where she spent her time, reading and writing. We were drawn together by common enthusiasms. I was able to translate for her—for she was still engaged in buying her land from the dozen or so peasants who owned it. And for her part she enjoyed coming up to the Abbey to see how work on my house was going, bringing with her an armful of books with sketches of architecture and garden-layout to add oil to the fire already raging among my villagers. With her blonde head and brown eyes she seemed to them something rare and strange—which indeed she was, being so solitary a creature; and when she kicked off her shoes to walk about the green grass of the Abbey, Andreas would nudge Michaelis at the coffee shop and say: 'There goes the nereid again.'

The nereid and I made common cause, exchanging figures and costings, worrying poor Sabri for advice, and in our spare time swimming together on the rugged rock-beaches round her land.

But Marie's design for living differed from mine, for she was an incurable romantic, and moreover a great traveller; her house was to have features of almost everything she had loved between Fez and Goa; recessed doorways with mouldings, Arab shutters, a fountain from Bundi, a courtyard from Castile. . . . The list changed daily but it was always an extensive one, and her enthusiasm was so touching and warming that it seemed cruel to tell her that the workmen in Cyprus could not execute designs so rare. 'Nonsense, we'll make them.' It went without saying that she was a person of fortune as well as a romantic; if Beckford had been alive he would surely have been among her many friends and correspondents—and perhaps he might have assisted at those early deliberations by the sea, or sipping Clito's country wine in the cool shade of his cave.

It was concern about her plans—for it is one thing to knock an old house about, but quite another to build from the ground—which made me so happy when Pearce Hubbard turned up, clad in his gold thread jeans of local weave, dark shirt and sandals. I knew him by name through many common friends, but we had never met. With his delightful insouciance (it seemed unfair to have the looks of a matinée idol, plus brains and taste) he burst in upon me as I was making heavy weather with a bank statement, and refusing to countenance any excuse, insisted that I must accompany him to Lapithos to meet Austen Harrison. He knew Bellapaix well and was a close friend of Kollis with whom he shared a passion for roses, and on this visit I recall he had filled the back of the car up with a wobbling forest of potted plants in the midst of which I sat, feeling rather foolish. As we bounced and swayed towards Lapithos he told me of his own Turkish house there and of how he and Harrison, for their sins, had become residents of Lapithos and owners of old houses. As architects their work took them about the world a great deal and Cyprus was a useful jumping-off place in which to have a drawing-office; it was also the ideal place to spend a summer, he added wryly, and he had sent his family out on several occasions. 'And now that you are here,' he added, offering me a fellowship in the wine and landscape, 'it's going to be splendid. I'm not here very much myself, but Austen spends a good part of the year in Lapithos. I know you'll like him and I hope he'll like you. He's an awful recluse—can one blame him? One wouldn't come so far from the haunts of man if one were a gregarious or clubby type. And his house will fill you with despair—may give you an idea or two. By the way, go a bit deeper, another ten foot for the end of the balcony, just to be sure. You don't want the whole thing to sit down one rainy day in the sludge and refuse to move—or to turn over on its side when you are giving an *ouzo* party on the roof.'

'Did the house seem fairly sound?' I asked nervously, though I had sworn not to try to cadge a free consultation from him. Pearce laughed. 'Depends on what you mean. An English builder would have apoplexy. But it's as sound as mine or Austen's—no, not quite: we've rebuilt extensively. How long do you intend to live?'

I was content with the implied reassurance and flattered by his approval of my general plan.

But all this was swallowed up in despair and envy when we entered Austen Harrison's house and found its romantic owner seated gravely by his own lily-pond, apparently engaged in psychoanalysing a goldfish. He was a noble personage, with his finely minted Byzantine emperor's head and the spare athletic repose of his tall figure. But the austerity was belied by a twinkling eye and brisk lively humours. One felt immediately accepted; and as I sipped a drink and listened to his conversation I suddenly realized that I was in the presence of the hero of *South Wind* or an early character from Huxley. He represented that forgotten world where style was not only a literary imperative but an inherent method of approaching the world of books, roses, statues and landscapes. His house was a perfect illustration of the man. He had taken over an old Cypriot wine-magazine, or perhaps stable, and converted it with a tenderness and discretion which made the whole composition sing—the long arched room lined with books, from whose recesses glowed icons; the shaded terrace with its pointed arches, the summer house, the lily-pond. All this was an illustration of philosophic principles—an illustration of how the good life might, and how it should, be lived. For him too the island life was only made endurable by friendly visitants from the world outside and I was delighted to find we had friends in common who came through almost every year and stayed for a day or two specially to make the pilgrimage to Lapithos. Of these

Freya Stark and Sir Harry Luke remain as forever identified in my mind with the place, for each of them had something special to give me.

Pearce Hubbard's own house was hardly less delightful. It was virtually next door, and it was here that we convened for that first memorable dinner by candle-light, given flavour and shape by good food and better conversation, and extended far into the night in a garden full of the scent of limes. Here they gave me news of other friends with a Cairo or Athens background who had just passed through or were due to arrive, each with his burden of information. Patrick Kinross, for example, whose book on Cyprus is not likely to be superseded as a brief and extraordinarily comprehensive sketch of the island and its problems, was due to visit them next week. Later Freya Stark herself would come. . . . It was clear that Austen Harrison had built himself a khan or caravanserai on one of the main highways of the world.

In them at least Marie found guides and advisers in the formidable task of building the 'perfect house for a writer to live in'; they tempered her enthusiasm without damping it, and kept her as far as possible within the golden mean. The three of them, in fact, shared one quality in common: they were all magpies. And travelling about as they all did they were able to indulge their taste, and bring back to Cyprus a bewildering medley of objects, from Egyptian *musarabiyas* to Turkish mosque-lamps. They were steadily stripping the Arab world of its chief treasures, as Pearce said, and soon their houses in Cyprus would have everything, except the mosaics of St Sophia. My own ambitions were more hedge-hopping and my means forbade me to indulge in such delightful fantasies—happily perhaps. But I enjoyed these treasures vicariously, so to speak, and appreciated nothing more than one of the great palavers which went on when one or other of the friends had arrived back in Cyprus with something exotic— Persian tiles, Indian fabrics, a Kuwait chest, or simply perhaps the design for a window or door triumphantly stolen from Fez, Algiers or Istamboul. Its position in her house which as yet did not exist, was a subject of the most earnest, heart-warming debate.

The Swallows Gather

We drove back that night from our first meeting with the 'hermits of Lapithos' with a profound content, and as the moon was late and high, turned off the road to spend an hour in the owl-haunted ruins of Lambousa, an old church standing in magnificent desolation upon the echoing stony beach below Lapithos. Here, walking about in the ruins, eating the sweet brown grapes we had stolen from Pearce Hubbard's table we talked of our houses, of the books we were going to write, and of the lives we should be able to live here in the sun: within reach of each other on this eloquent range of hills. The owls whistled and the sea banged and rubbed under the moon. We were full of the premonitions of a life to be lived which could offer, not merely leisure in sunlight, but a proper field in which to read and reflect, deploy words and study. Marie was to leave for India next morning (she always left like this, without a word of warning, to reappear after a month or two as suddenly) and felt disinclined to sleep, so we drove back along the silent coast and down to the little mosque, blazing like a diamond on the rocky peninsula opposite her wattle hut. Here we bathed in a sea still full of cold currents, smarting to the flesh, and drank the last of a bottle of red Chianti which we found in the hut. The dawn was breaking before we were ready almost, rushing out of the night-sea beyond Cape Andreas, a steeply mounting flush upon the bronze faces of the mountains. A dense dew lay upon everything as we drove back through the silent fields to Kyrenia for breakfast. There were to be many such mornings, many such evenings spent in good fellowship and wine, before the vagaries of fortune and the demons of ill luck dragged Cyprus into the stock-market of world affairs and destroyed not only the fortuitous happiness of these friendships but, more tragically and just as surely, the old tried relationships on which the life of the little village itself was founded.

But none of this was as yet apparent upon the face of things—and the brown smiling summer with its gross damps and fierce sun led us towards the languid flowering autumn of the year, hinting in the ripeness of figs and grapes, the emergence of snakes and lizards, of the winter to follow. Marie and Pearce vanished. Boris and Ines came. The work on the house was well advanced and I moved in, the better to supervise, to extract a poet's pound of flesh for every penny spent—I was getting short of money. But the plan was maturing and the place itself becoming even more beautiful than our haphazard plans and sudden afterthoughts had let me dare imagine.

The two floors of the house now began to represent themselves in their true colours as winter and summer floors. Below, a great fireplace, small kitchen, study and bedroom; above, the indescribable terrace which would later be shaded by its own vine; a large rambling old-fashioned studio room, a small hall with a fireplace, and an alcove set deep behind a pointed arch from the window of which my small daughter, if she sat up in bed, could gaze out at Turkey and see the fort of Kyrenia framed like a water-colour. Brick by brick, stone by stone, window by window, I watched it all put together by my friends with a sense of familiarity that one has sometimes when a poem 'comes out' of its own accord like an equation, without having to be tortured or teased. It all flowed from the magical black moustache of Michaelis, the brown fingers of 'the Seafarer', the lisp and stammer of 'the Bear'; and as the work went on my neighbours dropped in to appraise it and to exchange pleasantries with their friends and relations who were building it. Here, too, in autumn came visitors and there was a fine fire of flesh-rosy carob wood to greet them, whose flames jumped and glowed on the old doors and mouldings and screens. A few shelves of books too gave the sense of permanent habitation.

In that warm light the faces of my friends lived and glowed, giving back in conversation the colours of the burning wood, borrowing the heat to repay it in the companionable innocence of unpremeditated talk. Freya Stark, whose journeys to the wilder parts of Turkey brought her happily to Cyprus *en route*, illustrated for us the wit and compassion of the true traveller—one, that is, who belongs to the world and the age; Sir Harry Luke, whose gentleness and magnanimity of soul were married to a mind far-reaching and acute, who was fantastically erudite without ever being bookish, and whose whole life had been one of travel and adventure; Patrick Leigh Fermor and the Corn Goddess, who always arrive when I am on an island, unannounced and whose luggage has always been left at the airport ('But we've brought the wine—the most important thing').

They brought with them fragments of history and legend to set against the village lore; Sir Harry meditating on the double-sexed Aphrodite whose priests wore beards and whose worshippers inverted their dress—and wondering whether the extraordinary number of hermaphrodites on Cyprus did not perhaps betoken some forgotten race, bred for the service of the temple. Through them I caught a glimpse, not only of Cyprus as she is today, but of the eternal Cyprus which had for so long attracted the attention of travellers like them. And the biography of a saint heard from the lips of Sir Harry married like a cloth with the same story heard from Michaelis in his dialect form, so that my notebook became cross-hatched with material drawn from both. Let me add a page or two from it, since it lies to hand.

(a) From the balcony, towards four, by westering sunlight: plum-dark mountain roses: green wooden table in the rain: slurring of bees: chime of tea-cups: H.L. talking well about King Harry and the building of the Abbey which lies below anchored against the side of the cliff, bruise-grey. 'Both Latin and English are poorer than Greek in having only one word for life, "vita" and "life", whereas Greek has two, "Zoe" and "Bios".' He described the way the Levant had undermined the Gothic north —religion foundering in licence. Even the good fathers of the Abbey lapsed, were found to have several wives. A bishop had to ride up here on a mule to tick them off!

(b) The only oath binding to vampires, according to Manoli, is 'by my winding-sheet'. But Cyprus is not rich in vampires, is richer in saints. Estienne de Lusignan in his 'Description' says there are 107 island saints, not counting those whose names he does not know, and of foreign saints whose bodies rest in Cyprus,

315. There are six monasteries in happy possession of some wonder-working icon or holy relic.

❀

(c) This morning woke, believing that the house was on fire, but it proved to be the sound of silkworms feeding in Lalou's little house—a noise like a crisp forest fire travelling through dry scrub as the little creatures gnawed their way through the great parcels of mulberry leaves. Lalou says that the white mulberry in my garden is excellent for feeding. Up to the second moult they are fed with leaves from the ungrafted mulberry. They have never heard of lettuce leaves for feeding silkworms, it seems.

❀

(d) Scene of the wildest comedy next-door when Frangos in an excess of high spirits picked up the cherished motor-bike of his son-in-law and proceeded to juggle with it. He tripped on a terrace and suddenly the machine flew into the apricot-tree where it lodged precariously—it is only a two-stroke. Screams, yells, drama. If it fell out it would be broken. Ludicrous attitudes of Frangos climbing tree with rope to snare it before it fell. Son-in-law in tears. A safe landing, however, with a smart blow on the shin for the son-in-law which put Frangos in a good humour for the rest of the day.

❀

(e) The silkworms die with a dreadful crackling and sobbing and a noise of sinews being ground; the family sit round the great copper cauldron and skim off the product on to hand looms—great spools of butter-coloured silk thick as a man's thigh. And Lalou sings in the high true voice. 'Though my lover come from never so far away, my heart will recognize him by his smile.'

❀

(f) Last night the sound of the front door closing upon breathless chuckles and secretive panting, then the voice of Paddy Leigh Fermor: 'Any old clothes?' in Greek. Appeared with his arm round the shoulders of Michaelis who had shown him the way up the rocky path in darkness. 'Joan is winded, holed below the Plimsoll line. I've left her resting half way up. Send out a seneschal with a taper, or a sedan if you have one.' It is as joyous a reunion as ever we had in Rhodes. After a splendid dinner by the fire he starts singing, songs of Crete, Athens, Macedonia. When I go out to refill the *ouzo* bottle at the little tavern across the way I find the street completely filled with people listening in utter silence and darkness. Everyone seems struck dumb. 'What is it?' I say, catching sight of Frangos. 'Never have I heard of Englishmen singing Greek songs like this!' Their reverent amazement is touching; it is as if they want to embrace Paddy wherever he goes.

(*g*) 'Enosis and only Enosis.' I was able to test my theory of Greek character again tonight. Returning late I was hissed at from a dark doorway. 'Don't go up now. Manoli is drunk and might do you harm. He is waiting up there.' It sounded alarming but I pressed on up the dark road. Manoli was standing in the rosy glow from the tavern door, swaying a bit and twirling his moustache. 'Ah,' he says as he catches sight of me, 'Ah! Here is the foreigner.' His wits are all awry and he looks vaguely reproachful, that is all. I catch hold of his arm and whisper in his ear: 'Never say that Greece and England drew the sword upon each other.' He suddenly seemed to come to himself. 'Never,' he repeated indistinctly. 'Never, my friend! Never!' Crossing himself. And before he can muster enough national feeling to change his mind I slip past him into my own front door. Though they have written Enosis on every wall in the village, so far nobody had touched the walls of the house, three of which are on a public highway. I point this out to Andreas. 'Of course,' he says. 'That would be unneighbourly. And another thing. You know we all love the English. There is nothing anti-English in Enosis.''

(*h*) H.L. on St Hilarion, whose identity appears to be in some doubt. A pity, because the site demands a saint with a biography. He is, however, supposed to have retired to the castle and died there. His body was taken to the Syrian desert by a disciple and placed in a monastery he had founded. Neophytus Rhodinos says it was stolen by 'certain ascetics', while Makhairas hints that the body found in the castle was a later one. Where is it now? It is hard to say. Manoli has two fables of buried treasure, and a Princess asleep in a rock which he associates with the castle. H.L. quoted De Mandeville, however, and I looked him up: 'And in the castell of amoure lyth the body of Seynt Hyllarie and men kepen it right worshipfully.' Estienne de Lusignan, just to bewilder us, says the castle was originally built for Cupid; that demons and unclean spirits, his satellites, dwell there. St Hilarion's virtue drove them out, and his cult replaced that of the Love God. I prefer the Crusader name of Dieudamor.

(*i*) To Larnaca through an extraordinary landscape reminding one of Plato's God 'geometrizing': low hills, almost perfect cones with levelled tops suggesting the Euclidean objects found in art studios. Wind erosion? But the panel of geometrical mounds seems hand-made. And the valleys tapestried with fat-tailed sheep, plots of verdure, and here and there a camel-train and palm-tree. A strange mixture of flavours, the Bible, Anatolia, and Greece.

(*j*) The Mesaoria combines every extreme of beauty and ugliness; barren, sand-bedevilled, empty, and under moonlight a haunted waste; then in spring bursting with the shallow splendours of anemone and poppy, and cross-hatched with silk-soft vegetation. 'Only here you realize that things pushed to extremes become their opposites; the ugly barren Mesaoria and the verdant one are so extreme that one wonders whether the beauty or the ugliness has not the greater power.'

(*k*) Ownership of trees. To Zeus belongs the oak. Knowledge was 'the eating of the acorn'. Hermes owned the palm, and later Apollo both palm and laurel. Demeter the fig-tree—the sacred phallus of Bacchus was made from the wood. The sycamore was the Tree of Life for the Egyptians. The pine-tree belonged to Cybele. Black poplars and willows are especially connected with the winter solstice, therefore with Pluto and Persephone; but the white poplar claims Hercules who brought it up from the shades. I can find nothing about the mulberries and tangerines. . . .

(*l*) Above doorways a talisman of goat's horns, like horseshoes in an English village smithy. Frangos says this prevents the evil eye. The tall snake-boots worn by the men illustrate their respect and fear for the viper—of which they describe one 'fatal' variety: a short, fat-bellied, bile-and-sputum coloured reptile with a large head. When killed the 'bone of the head' is put in spirit and kept. The liquid is supposed to be a specific against snake or tarantula poison, and has the added power of curing impotence. Other customs, I have forgotten; but snake-lore here would be worth investigating. Snake an ancient symbol of knowledge ('Their ears have been licked by serpents'). H.L. on a medieval monastery where a breed of giant cat was cultivated specially to attack the snakes which infested the promontory.

(*m*) H.L. on Cypriot character. Anatolia has touched it with sleep. They are gentler, less strident than the metropolitan Greeks, and far more honest. The ancients coined the phrase 'Cypriot ox' because of their sleepiness. I find they have fine old-fashioned manners, unhurried and graceful. Samuel Brown in 1879 wrote of them: 'The Christian inhabitants, though Greek by language and religion, possess little of the intelligence, enterprise and restlessness of the Greek character, nor physiologically are they of Greek type. They, as well as their Mohammedan neighbours, are naturally indolent and unambitious, self-willed and obstinate, but peaceable, domestic, fairly honest and very easily governed. . . . Life and property are probably not more secure in any part of Her Majesty's dominions. How far the prevailing stupidity and apathy result from the system under which the inhabitants have lived for many generations is an interesting subject of inquiry. The education of the priests and laity is of the lowest standard. As the children appear bright and docile a system of sound elementary secular education would produce the happiest results.'

Artemisia thought poorly of them; but then she was a somewhat frightening woman, if I remember rightly, who pounded the bones of Mauselos her husband in a mortar and drank the powdered results in wine 'to give her strength'. An early form of bluestocking.

(*n*) To Famagusta with Marie and Pearce and an amusing friend who is bitterly critical of the administration. 'What good is it to have brought order and justice so-called if we have brought unparalleled ugliness? We have allowed the two walled towns which could have rivalled Carcassonne to be destroyed under our noses when a little town-planning would have saved them and earned millions from tourists. And look as you will you cannot find a single building, from a village pump to a town hall, put up by us which would not brand us as lazy vandals in civilized eyes.' I must say there is truth in this. But A.H. says it is the same all over the Commonwealth, unending ugliness, and the projection of England as Wimbledon.

What is the truth about our administration? It is hard to say. Sanitation and public health seem well found, to judge by this village; the building laws take account of them, though they seem rather out-of-date. Flies and anopheles are certainly kept down by the municipal health-people with commendable energy. And it is rather endearing to find scribbled on a mosque or church the last date of DDT'ing among the other *graffiti*. But there is one significant thing: in all the long harangues about the Government and its deficiencies there has never been any mention so far of dishonesty—only stupidity, arrogance, and ignorance. I have never once heard the word 'dishonesty' or 'bribe' and these would be the first charges to spring to the lips of indignant Greeks if there were a shadow of real belief in them. As for ugliness, if

we have built nothing good (and certainly there is one place outside Famagusta of an ugliness so soul-wrenching as to deserve a
Royal Commission) we have done excellent work in preserving
monuments. I am told this is entirely due to a quite exceptional
archaeological officer, Peter Megaw, who is a friend of Pearce's
and whom I shall meet. But all this must be measured against
funds. I have not seen a copy of the budget.

(*o*) My mother has arrived for a holiday, full of energy and
malapropisms, and totally convinced that yet another of the
family follies is in full swing. But the beauty of the house contents
her, and she is able to establish something like a regular domestic
routine with the help of Xenu, the huge porpoise of a maid from
the village of Carmi, whom we call 'the Kyria Eleison' from her
most repeated exclamation of surprise. Everything surprises and
dismays her; she is asthmatic and somewhat hysterical and blows
and whistles like a grampus.

This arrival is timely for another reason. I have been getting
somewhat low in funds and will have to turn aside to find work if
the grandiose projects designed for the top floor of the house are
to be completed this year. Unsupervised all would end in liquor
and fairy-tales; and while my mother is gregarious her knowledge of Greek is limited and keeps her somewhat tongue-tied,
despite the quantities of excellent country wine supplied to the
house by Clito at sixpence a litre.

(*p*) F.S. has left for Turkey with her calm, dispassionate voice
and quiet personal view of things. I can't help thinking her trip is
somewhat dangerous—but then they have all been. H.L. has
flown off round the world. Pearce and Marie have both vanished.
Mark Sarafian. Otto Manheim. Grisvold. Saunders. My brother
threatens to resurrect quite soon. This will put me in an embar-
rassing situation; I shall no longer be able to get free drinks on
his magnificent stand at Thermopylae. Lalou is to be married.
Her mother has given me wonderful material about the Cypriot

wedding. The whole ceremony is conducted to appropriate songs and dances on the archaic pattern. We have been formally invited by the old mother who visited us to sprinkle our hands formally with rose water before handing us a smartly printed invitation to the wedding. It is only the first of many to come, but it is a welcome sign that our neighbours accept us, and when I express my gratitude Andreas says quietly: 'After all, you come to us as a neighbour, not to make the "big gentleman" with us.'

(*q*) Another old friend, Maurice Cardiff, has returned to the island where he represents the British Council—surely an inspired choice, for he was part-editor and founder of the old Anglo-Hellenic review. He promises to find me some teaching to do. A close friend of the 'Lapithos hermits', he is a most welcome addition to the ranks of exiles; but more important, he has established firm links with the few Greek intellectuals on the island and is much beloved. Through him I met Nikos Kranidiotis the poet, who is the Archbishop's secretary, and G. Pol Georgiou, the only Cypriot painter of his generation who is of European significance.

(*r*) Among the grizzled muleteers who bring up loads of sand and gravel for the masons is one with a fine red jolly face whose son helps him in the work. Judge my surprise when yesterday I saw a copy of Eliot's *Quartets* sticking out of the pocket of his torn jacket hanging on a nail. He is a young schoolmaster, seldom in the village except during the holidays; but he is a poet and timidly showed me some verses which proved to have promise enough to be printed in the *Cyprus Review*. When I told his old father that his son, unknown to him, was a writer and had had his first verses printed he raised his dusty cap high in the air and exclaimed: 'Then praise be to the mother who bore him.'

(*s*) The quietness, the sense of green beatitude which fills this village derives not only from the great Tree of Idleness but from the Abbey; it intrudes an overflowing peace upon every little corner of the place. As all the houses face true north there can hardly be a window in the place which does not frame a corner of it, some gable or grey arch—unselfish and candid in death as its founders must have tried to become in life. How strange that so little should be known about it, and that no saint or hermit found it a fitting place in which to embody a legend. Half the village houses are built from the stone blocks of the place, stolen over successive generations and built into the walls and ovens and privies of my neighbours. Kollis is right about its being alive. Every Sunday its bell rings with a fine tang and the villagers dressed in their Sunday best troop down to prayer.

Meanwhile the work on the house went on unflaggingly under my mother's rather variable direction. She had a passion for folk-lore and ghost stories and I was rather glad she had never managed to learn Greek as all would be lost if she and Michaelis once got together. But she had taken to over-feeding the workmen in her large compassionate way, and now all sorts of delicacies were passed round on plates all day, together with innumerable cups of coffee, so that the lunch hour had begun to resemble a rather original sort of garden-party.

Together we shared some fascinating experiences—as when an English M.P. came in search of information and was induced to experiment with the white wine of Clito which bears the label '|*Swet White Dry*'. Unknown to ourselves, who were sitting over this excellent wine on the terrace, Mr Honey had begun a twenty-foot hole outside the front door to provide seepage for the village pump which was due to be installed that day. We bowed our guest out and almost into this pit before we saw it, and indeed had not my mother clutched the visitor's coat tails all might have been lost. But she earned her spurs by a classical malapropism. Talking of life in Europe compared to life in England, and making common cause with our guest who was a much-travelled man, she beamed and said: 'I'm delighted to find that we are both misplaced persons!' Or was it the wine? I shall never know.

Then there was Mr Honey's wanderlust. The terrible *cafard* of the village, induced no doubt by frequent potations underground, convinced him one day that he should never return. He was by this time fifteen foot down, and quite invisible, in the cesspit which was designed to look after the kitchen drainage. All morning a thin wraith of song had risen from the darkness—the only sign of life apart from a feeble scraping. He usually took his small son, aged seven, down with him on these excursions into the infernal regions. The boy was a clumsy little fellow, always dropping spades on his father's head. Today he rose to the surface, voided a basketful of black earth and said: 'My father will not come up. He says he is going through to Australia. He is tired of life in Bellapaix.' We tried to interrogate the darkness of the pit but only a confused series of sounds emerged, composed of snatches of song, belches, and some unhappy oaths. 'Honey,' I shouted, 'it is evening. Come up.' He groaned dramatically and shouted: 'Leave me to my darkness. I shall die here—or else emerge in Australia to start a new life. A new life!' he repeated in another key. 'Think of it, a new life.' 'The fool,' said Andreas, 'he is drunk.' The little boy nodded. 'He has had a bottle down there all day.'

Mr Honey belched feebly and shouted, 'It's a lie, by Saint Peter', but his strength was obviously ebbing fast. My mother became perturbed. She had been reading all sorts of things about fire damp and carbon monoxide. He might suffocate. 'He'll reach Australia by morning,' said Michaelis ironically and suggested dropping a pannier of earth on him, but I persuaded him against it. Honey was rather feeble in body—as well as infirm of spirit. 'I order you to come out,' I bellowed, trying the method of command, but the only result was some maidenly giggling. 'If you could see how you looked up in the sky you'd say you were a balloon,' said Mr Honey. 'Anyway,' he added, 'I hate the British and shall drive them into the sea single-handed, yea, alone.' I dimly saw a hand waving a bottle. 'Come up you fool,' I said. 'Hoity toity,' said Mr Honey. It was rather difficult to know what to do. Andreas produced a drum of water which he claimed would instantly revive the traveller, but I bade him desist for

Mr Honey was something of a treasure and I wasn't sure that he hadn't invented a new form of tourism. 'Let's leave him,' I said, 'until he is sober enough to come up. How, by the way, *does* he come up out of these pits?' The small boy indicated a make-shift windlass and a coil of rope; his task was to drag the baskets of earth to the surface and empty them. Occasionally a heavy one would crash down upon the gravedigger and a long spinsterish scream would come out of the pit, while all the workmen giggled and said: 'Honey's been beaned again.'

We tried the method of silence now, and that worked better, for no sooner did Honey imagine himself abandoned than all the fight went out of him and he began calling for his rope in piteous accents. I wound it round the boy, instructed him to carry a loop round his father's shoulders, and sent him down. Meanwhile I got one of the brawnier workmen to stand by with me for the resurrection.

There now ensued a somewhat dangerous scene, for my mother, for some reason best known to herself (perhaps she thought the gravedigger was ill or suffocating) appeared with a large glass of black coffee and vaguely handed it to Mr Honey as he surfaced. He for his part showed some reluctance to step on to *terra firma*. He seemed anxious to make a political speech—though this was hardly the appropriate platform for the rope turned round and round, and with it went the gravedigger with coffee in one hand, a wine-bottle in the other, and all the implements of his trade, including his small son, lashed round his neck. He was talking well, however, and it seemed a pity to interrupt him; but the impatient Andreas kept pushing him ashore with a mop, aided by the grunting maid-of-all-work who herself was apostrophizing the more approachable saints. Now he began to make a series of brilliant stage-falls, teetering for agonizing moments on the well before falling backwards into it, only to be brought up with a jerk by the rope. He fell like a golliwog, arms and legs spread. The coffee disappeared with a crash, the bottle followed it. Honey smiled foolishly and scored another parliamentary point, marrying it to a suitable gesture. 'My *dear* lady,' he kept repeating with gracious vagueness, 'so kind . . . so good. . . . Much regret ordering your execution. . . . Much regret British being pushed into sea . . . entirely their own fault . . . warned them years ago. . . .'

But finally we caught him: it was like fishing for a spider in a bath-tub: caught him, and carried him to the tavern above which he lodged and there spread him out on the great stone window-sill where he spent his leisure hours. He was luxuriously relaxed now and smiling beatifically. But he was barely sentient, though when at his request I lit a cigarette and put it between his lips he opened his eyes for a moment and thanked me. Rather sur-prisingly he said: 'I was with your brother at Thermopylae. What a fellow!' 'Indeed?' I said, anxious to have an eye-witness description of his death, but Mr Honey was fading into sleep now. The cigarette rolled from his lips into the road and lay there burning.

'He's so thin,' said Andreas, 'that if you wrapped him in a cigarette paper you couldn't smoke him.' Apparently little solid food ever passed the gravedigger's lips; he concentrated on more combustible provender. 'But he's a fine digger,' said Michaelis, and indeed this was true, for the holes—'Honeyholes' my mother called them—were completely circular and smooth. It was a great feat when one considered that after six foot or so he was working always in complete darkness. 'Peace be on him,' said Morais rather sententiously and with an air of disapproval, for he abhorred drunkenness.

Morais had become a good friend now, and could even take a mild teasing about his nationalist convictions with good humour. He was helping Michaelis carry the heavy S-bend for the lavatory plumbing when the latter called out to me: 'Hey, neighbour, look! Morais and I are bringing Enosis.' This was rather a good play on words for these great joints are called in Greek 'unions'. Morais managed rather a sheepish laugh.

I have one firm hold over my neighbours. I know more about Greece than they do. I am regarded with awe and respect because I have actually lived 'over there', among those paragons of demo-cratic virtue. Their idea of Greece is of Paradise on earth—a paradise without defect. And I have lived there, have Greek friends. . . . Now if I wish to bring pressure to bear upon my neighbour I simply say to him: 'My dear fellow, no Greek would do that, charge that, think that, etc. You astonish me.' And this phrase acts like a charm, for everyone is jealous of the good character of Greeks and tries to be as like them as possible. I am afraid I have become quite unscrupulous in my use of this weapon; when Pallis refused me water for my trees out of ill temper I brought him to his knees by comparing the Greek sense of 'philoxenia' with the Cypriot. He melted like an ice. When I suspect that I am being overcharged I have only to say: 'No Greek would try to profit from such stuff. They would give it away, particularly to a stranger.'

When Panos visits me with his family to offer me a vine he has had sent specially from Paphos for me, he is most amused by this gambit. 'I think if you told them no Greek wanted Enosis they would cease to want it too. Have you tried that?'

A Telling of Omens

'Under Ottoman rule, the Cypriotes had a clear majority of votes. Under English rule, the Cypriotes—counting both Christians and Mohammedans—are a minority of two in seven. . . .

'Under Ottoman rule, the representatives of the people had a majority of votes. Under English rule, representatives of the people are altogether excluded from the board. Formerly the Cypriotes had as much control over their own affairs as English people; now they are as helpless as a multitude of Russian serfs. . . .

'Such changes must be judged by the results; but for the time they have an ugly look. One hardly likes to see a popular franchise filched away, even though we get a cleaner street and stronger pier in payment for the theft. No rights are prized so much as local rights to which a man is born. The story of our city wards is full of warnings on that point. More than one Irish king has started on his downward path by tampering with the rights of city wards. No race, however weak, prefers a stranger in the chair of state.'

(*British Cyprus* by W. HEPWORTH DIXON, 1887)

But some of my visitors brought with them more troubling preoccupations which hardly seemed to find a place in that sunlit world of books and characters. One such was Alexis, an old Athenian friend—we had escaped together to Crete in '41 by caique and had been intermittently in touch ever since, though our work had taken us far apart. He was now at the United Nations and was passing through to Palestine. We dined together by moonlight at Zephyros, under the thick net of vines, and exchanged gossip about our common friends in different parts of the world. It was he who first voiced real concern about the shape things were taking in Cyprus. 'You see, the acceptance of the Greek case by Athens has altered the whole psychological picture here; it is a sort of moral endorsement for the right to Union which never existed before, and which if it isn't taken seriously may lead anywhere. And the F.O. seems fast asleep in London. Eden's failure to grasp the Greek offer is regarded by Athens as lunacy. After all, the only condition they asked was the change of one word in the statement: "The Cyprus case is closed"; had he agreed to substitute "postponed" for "closed" he would have evaded a hearing at UNO with all its possible secondary effects. Moreover Athens could then have refused to bow to Cypriot pressure and the thing would have simmered on here indefinitely.' It was distasteful in such scenery and over a wine which if it was not exactly vintage was at least of a good yeoman pedigree, to have to turn one's mind to the shallow bickerings of nations. Besides, I had come to Cyprus as a private individual, and had no concern with policy. 'How Greek is Cyprus, anyway?' I asked, thinking it of interest to hear an Athenian opinion. 'How Italian is Sicily?' he replied quietly. 'Have you had a look at the educational set-up and talked to the Cypriots? Language and religion —they are the determinants of national character, aren't they?'

'Does Athens want trouble here?'

'Of course not,' he exploded. 'But the tide has been rising there. The Cypriots have been appealing to the public through the clergy. The moral case is beginning to be widely recognized and with a short spell of international limelighting real strong feeling may be aroused. It's potentially most dangerous. The Greek Government could not go on for ever refusing to countenance the Cypriot case—because of the public. What they asked was a face-saver which would enable them to shut the Cypriots up. The formula they proposed carried no promises, no time-limit, nothing.'

'And now?'

'Now they'll take it to UNO.'

'With what result?'

'Perhaps none; but the case will have swollen to international size—which it doesn't merit; all sorts of new influences may emerge in the lobbying. I think you have got something potentially troublesome on your hands. The disposition both here and in Athens is for honourable settlement. A mere formula may do it. But you are letting it run on. Other factors lie in the background —Graeco-Turkish relations, for example. Aren't they of value? The Balkan Pact?'

'How typically Greek you are, Alexis. If I let you run on you'd deduce a world war from this one incident. We are politically rather dilatory, but the old ties are pretty strong, even here you know. You'd be surprised how much we are beloved.'

'Of course you are, you fool.'

'I mean that while everyone wants Enosis theoretically, there is no sense of urgency about it. In my village they would take a quarter of a century.'

'That's what I mean. The odds will shorten and tempers will rise as time goes on.'

'Perhaps. But people aren't blind either to the defects of Enosis whatever they say about the Government. It would mean hardships.'

'That is self-evident to us all. But you can't measure nationalist situations by a logical yardstick. You have got something here which could be set fire to.'

It sounded almost too preposterous, yet the logic of the thing was evident. But sitting there, over the sea, with a wedding-party at the next table but one singing Athenian songs and sending us an occasional bumper of wine, it seemed hardly worth an expenditure of thought and concern on the matter. 'I am sure the F.O. has weighed it up. You'll see. They will set a time-limit after a brisk haggle and we'll all subside into sun-bemused tranquillity.' Alexis smiled. 'God, how I wish you were right,' he said. He was in the swim of great affairs and could judge them better; I was a private citizen and could not follow their ebb and flow. 'Mine not to reason why,' I said. I turned the conversation in the direction of Michaelis and recounted some of my recent misadventures over the house. Alexis smiled, but his dark eyes remained thoughtful and I could see that I had not interrupted his train of thought, for no sooner had I finished than he resumed the thread of his political deliberations which even the magical moonlight breaking like surf upon the rocks below could not persuade him to abandon. It was disquieting that he should take the affair so seriously, and later when we drove home I turned his conversation over in my mind, comparing it with that of a young Israeli journalist whom I had encountered in the Abbey one sunny morning, taking pictures and discussing Cyprus with Kollis. He had said: 'The decision to take it to UNO was a grave error, though I suppose the Greeks had no alternative and were reacting to domestic pressure. I'm convinced they want to deflate the tyre, not blow it up any more—because it could go off.' 'Go off?' I echoed. 'Yes, like Palestine. I don't myself believe in Greek ill-intentions but they will need something stronger than the moral case if they are going to interest UNO which has so many other problems. You can't just point to a perfectly tranquil little island and ask for Union without more ado. The world must be convinced that the problem merits international consideration.' 'Are you suggesting they might start trouble here?' 'I'm saying that serious trouble could arise. There must be twenty Cypriots capable of blowing up something; or perhaps ten Cretans might take it into their shaggy heads to come over one day and show them how. The bulk of the people, as yet quite passive, would be forced to choose. We loved the British but we were forced by sentiment to rally to the cause when the storm broke.' Kollis looked acutely uncomfortable as I said: 'But you do not take into account Anglo-Greek amity.' 'It could not stand the test of open insurrection.'

He was an interesting young man and spoke almost perfect English with a slight slur. We drank a glass of wine at Dmitri's while he expatiated on his theme. He was obviously turning his ideas over in his mind before committing them to paper. 'As for the Government here,' he said, 'it is fast asleep. I had an interview with an official described as a Political Officer. Do you know what he said when I asked about Enosis? He said: "Well, old man, officially it doesn't exist, though unofficially it's a bit of a headache."' He drained his glass and stood up. 'There is nobody I have talked to who impressed me as having the faintest grasp of the situation. I wonder who does the Colonial Office reporting on it? There must be someone well briefed. There are two excellent Commissioners in the field, but both complained of neglect and lack of funds and backing. The general atmosphere is rather depressing, indeed I find it alarming. It's too peaceful to be true.'

My purely personal angle of vision, limited as it was by the horizon of my village, denied me such troubling reflections, yet I could not help but take them seriously since a disturbed island would mean a disturbed personal existence there. But here I consoled myself with the thought that, however dilatory we were, sooner or later we would find a frame of reference in which to contain the issue. Every factor was favourable to us. We were known and loved; belief in our fair-mindedness and political honesty was unshakable; and indeed it seemed to me that even a referendum held after an intervening period of self-government might result in something like a drawn match, particularly when one considered the Turkish vote of one in five. The situation as I saw it then seemed to me to offer us only a chance of getting closer to Greece and Turkey. The Turkish case, such as it was, was hardly formulated, and had achieved no telling mark upon world opinion. Of course the Turks would react sharply to the possibility of Greek administration and the substitution of the drachma for the pound, but with the moral sovereignty of the place conceded to the majority it might not even be necessary for Cyprus to leave the Commonwealth at all—so accommodating did the Athenians seem in their offer of bases in Crete. And I had ample evidence of the heavy qualifications under which the feeling for Enosis laboured—particularly among the middle classes who could foresee short commons ahead of them. Indeed, as with Morais, I felt that some frank and generous statement was the best way of disarming the Enotists. It was a pity that we were missing a catch or two, but then we usually did with our ponderous parliamentary methods. 'It will all come out right,' I said to the young man, feeling the buoyant warmth of the sunlight as it floated down through the leaves of the great Tree of Idleness, and he said nothing to dishearten me.

But if these considerations could be idly dismissed for the time being, it was not long before they appeared again in one or another different guise. I met a senior government official at Pearce's luncheon-table, for example, who addressed questions to me which rather took my breath away and followed them up with equally extraordinary assertions. He said, for example, that the Cypriots could claim no Greek heritage, since they didn't speak

Greek, that they were Anatolian hybrids. The Enosis feeling was whipped up by a few fanatical clergymen and had no genuine public support.... The sort of things which, on the face of it, might be open to argument, but which could certainly be tested in the field at first hand. These errors of judgement were the sort of things one always heard in the pubs frequented by the British community, and were perhaps not so important as I judged them to be. But what worried me was that officials in whom political power was vested should regard the whole problem as essentially a colonial rather than a European one, and apply the dusty yard-stick of other colonies to it. However negligible the Cyprus issue might seem it was after all soon to emerge on the plateau of inter-national relations; ignorance of the basic factors might prevent London using the tact, skill and brains which were needed to reach a settlement.

All this was given greater force and colour for me when I was commissioned to write a series of articles on the issue for an American Institute of International Relations bulletin—a dis-tasteful task, for I dislike writing about politics. Yet the money would buy me a door and a window for the balcony room, and I knew no better way of earning it. As my Israeli journalist had stepped into his car after shaking hands all round, a thought came to him. 'You English,' he said, 'seem to me to be completely under the spell of the Graeco-Roman period, and you judge everything without any reference to Byzantium. Nevertheless that is where you find the true source of Greek thinking, Greek *moeurs*. That is what you should all be made to study.' It was a prescient observation, and when I sat down to try to sort out my ideas about the Cypriot Greeks it came back to me with force. Certainly it explained much that I could not otherwise explain; it excused much. Even in a consideration of the Enosis problem the cultural heritage of Byzantium and its institutions illuminated everything. She was the true parent of Modern Greece

For Byzantine culture was something more than the sum of the elements it drew from languishing Hellenism and the influences of the Near East. It was an entity *per se*, not merely a colourful composite made up of assorted fragments of different cultures.

The 'Eastern Roman Empire' is in a sense a misnomer; for in 330 when Constantine the Great shifted the capital of the Roman world to Byzantium, he founded a spiritual empire quite unique in the style and resonance of its approach to problems, in its architecture, laws and literature. How is it that the West in its passionate romantic attachment to the Greek and the Graeco-Roman has ignored it so completely? It is difficult to say. For somewhat over eleven hundred years from its fateful founding to its fall in 1453, Greece was a part of that great octopus, whose tentacles touched Asia, Europe and Africa; and while the West was passing through the Dark Ages which followed the end of the Roman Empire, Constantinople sprang into exotic bloom and irradiated the world of science and politics with a new style of mind, a new vision. A true child of the Mediterranean, its spiritual temper was shown in its religious and artistic spirit. Politically it was characterized by a belief in the unbroken, indeed unbreakable, unity of Church and State—and the Greek Orthodox Church, its basic institution and mentor, has continued to flourish within the modern Greek state. Byzantine man could conceive of no political idea which did not assume the complete unification of Church and State; and the basic social unit of this great culture was expressed in a body of believers, composed not as a geographical entity, or on a racial pattern (for the Byzantine could belong to any one of a dozen), but purely as a sovereign consensus of Christian opinion. This opinion found its voice without any of the so-called democratic processes we know, without elections or the concept of majority rule as a purely procedural construct—a means of locating and probing the people's will. Assent or dissent was expressed at annual meetings in church whose object was to decide on both secular and religious affairs and transactions. A rare bloom, this; and the Greek churches and communities kept it alive through four centuries after Byzantium itself had gone down to dust and its children foundered deeper and deeper in the darkness which Turkey brought upon the world she inherited.

Darkness? These things are relative. What does amaze one however is that the Turks, perhaps through lack of a definite cultural pattern of their own, or of one worth imposing on the Greeks, left them freedom of religion, language and even local government—and indeed vested in them a large part of the Imperial administration: a recognition perhaps of the enviable qualities of restlessness and imagination which they themselves lacked. When modern Greece, therefore, emerged once more into the light of day as a geographical entity in 1821, it was as a step-child of Greek Byzance. For nearly four hundred years the Orthodox Church had served as a repository for the native genius or ethos of these latter-day Byzantines. Language had been carefully preserved so that apart from a few Turkish suffixes and a few score borrowed words Greek was still manifestly Greek, and the average Greek community emerged from the Turkish occupation less changed psychologically, say, than the British did from the Norman. Much that was Turkish in the way of manners, cookery, and so on was retained, but even this residue was soon infused with a liveliness quite foreign to the stately old-fashioned Turkish style with its contemplative and luxurious indolence. The clearest contrast offered us as a field for study is the Greek version of the Turkish shadow play which also emerged, live and kicking, in the person of Karaghiozi, from the Grand Turk's ear.

Things were no different in Cyprus; the long persecution of the Orthodox Church by the Latin culminated in the famous Bulla Cypria in 1260 which made the Latin Archbishop the supreme ecclesiastical power in the island over all clergy; the Orthodox bishops were mere dependants of the Latin bishops and at ordination were forced to take an oath of obedience to the Holy See. Paradoxically enough the powers of the Orthodox clergy were only restored in 1575—by the Turks themselves. Presumably they had seen the patient unobtrusive struggle of the Orthodox against the Latins, and wished to make common cause with them. At any rate when they came they were welcomed by many of the Cypriot peasants who had groaned under the harsh military dictatorship of Venice, and under their rule serfdom disappeared and a fair measure of local autonomy was enjoyed by the people of the island. And later?

'The unexpected phenomenon was now seen of the supreme

power and authority over Cyprus passing into the hands of the Archbishop of the Orthodox Church of Cyprus after about 1670, he being now regarded as the ethnarch or leader of the Greek-speaking section of the inhabitants. The original cause which brought the Orthodox prelates out of their previous obscurity was the desire of the central government in Constantinople to devise some local check upon its extortionate and not always submissive local officials; but by the beginning of the nineteenth century the influence acquired by them had become so paramount that the Turks became alarmed. In 1804 a rising against the Archbishop was quelled. In 1821, however, a more serious disturbance occurred and the authorities arrested and executed the Archbishop, bishops and leading personages of the Orthodox communion on the charge of conspiring with the insurgents in Greece, then struggling for their independence.'* From this one could see just how deeply hidden, and in what depths of unconscious historical process, the roots of Enosis lay hidden. Could it be extirpated if it could not be satisfied? I could not find it in my heart to believe such a thing possible. But it might be accommodated and even turned to our advantage; accommodated, that is to say, psychologically. . . . How could this best be done?

The absence of a political life of any sort in the island was a major weakness, and the current political scene divided itself neatly into two panels—Right and Left. It was significant, indeed very significant, that even the flourishing Communist party dared not ignore popular sentiment on the ethnic issue, and was forced to keep the Enosis plank as its foundation. This seemed irrationality bordering on lunacy when one considered what short shrift the Athens Government would have to give to the party and its adherents should Enosis come. Was the national call so powerful a vote-gatherer that even Marxists must respect it or see their party founder? It seemed so.

And then a constitution? The Greeks feared it, for as Panos said: 'We fear that any delay would spell the death of Union. We could easily be led away by political differences. Our unity would be impaired by a long period of waiting. If we accepted any

* Cyprus Handbook, 1919.

interim state of things we would founder in apathy and self-division. This is where the English could be so strong, if they produced a constitution so liberal as to be unexceptionable.' But there lay the rub. Unless Enosis itself were a reserved subject (which no Greek would accept) the legislature would always be overturned by the folly and exaggeration of the Unionists, who would clamour for immediate secession to Greece and dissolve the chamber. That explained the narrowness of the constitutions which Britain offered—they could not be broader and workable. An unsatisfactory hedge of thorns for us to climb through!

These conclusions did not come altogether, but singly and from many sources; the picture I formed was a composite made up of many fragments of gossip and thought, of many stray meetings in coffee-houses or along the hospitable sea-shore. I tried to condense them simply for the sake of clearness so that my essay for the bulletin should have the balance and perspective of a real document—not an ephemeral production. But even in this I did not feel directly concerned; my angle of vision was a selfish one.

I had also at this time begun to teach English to the students of the Nicosia Gymnasium—a task which though arduous was most interesting, since here one could feel the true temperature of nationalist feeling among the older students, who hardly a year later were to be among the terrorist groups. They could not foresee this, as yet, however, and their vociferous enthusiasms led them no farther than public demonstrations of faith in UNO. The thought of violence in Cyprus was far from everybody's mind. The Archbishop was a man of peace and everything would be settled peacefully. In answer to the question: 'What will you do if UNO rejects the appeal?' there was at that time only one answer: 'We will take it back. We will have peaceful demonstrations and strikes. We will mobilize world opinion.' Nobody ever replied 'We will fight,' and if one suggested it oneself as a question a look of deep pain would appear on the nationalist countenance, the voice would fall reproachfully as it replied: '*Fight*? Against Britain whom we love? Never!' Despite the mounting tide of feeling the mouthpieces of the movement never ceased to underline the phrase: 'Enosis contains no anti-British barb. We

love them and want them to stay as friends. But we want to be
our own masters.' But there were warnings, too, which bade us
hurry if we were to contain the high spirits of the people and
canalize them productively.

The Nicosia Gymnasium was a large rambling building inside
the old Venetian walls; together with the Archbishop's palace
it formed the spiritual nerve-centre of the Greek community.
With its rococo-Doric portals it looked, as all Greek gymnasia
do, like a loosely adapted design based on an early illustration of
a Doric temple by Schliemann. But it was a handsome place with
its broad roadway and feathery green pepper trees, and the little
Church of Saint John opposite was a delightful example of
Byzantine architecture.

By electing to live in my own village rather than in the capital
(which might have been more practicable) I retained a link with
the rural community, even though my hours were such that I had
to leave the house at about half past four. I rose, therefore, with
the shepherds and scrambled down to the Abbey with the first
wave of sheep or cows to where my little car stood, white with
dew, under the Tree of Idleness. Light would just be breaking up
out of the sea, and against it the rosy spars of the Abbey ruins
outlined themselves in sulphurous streaks of bronze and scarlet.
The dawns and the sunsets in Cyprus are unforgettable—better
even than those of Rhodes which I always believed were unique
in their slow Tiberian magnificence. As I breasted the last rise
where the road falls like a swallow towards Kyrenia I paused for
a minute to watch the sun burst through the surface mists of the
sea and splash the mountain behind me with light. Usually I had
someone with me—a shepherd cadging a lift to some distant
holding, or the sleepy postmaster hurrying to Kyrenia for the
first sorting. We smoked in silence and watched the slow con-
flagration of the world from this little table-land before humming
down the breath-taking declivity into Kyrenia. A quick loading
of oil and petrol and I would start to climb the range, the sun
climbing with me, balcony by balcony, ridge by ridge; until as I
breasted the last loop of the pass the whole Mesaoria would
spread out under the soft buttery dawn-light, languid and green

as a lover's wish; or else shimmer through a cobweb of mist like the mirage of a Chinese water-print. And always, far away, at the end of the great plain rose the two steep fingers of Santa Sophia which marked the capital.

My links with my village were also fortuitously preserved in another way—for some of my villagers had sons and daughters studying at the Gymnasium, and there were at least three or four of them waiting for me when I arrived, ready to carry my books and claim friendship with me because their fathers were my friends.

This indeed was the perfect laboratory in which to study national sentiment in its embryonic state—indeed a Greek island within Cyprus, with its spiritual and political aspirations condensed around the person of the Ethnarch (who was often visible, pacing the old-fashioned balconies of the Palace with an air of gentle reserve) and embodied in Greek language and Greek institutions. Here, too, bloomed that extraordinary flower of chance, the quixotic irrational love of England which no other nation seems to have, and in a fantastic sort of way it flowered in blissful co-existence with the haunting dream of Union. It was almost impossible to believe one's ears at times, so contradictory and so paradoxical did the whole thing seem. The portrait of Byron, for example, in the great hall, at the head of the whiskered team of shepherds and farmers whose efforts brought freedom to Greece. On the headmaster's desk stood a portrait of Churchill gravely listening to his fervent denunciations of British policy and its injustices to the Cypriot people. 'We will never flag, never give in,' he assured me, glancing at the portrait as if to draw moral strength from the grave toby-jug face with its sulky reproving glare.

Modern Greek history can hardly explain the fantastic romance which the Greek mind has built up around the story of the 1821 Revolution; England 'sent her greatest poet to help them raise the flag. He died for Greece and England—they are both not countries, but symbols of liberty incarnate.' (This from a school essay.)

I was swept along on the tide of these feelings whose bewildering polarity and succession of moods followed one another so fast that there was hardly time for one to cohere before another took its place; from the Girls' Sixth form, plunged in anti-British anarchy, I crossed the road to hear a classics student reciting Byron with tears in his eyes. They were admirable children, each wrapped in the bright silken cocoon of a dream; sleepwalkers who were awakened only by the crash of a pistol or a bomb, and who then gazed about them wonderingly to find that all these brilliant words and thoughts had a resonance only in death, and that the stark geometrical designs of commerce and policy cared nothing for these flowing free-hand poetical designs of a perfect world where Union with Greece meant something not unlike the mystic's Union with the Infinite. The tragedy is that it need not have happened.

Need not? It is easy to be wise after the event. Yet in all honesty I cannot be sure whether my own approach to the problems of Enosis would have been more fruitful if it had been embodied in a policy and applied. But in these early days, under the spell of the summer sun and the unpremeditated kindness everywhere, there hardly seemed to be the need for undue haste and worry.

The Greek educational system itself is an oddity. It was designed by the Germans with a thoroughness and efficiency which is spell-binding. The curriculum might have been designed to keep the student awake all day and all night—so overloaded was it, and so crammed with subjects. In the hands of Greeks, too, it had acquired a few subtle modulations without losing its basic form. Teachers were issued with a huge register graduated and squared in which one apparently entered every breath drawn by one's charges. Intensive tests and checks had to be listed therein and a complicated system of marking adhered to—based apparently on the Queensberry rules. As the curriculum was so vast there was no time to expound. Blocks of printed matter were hurled at the students to learn parrot-fashion. The results were carefully noted on a sort of temperature-chart and then transferred to the register. As there was always a riot if students found their marks falling below the required pass standard one began to fudge them—if only for the sake of peace and quiet. The teacher's life was a rather tricky one, for the student regarded it as his right to complain to the head if he felt that he was being victimized—and everybody who did not get ten out of ten felt immediately victimized. Many were the storms, the public inquiries, the denunciations, while more often than not the parents of a protesting child would appear at the hearing and wave threatening umbrellas at the responsible master. It was marvellous, and the situations which arose would have delighted the heart of a Dickens. But the professional teacher in the Gymnasium lived a life of acute mental unease. Twice I heard of cases where the teacher undermarked, i.e. victimized, the daughter of a rich and powerful man, and brought down the father's wrath upon the unfortunate headmaster. 'Tread softly, tread lightly, piano pianissimo' was the watchword.

The composition of the classes was pleasingly democratic, though, and very reminiscent of a Scottish school. There was absolutely no class feeling; Andreas' son in his tattered clothes sat next to the son of Mr. Manglis, my millionaire, and they were firm friends. But then in this sense Greeks have always been the world's greatest democrats.

I was exposed to three of the school's many classes—the two Sixth forms, male and female, and one which roughly corresponded to an English upper fourth. Epsilon Alpha. This was full of incorrigibles aged around fourteen who spent their time in a variety of ways—but never in listening to me. To achieve silence was impossible—a soft but persistent susurrus like a slow puncture was the nearest one could get to this—and the normal was a growling wave of chatter which rose and fell like a sea. I tried, as an experiment, sending talkers out of the room one by one, in order to see at what stage the class became controllable. I was left at last with three students. As no corporal punishment was permitted in the school it was impossible to do more than gesticulate, foam, dance and threaten: which is what my Greek colleagues did for the most part.

Stigma Gamma was the appropriate title of the Girls' Sixth, and here I began my ministrations at seven each day, entering the large unheated classroom with a shiver. They rose politely enough and repeated a prayer under the prompting of the head girl. Then I read out their names from the register—like the dramatis personae to a Greek tragedy: 'Electra, Io, Aphrodite, Iolanthe, Penelope, Chloe'. Like the boys, they were a mixed group in the social sense; Electra's father was a gardener in Kythrea, Io's father a judge, Penelope the daughter of a shoemaker. They comprised a cross-section of Nicosia and the surrounding districts. But they were uncomfortably united in one thing, besides Enosis, and that was a passionate, heart-rending determination to marry their English teacher. Every morning my desk bore half a dozen offerings—Electra brought black roses and white, Chloe a special kind of meat ball made by her grandmother, Aphrodite a volume of poems I had mentioned. If their devotion had been accompanied by greater self-control in class life would have been easier; but no sooner had I opened the proceedings than each started to do work of her own. One sewed secretively, another made darts, a third made a catapult from a paper-clip, a fourth decided to enter up her diary for the day ('Today he looks cross, my teacher, his jaw is set, his brow grim, but I love him all the more'). Reprisals were always accompanied by agonizing tears as the expelled creature betook herself to the library where she ran the risk of being found by the headmistress. Heaven alone knows what punishments a girl-student might be liable to undergo. I never dared to ask. I maintained throughout a decorous reserve which always hovered on the edge of laughter. Aphrodite, appropriately enough, was the most spirited and most difficult of the girls. Her father was a rich confectioner of the town and she had all the confidence and repose which comes of never having been short of money. She was indeed as beautiful as her counterpart in myth was supposed to be; but she was something more—she was a writer. She read poetry to herself in a low murmuring voice and behaved for most of the time as if she were succumbing to ether. But these dreamy Chopinesque moods alternated with moods of anarchy. Invited to the blackboard, she had a habit of passing behind the back row of girls and with one flowing movement, invisible as a conjurer's pass, of tying their pigtails together—so that by the time I was studying her blackboard technique a riot had broken out among the back benches, where six girls found themselves yoked like oxen. Invited to write an essay on her favourite historical character she never failed to delight me with something like this: 'I have no historical character but in the real life there is one I love. He is writer. I dote him and he dotes me. How pleasure is the moment when I see him came at the door. My glad is very big. How pleasure is that moment. As all people are dreamed so am I,' and so on. Her essays were a perpetual delight; but they were not the only ones. Dimitra also wrote some which were memorable, though she always verged upon self-pity. 'I am orphan and have never been enjoyed,' was the beginning to one. She also was afflicted by the verb 'dote', as indeed the whole class was. This was the unfortunate fruit of a day when Aphrodite asked me slyly why English had only one word for 'love' when Greek had several; in my attempt not to let the Empire down I produced 'adore' and 'dote'. The latter stuck like a burr. But unfortunately each girl elected to marry it to a different preposition so that my essays the next day were full of heart-rending examples. Electra described the King and Queen of Greece 'doting at each other'; while Chloe wrote: 'When they married they were in a great dote. He was so excitement and she was so excitement. They were both excitement.' Which was fair enough I suppose; only it was difficult to see how on earth to correct such work intelligibly. Driving home in the afternoon I used to brood on these problems, mentally conjugating 'dote' like a Bach fugue, 'I dote, thou dotest, he dotes. . . .' On Independence Day I found the blackboard shrouded with crape and with the legend on it 'WE DEMAND OUR FREEDOM.' Everyone was looking extra-ordinarily tense and self-possessed. After prayers Aphrodite stepped forward and handed me a petition signed by the class insisting on the right of the Cypriot people to be free. I thanked her. 'You understand us, sir,' she said, and her voice had a distinct tremor in it. 'So you will understand this. . . . We do not wish to be impolite or embarrass you. . . . We love England. . . .' I laid it silently beside the black rose from Kythrea and the meat pie and the confiscated knitting, hair-slides, ribbons and copy of *Endymion*. It seemed to me to symbolize the situation perfectly.

The boys were quite as colourful, though in many ways more exigent. I am thinking of Stephanides, the wine-merchant's son with his battered grin and pocket comb, of Kallias, of that fat ruffian Joanides, of Spiropoulos and Grikos and Aletraris. . . . It cost me something to hold them in check. Yet they were an easy-going and polite lot of youths, no better and no worse than their counterparts in Europe, and all bedevilled by the national dream. Handsome Leonides, for example, who stayed behind one day and asked me whether I would assist him in writing to a pen-pal in Glasgow. Her letter and photograph were produced after much blushing and scraping of the floor with his toe. It was an odd letter from a factory-hand who was dying to know about the world and thought that a pen-pal was the best way to find out. She asked Leonides whether everyone was black in Cyprus and wore nightshirts. These questions did not hurt so much as astonish him. 'I thought such an advanced race as the English would know this sort of thing. If I, a Greek, know that they are white in England and only wear nightshirts in bed, how is it that she . . . ?' I answered these questions as best I could, and drafted a reply or two for him, leaving one or two of his characteristic mistakes; but here again I noticed in his draft the word 'dote' which proved that he had somehow been in contact with the Girls' Sixth. When I accused him of it he blushed and grinned. 'It is Aphrodite,' he admitted at last, overcoming a formidable resistance. 'We ride home together on our bicycles. We are doted on each other, sir.'

Kallias was a strongly built youth of eighteen, with good shoulders and a classical head on them. His curly hair was always crisply trimmed and brushed ack from a broad forehead with well-placed blue eyes. His manners were perfect and he always threw his moral weight on the side of good order in class—for which I was deeply grateful. I had heard he was the school's greatest athlete, and certainly he was deeply respected. It was all the more surprising one day to see him being inattentive and to be forced to confiscate some papers. These proved to be of interest. The first was the draft of an essay for me in which he had been asked to write a letter to a public figure he admired—some world-renowned musician or politician or what-not—in English. His offering read as follows:

My Dear Reg Park:

I am admiring you for my health. You are the best body-builder in the world and the crip-dumbels for chest and arms are the fruit of a superb imagination. In my dreams I am always found in London and am much enjoyed. . . .

Among the other fragments was his identity card with a picture on it proving Kallias to a be founder member of the Weight-Lifters' Association of Great Britain, and a half-completed form for a course in Dynamic Tension in which he had been asked the following questions: 'Are you ruptured? Constipated? Breath Bad? Tongue Coated? Pains in the back? Do you tire easily? Are you married?' To all of which he had replied in the negative. . . .

In these classes, too, I encountered the same shifting wind of popular opinion which hovered between anti-British intransigence and the old ineradicable affection for the mythical Briton (the 'Phileleftheros') the Freedom-lover, who could not help but approve of Enosis as an idea. Had he not virtually created Greece out of the black dust of foreign tyranny? And then, of his own free will, sealed the gift by handing back the Seven Islands? What could be anomalous in the desire of Cyprus to share the same fate? Even the great Churchill had said it was to be so one day. . . .

This was roughly the line of thought. But of course all this feeling was kept permanently at the boil by official direction, by the press, by the heady rhetoric of local demagogues and priests. I asked a teacher why such pains were taken to keep the young people in a state of ferment. 'Because,' he said, 'we must mobilize opinion for our appeal, and everyone is so slack in Cyprus. Solidarity of opinion is not enough—besides it is there, it exists. But suppose we have to take peaceful action to back up our case, demonstrations, strikes, and so on? Students would play a large part in helping to form world opinion.' 'And if they get out of hand?' He smiled. 'They will never get out of hand, we have them *there*.' He took up a handful of air in his clenched fist, showed it to me, and replaced it. In those days it cost little to be a hero in words or on paper.

Paul was seventeen, an orphan. He lived in the school lodging-house, and spent all his spare time in the library studying the ancient Greek poets. His father had been killed in Italy serving with the British forces and the boy still proudly owned a service medal which had been sent to him after his father's death. He was a thin, solitary boy, burning with hunger for some chance of advancement in life, which he felt to be closing in upon him. He thought perhaps he would like to be a teacher somewhere, perhaps in England. He was never troublesome in class, and indeed did not seem to have many friends. His work was tidy and pains-taking, and the teacher who was resident supervisor of the School Lodgings told me that he often found him studying in the small hours of the morning. I won his respect by telling him about the modern Greek poets, some of whom I knew, and show-ing him the work of Seferis, which astonished and somewhat frightened him. But he was enthralled, and borrowed nearly all my books with the same inarticulate, fervent hunger with which he addressed himself to the blackboard when I wrote on it.

One day he stayed after the class had gone, ill at ease, and pre-occupied. 'Can I ask you a question, sir?' 'Yes.' 'You will not be annoyed?' 'Of course not.' He took a deep breath, sat down at his desk, composed his long spidery fingers and said: 'Will England force us to fight for our freedom here?' I registered astonishment. 'I have been reading an essay,' he said, 'in which it says that freedom has never been given, but always taken, always earned at the cost of blood. A people that is not willing to accept the price is not ready for Freedom. Perhaps England understands this and is waiting for us to prove ourselves ready to die for freedom?'

The paradox, of course, was that in the technical sense they were freer under Britain than the Athens Government could afford to let them be—but who would believe that? And then, again, while they enjoyed almost perfect civic freedom, they had no say in their own affairs from the point of view of popular suffrage—an intolerable state of affairs for the heirs of Byzantium. They existed under tutelage, under laws composed by some invisible body of lawgivers in Government House, which none of them had ever seen. This was a crucial point purely psychologically—and it gave the island life a strange flavour of stagnation, though the administration was just and conceived with conscience and regard. A *feeling* of foreignness, of alienation from themselves, persisted: somewhere, dimly, they felt that this weird, padded, essentially suburban life was not theirs. Somewhere the values they sought would be found to depend on the spare, frugal Mediterranean pattern of things—the light-intoxicated anarchy of Greece always leaped at them like a panther. But the more we talked of these things, the less easy was it to pin them down and formulate them—for they depended on values inherent in a whole way of life, the Byzantine way, not the European. And yet what they most wanted they also feared. A Greek life was the life of a lean wolf, offering no security or material advantage; unsound in administration, torn by the fluctuations of poverty and self-seeking; terribly insecure. 'How *can* the Cypriot want Enosis?' the English residents of Cyprus who knew Greece kept asking themselves. One can well understand them. Military service in the Greek armed forces? Crippling taxation? Bankruptcy? Poor administration?

Surely it was all founded in a childish bad dream from which they would awaken one day and realize that they could enjoy perfect Greek freedom within the Commonwealth—enjoying the best of both worlds? Was it not all due to a lack of education?

These are the sort of questions I inflicted on Maurice Cardiff in his lovely Turkish house on the outskirts of the town where I enjoyed a free lunch several times a week—a real blessing, for my budget was a slender one. But he himself, with his long experience of the Balkans and his knowledge of Greece, had already asked them of himself and answered many of them; though his findings fell for the most part upon deaf ears.

To my vague and questioning remarks he responded with concrete ideas, concrete assessments of a situation which he regarded far more seriously than I: his work gave him a stake in it. Our tenure in Cyprus had perhaps been one of folly and neglect—but both words could be summed up in the phrase 'poverty'. Financial and political poverty had gone hand in hand. He nodded when I suggested that the administration had never had the brains either to see what bubbled beneath the deceptive surface of Cyprus life or the money to do anything about it. How could we answer Cyprus in the demands she made unless we could give her what she felt, obscurely, dimly, we had to offer—a stake in the larger world? The youth of the little island was bursting with brains, talent, and an industry honestly comparable to that of the Germans or Italians. There was no outlet for it. Our educational system was vestigial, limited, more out of date even than the gymnasium system in which I was working. Yet it was staffed by devoted and loyal men, who had spent years teaching the lesser breeds their alphabet.

The one clearing-house for ideas which the island lacked—apart from a Senate—was a university; but even this was not enough. In Nicosia there was not even a public swimming bath let alone a theatre, or a bookshop where one could buy a French newspaper. . . . These things came to me with the force of a revelation. Yet they were there, self-evident: and factors which contributed to though they could not cause the general air of suffocating inertia which pervaded everything.

In a sense it was our failure to project the British ethos, to make available to the Cypriot the amplitude of our own civic and cultural resources, which had contributed to his sense of neglect, to the frustrated feeling he had of being an outsider. The basic failure lay somewhere in our inability to include him, and his set of values, in the British family. In England he could be a waiter; but in Greece—'starving Greece'—Cyprus had a stake, indeed had given the Foreign Office a head, not to mention two generals, and a host of administrators, lawyers and so on. They 'belonged' there; to the British they were a 'bunch of Cyps'—as one might say 'Chimps'. At least these were the impressions which I gained from those long afternoons when, ashamed of trading on Cardiff's warm-hearted hospitality, I spent my lunch hour in the fragrant smoke and turmoil of the great market, enjoying a *kebab* from a meat-stall, or a pie whose filling detonated between one's teeth with the savour of garlic and sage as one bit into it; afternoons spent rambling round the great Mosque with a fellow-teacher or student—or for contrast spent lunching in one of the hostelries where the British business community gathered and where one could surprise public opinion in its raw, unfermented state over a glass of Pilsener. All these elements fused slowly together to give me a composite picture of Cyprus as she was today, and to explain why she was in the state in which she found herself.

And these experiences I took to the quiet courtyard and rush-grown private water-tank around which Cardiff's old house had been built, to discuss them with him over a glass of *retzina*, recently received from Athens, or some of the light good table-wine of Cyprus; and indeed to temper the preoccupations which grew out of them with the more congenial private gossip about common friends and the books—the endless books—with which we passed our innermost time.

By now he and his wife Leonora were frequent visitors to Bellapaix; they brought their friends—and often found other common friends camped at my mother's convivial fireside, trying their skill upon some choice offering of Clito's. My return to the old house in the hills every night was a perpetual joy: not only to know that a new outwork of bricks or a window-frame had been laid in my absence, but also to have the excited uncertainty about whom I should find already there, sitting in the firelight, waiting for me. Sometimes it was Marie, freshly back from Paris or London, loaded with books; or Ines with her falcon's beauty strumming the guitar and singing some magical passage from *flamenco*; or Sir Harry gravely discoursing on chapters in Cyprus history which lay outside the dull dusty present—the severed head of Oneseilos buzzing with honey-bees, or Berengaria being crowned in Limassol, or that odd King of Neo-Paphos who invented an early form of fan by anointing himself with Tyrian oil, which his doves adored, in order that their fluttering wings should keep him cool during meals.

And the Abbey itself was there, fading in the last magnetic flush from the horizon, with its quiet groups of coffee-drinkers and card-players under the Tree of Idleness. At full moon we dined there, barefooted on the dark grass, to watch the lights winking away along the fretted coast and the great bronze coin shake itself free of the sunset-mist and climb with slow, perfectly punctuated steps into the nether heaven, bubbling into the great rose-window of the eastern wall like a visitant of the Gothic world. Here in the striped darkness, dotted with pools of luminous moonlight, we walked and talked, the smell of roses and wine and cigars mingling with the humbler scent of the limes, or the whiffs of bruised sage coming to us from the face of the mountain behind where Buffavento rose slowly to meet the moon, like a mailed fist. And somewhere upon the outer silence would come the haunting liquid music of a flute perhaps, its five-tone scale like a thread spun upon the silent air between the pines.

How could such a sun-bruised world be transformed, be any different? It was hard to believe, listening to the silence-ennobling voice of Pearce or Marie upon the darkness of the old cloisters. Or at midnight taking a car and riding along the deserted coast, clad in nothing but bathing-costumes, to where the deserted mosque lay, perched over the water, solitary as a sea-bird, its shuttered windows flaring at the moon. . . .

Twice encamped on a moonlit beach I was woken by the sound of a guttering caique-engine and the voices of fishermen (as I thought), who had drawn inshore to mend their ragged *seines*; and once, under the shadow of a great carob-tree near the mosque, I saw two lorries drawn up off the shore-road, silent and without lights, and full of men who were not smoking. They were teams, I thought, of carob-pickers getting away to an early start in order to deal with some remote holding perhaps. I had forgotten these things almost as soon as the little car rolled off among·the olives to breast the main road for Kyrenia. They constituted a firmly closed door—closed as irrevocably as the Cyprus question was in the minds of our mandarins in London—and only to be abruptly opened by the crash of dynamite months later.

The house grew, Marie's wattle encampment became a settlement, a walled garden full of premature trophies which would grace the house when it was completed: Indian peacocks, parrots, carved chests, inlaid lamps, infant palms. The hermits of Lapithos made friendly incursions to advise and counsel—and inevitably left her brimming with new ideas. Lamplight, wine and good conversation sealed in the margins of the day so that one slept at night with a sense of repletion, of plenitude, as if one were never more to wake.

It was now too that I met the Colonial Secretary of the island at Austen Harrison's lunch-table, where he proposed that I should apply for the post of Press Adviser, then about to fall vacant. There was much that needed doing in the field of public relations and it was felt that someone knowing Greek and having a stake in the island's affairs might do better than a routine official. The idea was exciting, and indeed would solve all my problems, giving me the scope to finish the house as it deserved to be finished and the leisure to explore all that remained as yet unknown in the island. Indeed it seemed an unhoped-for stroke of luck and I suspected that the original idea had not been the Government's but had originated in the mind of Austen Harrison or Maurice Cardiff, both of whom were most anxious about the shape of things and eager to see some sort of solution to a problem which threatened the ordinary day-to-day life of the island which we all treasured so much.

Moreover at this time I felt that perhaps such errors as there were might lie in assessing the situation on the spot, in lack of adequate reporting on it. I had no means of knowing what sort of liaison the Government maintained with London, but I knew that in the field their information was largely based on reports from their own departmental officers which, while factually accurate, lacked political pith and the sort of interpretations which are essential if high-level dispatches are to be what they should be—namely guides to action. More than this, the problem of Cyprus as it was developing was one of several dimensions, and the effect of a coffee-house conversation in Nicosia could not be evaluated unless one could see it from three angles at the same time, namely from Athens, London and Nicosia. How could semiliterate peasants, with a purely parochial outlook, be expected to do this?

In this field I might certainly be of use to the Government and play a small part in bringing about the sort of solution which I felt, we all felt, must be round the corner.

I was full of optimism, living as I did in both worlds—the noisy urban world of Greek Nicosia with its mounting tide of strikes and demonstrations, its demagogues and self-elected heroes whose shrillings filled the still cloudless air like the whizzing of gnats round some stagnant pond; and the no less Greek world of the village, lumbering quietly among the foot-hills, with its ancient bemused courtesies and unworldly kind-nesses. Asleep.

Even the signs and portents of the day were less disquieting because always the fine manners of the Cypriots were there to disprove the noisy contentions of Athens radio—whose en-venomed shrillness had not yet reached meridian. The villagers listened with a kind of uncomprehending pleasure to the strange, yet familiar accents of this metal God which tried to convince them that they were other than they were—peaceful, order-loving, and secure in life and person. They listened as uncompre-hending children might listen to the roll of distant drums which competed with the gentleness and timidity of their hearts in their insistence on other values based in hate, in spite, in smallness. Who was the enemy, where was he to be found, the tyrant who had liberated Greece? They watched me with speculative curi-osity as I walked up the main street with the three small sons of my builders, one carrying my books and paper, another a loaf of bread, a third the mended primus I had retrieved from Clito that afternoon. . . . Try as they might they could not marry the two images. Wherein did my tyranny lie, I who was so polite and who was teaching my daughter Greek? It was a great puzzle. And if they accepted me, were they not to accept the other Englishmen they knew—each Cypriot had a dozen personal friends among the tyrants whom he had come to respect and love. And even if they tried to hate the Government, the very abstraction resolved itself into the faces of officers whom they knew, servants of the crown who spoke Greek, who had built them a well or a road. The problem was to locate the enemy, for Athens said that he was everywhere, but in the island itself he had dissolved into a hundred fragments whose context was personal meetings and personal affections. The villagers floundered in the muddy stream of undifferentiated hate like drowning men. They were glad to hear the Government abuse like children who exult when one, bolder than the rest, cheeks the headmaster. It was exciting. But they were also assailed by the undertow of misgivings and anxiety when they heard the demagogues speak of bloodshed, of fighting, and of sacrifices. They too were sleepwalkers whom the bombs awoke, and whose resolution was hardened deliberately, day by day, by those who understood to the full the technique of insurrection.

Walking up the dark road with me one night Andreas said: 'Tell me, sir, soon England will solve all this and we can be at peace—is it not so? I am getting worried about the boys; at school they seem to spend all their time singing nationalist songs and joining demonstrations. It will all end soon, will it not?' He sighed, and I sighed with him. 'I am sure we will come to understand one another,' I said. 'I don't say you will get Enosis because of our responsibilities in the Middle East; but I'm sure we will come together.' Andreas pondered. 'But if we have offered every facility for bases does that not satisfy England? Must she maintain sovereignty over Cyprus? Why? We say to her: take as much as you want, build what you like, stay for ever, but let us have our island. At least if not today, tomorrow, in twenty years. . . .' The question of sovereignty was always the basic complex and I had been forced to design a sophistry to meet it. 'Your brother has a piece of land, Andreas. You love him. He loves you. He tells you to borrow it and build a house on it for your family. "Build what you like," he says, "and it will remain yours for ever." Now, while you love and trust him—who knows? Strange things happen in the world. Would it not be wiser to keep the title-deeds of the land before spending your capital in building on it? That is what England feels.'

This answer he found at once satisfying and troubling. 'I see,' he said slowly. 'We have a proverb,' I said (it was in fact a

Turkish proverb retailed to me by Sabri), 'an Englısn proverb
which says: "In business never trust anyone—not even your own
kin."' Andreas smiled at this. 'I thought you were a more trusting people,' he said. 'Now I know why you are called Foxes for
your cunning,' and he presented a forefinger briefly at his temple
as a tribute to the perfidiousness of Albion.

The Winds of Promise

'The fox in her sleep dreams always of chickens.'
'If the baby doesn't cry, Mother won't suckle.'
'One does not go to Hell to light a cigarette.'
(Cypriot Greek Proverbs)

My appointment, somewhat to my surprise, was ratified in the late spring, and I was bidden to the Government Lodge in Troodos for my first meeting with the Governor. Marie elected to drive me up the mountain switchback as her racing car made much better time than mine on the steep gradients, and we set off one faultless morning, to sweep across the Mesaoria towards the foothills before the sun had fully breasted the bastions of the Gothic range and set the dust rising from the brittle and arid soils in which, by high summer, nothing more would grow until the autumn rains. The ugliness of the plain was, so to speak, at the height of its beauty—a range of tones vibrating with the colours of damson, cigar-leaf, putty and gold-leaf. Here and there upon a skyline, diminished by distance and somehow made the more significant for being so isolated and so small, a team of camels oozed across the dusty screen. Their riders wore coloured turbans, spots of cobalt or crimson or that resonant dark blue—a vitreous marine blue—which is so characteristically Turkish in tone.

We ringed the black elephantine bastions of Nicosia, stopping only to buy a bag of yellow cherries, and set off like the wind across the plain once more, trailing our banner of dust, to where in the foothills the road began its harsh and sinuous ascent into the cool airs and oak forests once dedicated to Jove. We were in good heart, for despite the disquieting newspaper reports of demonstrations and speeches, rumours were in the air of new approaches, new assessments.

The mountain villages are beautiful—and today Kakopetria, for example, folded in upon itself, coiling round the rim of a mountain torrent, shaded by enormous white poplars, looked hauntingly peaceful; but higher up, the rocky banality of the range is unrelieved by any man-made features—while a village like Amiandos made us catch our breath in pain. It lies against the side of a mountain which has been clumsily raped. The houses, factories and shacks are powdered white as if after a heavy snowfall; mounds of white snow rise in every direction, filling the cool still airs of the mountain with the thin dust of asbestos. Men and women walked about in this moon-landscape, powdered into ghoulish insignificance by the dust. A man with a white wig and white moustache shouted 'Hullo' as we passed.

The little lodge that Rimbaud built lies, as do most of the Government quarters, in an unhealthy-looking ravine choked with pines, and denied any one of the thousand magnificent views in which the range abounds. It seemed like an H.Q. carefully chosen against the fear of air attack. The building itself has nothing to commend it except the memory of its author whose work is commemorated in a finely worded plaque, for it is of traditional Public Works design, and resembles any one of a thousand such villas in the Indian hill-stations. Indeed the whole of Troodos looked like some unlovely and ill-considered hill-station, with its primitive latrines and general air of hopeless desolation. The thought of spending a holiday there, even in one of the three or four well-found hotels, would hardly commend itself to any but the bed-ridden. One would yawn oneself to death.

The Governor was a large, quiet and deeply attentive man with a record of excellent public service, well briefed in the island's past history and anxious to make some considered offering towards the present discontents, if only they could be isolated and analysed. If he had a faintly aggrieved air it was because he suspected he was being made a fool of—for he had been reading the nationalist press only to learn with pain and astonishment that our rule in Cyprus resembled something thought up by Attila, and that we were dedicated to plucking Hellenism out by the roots and decreeing a 'perpetual enslavement of Greeks'. 'Where do they get all this stuff?' he asked. It was easy to answer though not to excuse; the fires of Enosis could not be banked unless every Greek peasant could be made to feel enslaved, and what facts would not bear out emotions based on fictions might achieve. Most of this fire and brimstone came from the pulpit, but quite a lot came from people politically on the make, like the Mayor of Nicosia, who exhibited much of the weird polarity of feelings I had observed among the students of the Gymnasium. In other words, while he wanted Enosis he didn't want it immediately; and while he hated the foul oppressor he sincerely and genuinely loved England, and his well-merited O.B.E. was a much-cherished decoration. (After almost every speech the English newspaper attacked him and suggested that he return it as an earnest of sentiments expressed; but he did not comply with the demand.)

The Governor himself was in several minds about the situation; on the one hand people assured him it was serious, on the other the day-to-day transactions arising out of it suggested the crazy discontinuities of some Irish farce. One thing, however, was clear: all this blasting and bombardiering was conducive to disaffection, and this must be stopped. He was advised that a serious warning should be issued to the press and public to toe the line, accompanied by the offer of a constitution, and the wheels had been set in motion to effect this. I asked if I could see the text, but as my appointment was not yet effective, this might have been a breach of privilege. I told him, however, that at the moment it would be wiser not to give any excuse to make the Greek appeal one that could point to evidence of illiberality within the island, or of victimization. Moreover, dealings with the press were always tricky, as the press constitutes a world-freemasonry, and nothing could more quickly influence public opinion for or against a measure than the attitude of the press. We talked soberly along these lines before I took my leave to find Marie idly eating cherries under a pine and flipping the pages of an architectural manual.

I had found Sir Robert moderate, just and painstaking; and if I had any reservation at all it was only that I felt that the problem was not being regarded as a European political problem but as a purely Colonial one. The angle of vision was one which took no account of Athens and Ankara—and here, it seemed to me, were the two nodes of the thing which determined the *international* aspects of it. Colonial officials, trained to direct rule, will always find this difficulty in dealing with problems outside the rule of order, and which in the final analysis can be bent to compliance by the use of force. Those who work in sovereign territory have to cultivate a suppleness and dissimulation, a tactical mind and a reserve because no issues can be forced: they must be engineered. The difference is between the craft of a fly-fisherman and someone who dynamites from a rowing boat.

The key to the whole thing was the acceptance by Athens of the Enosis case as meriting international consideration. As far as I could see most of the officials were still thinking in terms of the riots of '31 which did not spread into island-wide disaffection precisely because this factor was missing—Greek acceptance. In a sense everything now was vitally changed; yet our political approach had not appraised the change. It was summed up for me by the words of a fellow-official at the lunch party which followed: 'I've seen all this before. You'll see, we'll let them go so far and then simply smack them down.' The trouble was that the hypothetical smack would echo now at the United Nations, in the ears of those whose attention could be more quickly drawn to 'colonial oppression' than to an Indian famine; above all, it seemed necessary to provide no martyrs who would foster the Greek case. The island was, in fact, quiet despite the strikes and demonstrations; the press was free; there was nobody in prison for a political offence; life was normal. Moreover the Greeks were apparently presenting their case with such an overwhelming politeness and friendliness that the whole thing might pass over the heads of the public world in silence. It was essential not to envenom it any further until the results of the appeal could be judged.

Judge my surprise then when I came down the hill one August morning to find that the Bow Street runners had affixed to the door of the tavern a majestic document couched in Mandarin which offered a constitution together with a serious admonition against disaffection—all in the *style pompier* so beloved by jurists, and officials. Neither admonition nor constitution was very clear, and as I joined a bearded group of shepherds round the placard all lip-reading with ferocious concentration, I could not help sharing the sigh of sheer bewilderment that went up. 'What does it mean?' said Dmitri in heavy bewilderment. 'Does it mean we can't speak of Enosis any more without going to prison? Sing the Anthem?' I could not enlighten him; yet that is what it appeared to mean, though the terms were wide and vague. Moreover the constitution appeared to be the draft of a draft, intended to allure rather than confuse: yet containing as far as I could see no concrete formulae susceptible of acceptance or rejection. The whole thing had a puzzling sort of air.

In Kyrenia I saw small groups clustered about other copies on doors and boards—the text took about ten minutes to read. All was bewilderment.

In Nicosia amazement was tempered by an irrational amusement. 'Does this,' asked a journalist, 'mean that we cannot quote dispatches from the English press containing the word "Enosis"?' I was heartily grateful that I had not yet taken up my duties, since I could not have answered the question. A junior official whom I met, however, seemed in high spirits. 'Have you seen the proclamation? That'll show them! Stop all this nonsense once and for all. Then we can get back to the job of just jogging along." Jogging along! The dream of everyone whose career depends on gravitation rather than aptitude. The Empire just jogging along down a country lane among the hawthorn hedges, in blossom time. . . .

I jogged along to the wine company for which I had been doing some copy-writing, to draw my pay and pay my respects to my millionaire. I found him regarding the daily newspaper on his desk with an air of carefully controlled hysteria. 'Have you seen this?' he whispered. I nodded. He prodded the document with his finger carefully, as one might prod an animal to see if it were quite dead or not. 'Not a month ago,' he said, 'I lunched with Hopkinson in London and assured him that, despite all appearances to the contrary, Cypriots would seriously consider a constitution provided it were really liberal. But this is something for Zulus.'

His view was fairly general, as far as I could see, among those who genuinely wanted to set a term to agitation: who were, in a sense, on our side. At this time there were very many; and this temperate view of things must have been shared by at least half the peasants. I deduce this from one fact: I never saw the slogan ENOSIS written up anywhere without finding immediately underneath it some reference to 'Heretics'—i.e. those who were against it. At first it was 'A MURRAIN ON HERETICS'. Later it was to become 'DEATH TO TRAITORS'. Death in word and in fact.

At the Secretariat all was silence and emptiness. The Government by tradition spent the summer in the mountains and it would have been deemed loss of face to concede the necessity of staying in the capital for the trifling crises of the moment. There was nobody here to consult save the officer of the watch, so to speak, who was linked to Government House in Troodos by telephone. He had no views on the Proclamation, and appeared not to have been informed of its existence; he had no glosses to offer upon it, and contented himself with giving me detailed instructions as to how to reach my satrapy—the Public Information Office, which was then located opposite the law courts on the edge of the Turkish quarter, in an old building full of mirrors: a place which would have delighted Pierre Loti.

This too was closed and the staff on holiday, so I took myself by sunlight to the hospitable porch of Maurice Cardiff where I found him admonishing a vine which showed signs of escaping from its trellis. 'Am I mad,' I asked him, 'or is this Proclamation rather a risky thing to do?' He laughed. 'We are all mad,' he said. 'It's clear you don't understand Cyprus.'

'But seriously.'

'But seriously.'

'I mean if I were a nationalist leader longing to give UNO some examples of illiberality I would immediately provoke a demonstration and get several hundred schoolboys locked up. It would be an admirable political gambit. Unless you think the Government is only blustering and would be too timid to act.'

'Worse than that. The Cypriots themselves are too stupid to take advantage of it. You'll see.'

The phone rang and I was left pondering in the sunlight, inhaling the deep scent of magnolia blossom. He returned with a grimace and said: 'You may see martyrs yet. The press has decided to go on strike for a week; there are to be demonstrations. Perhaps they'll have some martyrs to take to UNO after all.'

These were depressing enough omens for a newly appointed official to ponder on. I was grateful that my duties were not to begin for a few weeks. I went down to the Turkish quarter and sat down among the carters and bus-drivers for a coffee and cognac in the very shadow of the Bedestan, the most haunting corner of Nicosia. Here I was joined by Stephanides and Glykis from the terrible class Epsilon Alpha. They appeared not to have heard of any Proclamation—but as neither enjoyed reading it was not surprising. 'My father tells me The News at night,' said Stephanides, and added under his breath, 'when he doesn't drink too much.' He thought the world of his father.

I remembered how the old man one day, wiping his hands on his leather apron, had winked and said: 'Enosis? Yes. I could settle it this afternoon. Cede the place to Greece on condition that you can lease it back for a hundred years at a nominal rent. Crown the King in the Cathedral and tell everyone to shut up— *He'll* do it for you.' It sounded easy, and yet in these days a comic opera solution would have been not beyond the bounds of possibility. But once it had become an International Problem . . . what then?

'Well,' said Glykis tilting back his cap and gazing up at the irrational beauty of a Gothic cathedral which sprouted tall minarets, symbolizing at a single blow the beauty of Cyprus which rests upon incongruities, 'well! The Lusignans were here for three hundred years and Venice for eighty-two. The Turks stayed three hundred, the British seventy-eight. What does it all mean?' What indeed?

Lying across the sea-routes of the world she had always been the direct concern of any maritime power whose lines of life stretched across the inhospitable and warring East. Genoa, Rome, Venice, Turkey, Egypt, Phoenicia—through every mutation of history she was sea-born and sea-doomed. And now for us she was no longer the galleon she had been to Venice but an aircraft-carrier: a ship-of-the-line. Could she be held? There was no doubt of it, if she must be; the problem was not there. It turned upon another point. Could she be held by *force* and not guile?—because in default of political accommodations we would find ourselves in the situation of Venice. I didn't know.

Troublesome as gadflies, I chased away these thoughts with their annoying persistence, and turned my back on the capital and its buzzing coffee-houses, taking the long curling road towards the Gothic range, its mountains drawn back like harps against the noon-tide sun. The bright uplifted blade of the sea greeted me as I pierced the blank stone wall of the pass, dispersing these gloomy intimations of a world outside this tangerine-scented sunshine which would so soon close down upon us with the ring of an iron door.

Escaping to Bellapaix was like entering a walled garden; on the last crown of the road there was a small reception committee of ardent nationalists aged about nine who danced along beside the car shouting: 'Union' in heartrending accents, and never failing to add as my identity was established: 'Yasu, neighbour.' They would race each other breathlessly to the Tree of Idleness in the hope of carrying a parcel up the hill for me—for my mother's liberality in the matter of home-made cakes and doughnuts was by now proverbial. The last turn of the road was like coming to rest in a favourite painting, opposite the café under the great tree; for as the engine stammered into silence the massive volume of the Abbey's quietness welled up around one like music, encapsulating the voices of the village, the clink of glasses, the slap of cards, or the more distant sound of ravens in the trees. And detaching themselves from the groups of quiet coffee-drinkers came my friends, one by one, to bring me a rose, or a new idea for tiles, or a letter which had just arrived.

At the house I found my brother had arrived with his wife and a mass of equipment—including everything except bags of salt and coloured beads to suborn the natives. He was somewhat aggrieved to find that I had buried him at Thermopylae but on the whole took its implications very well; after all, it meant free drinks, the proper reward for family heroism. The village rejoiced in his resurrection, and even Frangos was not so huffy about the deception as I had feared. Moreover, within a matter of days, he found to his own surprise that his Greek—which he had imagined gone—returned hand over fist, and this gave him direct access to the affections and understanding of our neighbours and friends. Moreover, with film and sound equipment, he now began an exhaustive survey of the village and its life so that everyone began to nourish absurd dreams of Hollywood contracts and stalk about with an air of deliberation, 'acting'; even Mr. Honey whom I would never have dreamed was so frivolous.

It was time, too, for a change of domicile, for my new duties would forbid my being so far beyond the reach of a telephone; and though sorry to go, I was glad to surrender the house to my brother and to count on enjoying the week-ends spent there. If my sadness was mixed with relief it was because I knew that the minute he started collecting the whole place would be alive with lizards, rats, snakes, and every foul creeping thing the Creator invented to make our lives uncomfortable here below. No one who has not smelt an owl at close quarters, or seen a lizard being sick, will have any idea what I mean!

The Satrap

'No sparks in last year's ashes.'

'A fool throws a stone into the sea and a hundred wise men cannot pull it out.'

'If the stone falls on the egg, alas for the egg—
If the egg falls on the stone—alas for the egg.'

(Cypriot Greek proverbs)

———◇———

The Information Office had a beguiling air of good-natured shabbiness, and its awkward mirrored rooms gave one the impression of entering an abandoned barber's shop on the Rue Cherif Pacha in Cairo. I had been led to believe that much needed to be done, but I was unprepared to find so few of the means for doing it. My inheritance seemed in pitiable shape; a cellar full of discarded blocks and photographic equipment so shabby and mouldering as to be a disgrace; an aged film van or two; a moribund house-magazine; and various other odds and ends of little practical use. Absolutely no briefs save the Colonial Report a year out of date; and a mountain of posters showing pictures of the Queen decorating coal-black mammies with long-service medals—the very thing to make Greeks and Turks, with their colour-bar, dance with rage.

But nobody bothered to hide its shortcomings, and these purely operational limitations were easy enough to remedy with a little time and money: but both were short, it seemed. 'It's customary to knock administrations,' said a colleague, soberly sucking his pipe. 'But when you see the revenue you'll understand that most of our troubles come from trying to live on our income. Anything we've borrowed has gone into long-term projects. Building for eternity, old man.'

Apart from these remediable deficiencies, however, there was another which caused me uneasiness: there were no policy files.

There were mountainous files of factual reporting on districts and personalities. There was nothing vaguely resembling a policy line which one could study and interpret. For the first time I realized that we had no real policy, save that of offering constitutions whose terms made them unsuitable for acceptance, and of stone-walling on the central issue of sovereignty. This too was all right: Enosis had been a staple feature of Cyprus life since our arrival in Cyprus, and was likely to go on being so. Irrationalities of the kind did not deserve to exist—consequently Enosis didn't exist. The local radio station was forbidden to mention the Archbishop or his case on the air—an absurdity so patent that I could hardly credit it. Were the proceedings at UNO also going to remain un-mentioned by the domestic radio—presumably UNO did not exist either? And what of its credit with our public—which I must say, to judge by the village, was quite high? Most of these points called for quick decisions which would have been easier to make had I been able to discover what the formulated policy on the island was. Should one for example behave as if the Greeks were Greeks? The Greek National Anthem—should it be played on Independence Day while Athens was broadcasting scurrilous and inflammatory material, inciting Greeks to rise?

There seemed to be no clear line on all this so I was forced to steer a course between vague amiabilities and reproaches for the time being; counsels of moderation borne upon the wings of hope. I based everything upon Anglo-Greek amity, sure that at least here one had a responsive chord which could be touched, sure, too in my own mind that here was a foundation strong enough to allow a real policy to be constructed over it.

My fellow-satraps ('Wicked Satraps of the Cyprus Govern-ment'—Athens Radio) were an amiable and good-tempered crowd, liberal in instinct and scrupulously fair in their general dealings with the world; but they saw no undue cause for urgency or brainwork on policy matters. They embodied the remorseless weight with which the Commonwealth moves down its appointed grooves, governed by the law of inertia. It is absurd to expect the qualities of ballet dancers in public servants or to despair when one doesn't find them.

The Satrap

One of the slogans of the day was 'Potterism', an opprobrious expression coined by a bibulous and witty journalist, a frequent visitor to the island whose articles never failed to cause me concern, though they were never quite so clever as his private strictures on us all. He maintained that all administrators belonged to a cohort of mindless and faceless men who should either be numbered or described collectively as 'Peter Potter, O.B.E.' 'It's Potter again,' he would cry, on being informed of some stroke of policy or some new government statement. 'It's that man again.' Potterism, according to him, was characterized by the semi-detached mind, and all Potters were rock-cake and lemonade administrators, small-car aficionados, sambo-rulers—and heaven only knows what else. It is easy to criticize, but harder to turn the other cheek, and while I accepted these broadsides on behalf of my fellow-satraps I returned them whenever I could, aiming a shaft or two at the press corps. A Press Officer is, after all, the administration's whipping-boy, and after years of press work I had grown the skin of a rhinoceros so that even the persistent attacks on me in the local English paper were hardly more than amusing.

There was so much to do that there was no time for ill temper, though now and again I was snappy from sheer fatigue. The basic problem was to convince the administration that the situation might easily become an emergency; this was no time to jog along. But this I completely failed to do. I found myself imprisoned in the rigidified formulae of the Colonial Office. With the best will in the world (and there were many people ready to cut red tape and take swift personal decisions) it was impossible to make headway through the Sargasso Sea of paper in which we were entangled—all of us, not least the Governor. The submission of estimates, the minuting of files, the endless committee-meetings, were galling to someone who had just seen the Archbishop preaching in Saint John's, and heard the ominous growling of the crowd. Public disorder was gradually mounting, octave by octave, and it was obvious that the need to contain it would soon be forcing active decisions upon us. The Archbishop had just held an island-wide ceremony at which he had formally and deliberately committed sedition from the pulpit. The Government had saved its face by quibbling over interpretations of the Sedition Law, obviously dismayed by the sharp reactions to the Proclamation from the world press—upholders of free speech (when it pays). Worst of all, the stormy petrels of journalism were beginning to arrive and there was not a stitch of background material with which to feed them; I set the whole staff to dredging for factual data from the various departments, many of whose directors were on leave or absent for conferences. Briefing proceeded by word of mouth, and here at least I had reason to congratulate myself, for by an inspired stroke the Colonial Secretary had appointed an officer to me whose brains and initiative were exceptional—Achilles Papadopoulos. He was typical of the best Cypriot product; one of three brothers, he came from the poverty-stricken village of Pitsillia in the hills. His father, a grey dignified old peasant, used to visit us sometimes, just for the pleasure of gazing at his son who had reached such dizzy heights of success in the Government as even to be decorated. Achilles loved the old man, as indeed we all did, and always made him comfortable on a chair and ordered him a black coffee. Each of the three sons was remarkable in his own line; for the elder and the younger both occupied positions of respectability. Whenever I was assailed on the subject of Potterism I could not help thinking that a system cannot be entirely bad if it has provided a career for such brilliant and hard-working boys as Achilles, who in one generation had stepped from the peasantry into what passed in Cyprus for the gentry. He was well worth his place in the ranks of the satraps and throughout this difficult period handled the bulk of the work, though he was new to it, with intelligence and precision. He also wrote lucid and unexceptionable English, which was a relief.

I had now moved from the village to a shabby little concrete villa, the best accommodation that could be found at short notice in the capital. It was a dispiriting sort of place, but suitable to the times which did nothing to allay my misgivings about the future of all of us. My recommendations for my office were treated with consideration and dispatch, but I had already learned to interpret the hollow laughter which greeted me when I spoke of securing supplies and staff in a few weeks. I had not yet learned that the Crown Agents in whom the whole marketing business of the Colonies is centralized were the most dilatory body in the world. They must have read my letters with knotted brows in London for there was not one which did not appeal for something to be sent to me by air. By air! I might as well have addressed love-letters to the Dalai Lama. Nor could the local market supply the demands we made—and here the terrible shabbiness and inadequacy of Nicosia were amply illustrated. It was not only that it lacked a theatre, a swimming-pool, a university, a decent book-shop; it seemed absolutely innocent of technical trades and skills of the type that any provincial town in England could show—printing, blockmaking, fine-grain developing, designing. . . .

I realized now why the Cypriots regarded Greece as so far advanced. It was, if one compared capital with capital, Athens to Nicosia. With all its anfractuous and crazy anomalies Athens was Europe. Nicosia could only be compared for twentieth-century amenities with some fly-blown Anatolian township, bemused and forgotten on the central steppes. On all sides we were confronted with modern towns like Beirut and Alexandria. The comparison was unfair, of course, but it was inevitable, and one made it mentally a hundred times a day. Nicosia was a town which had been left becalmed by the Turks, to drowse away its life on the dusty Mesaoria; what had been done to awaken it? There had been no need until now.

While my village was only an hour away, it seemed to be situated in another world, for the foreground of my life was already beginning to fill up with new faces, journalists, M.P.'s, dignitaries of various calibres, each of whom had to be welcomed and briefed. Some wished to interview mayors, others to talk to peasants, others still to nibble at the crowded hours of free time enjoyed by the Colonial Secretary and the Governor. The Administration suddenly found itself spotlighted on the world scene, subjected to the darts and probes of the world press, whose representatives crowded the grim Tyrolean bar of the Ledra Palace Hotel, circling over our corpses like vultures. 'There is nothing Potter fears except a P.Q.,' said my friend, and there were plenty of them now, to which we had to find effective answers or oblique retorts ('leg glides'). We were like men who, becalmed for a long time without food and water on a balsa-wood raft, suddenly find that they have drifted into the middle of a sea-battle. The few inches of space the island had enjoyed hitherto in the world press had now swollen out of all recognition, had proliferated like a cancer into feature-articles, political treatises, supplements and leaders.

Disorders increased under the stimulus of rhetoric and the envenomed insinuations of Athens Radio, and we were already floundering in a sea of upheavals caused by the students and apprentices of the five towns. Under all these stresses, the Administration began to show some justifiable annoyance and there were calls for action. But here we came up against another factor to which I had been blind hitherto, but which was perhaps the real determinant of the situation as it developed. The state of the police force was deplorable: underpaid, inefficiently equipped, inadequate in size, it was totally unprepared to meet the needs of the day. Indeed, it was already showing signs of strain and a marked inability to deal with civil disturbances organized by students. I am not revealing secrets—for the findings of the Police Commission of 1956 have been published as an official document and no historian concerned with cause and effect can afford to neglect it. It is the key document to the years 1954–6.

'You complain,' said Wren, 'of neglect in your own department. You should see mine!' But he was too loyal and too single-minded a person to say more. We were both newcomers to the satrapy faced with the need for drastic changes and conscious that time was ebbing. We met with our woes at the great square desk in Government House to lay them before the Governor. The enormity of past neglect must have been visible not only in our demands but upon our faces; in Wren's case he was faced with the task of trebling his force overnight if he was to contain the present discontents. The Police Force had remained almost unchanged, except for a change of title, since 1878! I heard him describe the state of his inheritance in that quiet and unemotional voice of his —a voice without rancour or any of the smaller envies—and I marvelled at his coolness. He was someone rather exceptional in the world of the Police, and had the fine spiritual head of a grammarian or a philosopher. He, like myself, found himself in the toils of that small committee of minor dignitaries which presided over estimates, and which chipped and pared at them without the faintest knowledge of the particular needs of the department concerned, and certainly with no imaginative grasp of the current urgency of our needs. The Governor was far from deaf to our appeals, and nearly always threw his weight in upon our side; but he himself was tied hand and foot, not only by the rigidified machinery of the Regulations (which represented diagrammatically would resemble something like a wrapped mummy) but by the timeless inertia of the Treasury.

From all this followed another unpalatable fact—and one which from the point of view of Public Relations I found alarming. What the police could not enforce the military would have to undertake at gun-point. . . . It seemed to me that if we were contending with Athens for the compliance (not even loyalty) of the Cypriot peasant and the maintenance of order, there was no quicker way of igniting the villager than by shooting a couple of schoolchildren during a riot. I said nothing about the creation of martyrs or the reaction of the world press—for these were self-evident factors. But here I found opinion divided. Some officials thought that sharp action would give the Cypriots a lesson and quell disturbances, which would only mount in intensity the longer they were allowed free play. They did not believe that the Cypriots had any real fight in them; but inability to see Cyprus detached from the colonial framework blinded them to the fact that Cretans might come over and set the island an example—and this was certainly to be feared. This classical piece of ignorance was impossible to dispel among officials, none of whom had any knowledge of European politics and the Balkans. They regarded Cyprus as if it were Tobago—their only referent. Few spoke Greek or Turkish, and while many had spent years in the island, few had ever visited Greece or Turkey. Perhaps this was not very serious—though it seriously bedevilled judgment on the spot; for they lived by the central colonial proposition which, as a conservative, I fully understand, namely: 'If you have an Empire, you just can't give away bits of it as soon as asked.' I differed with them only in believing that in Cyprus we had an issue which could be honourably compounded, and should be treated diplomatically with the traditional skill and experience which were available to us; and that we should lose by force everything that could be gained by diplomacy. In a sense this assessment of things excluded the Cypriots—for I had already recognized in them the martyrs of a situation which was only partly of their own making. I based my views on what I knew to be true of Greece—namely that the Enosis proposition touched the very quick of the Greek heart and that whatever was said about it (however hysterical) was deeply felt. And here too I did not think of incitement and intervention in Cyprus as the work of a Government or an official organ, but the spontaneous efforts of those whiskered island lunatics I knew in Rhodes and Crete, any three of whom could constitute a self-appointed band of 'heroic liberators'. Cyprus was wide open by sea, its police force practically non-existent. Twenty Cretan shepherds with a load of abandoned war equipment such as litters the waterfront at Salonika could do a tremendous amount of damage in a very short time. . . .

But now my journeys began and I became an experienced conductor and pilot for visitors. My map of Cyprus became cross-hatched with visions of its landscape under sun or cloud, in various weathers, at moonrise and sunset: in the grim mountains of Troodos, or the smiling vine and mulberry lands above Paphos, at Salamis and Jalousa, Myrtou and Famagusta.

But though I had deserted the village it retained its hold on my attentions and affection in the person of almost daily visitors to the ugly little house; they arrived in a roar of dust at the door, where the good Dmitri deposited them from his bus, to spend an early breakfast-tide with me. Mr. Honey brought me cyclamen bulbs and a report on the bitter lemon trees which needed grafting; Andreas brought a pocketful of new tiles of an Italian type which had recently been imported and with which he wished to beautify the bathroom; the *muktar* brought me an encouraging account of my brother's dancing at Lalou's wedding, which had

surpassed in grace and agility all the young bloods of the village
—and which had been due to *ouzo* as far as could be judged; and
Michaelis brought me his eldest son for whom he wished to find
a post in the Government service. Anthemos brought fresh vege-
tables from his garden. And surprise among surprises, even old
Morais turned up one day with a bunch of flowers and a great bag
of nuts.

Nor did the scholars of the Gymnasium abandon the link I had
severed when I left my teacher's post; every morning a couple of
grubby youths would bicycle up to the door with some urgent
request—to write a letter to a girl or an application to a Correspondence College, or for help with a piece of homework.

Neither the failure of the Greek appeal nor the mounting tide
of strikes and school-lockouts seemed to have affected their
sunny good-nature, or the profound belief that the politics of the
greater world outside would, like some stage-curtain, part suddenly one day to allow some happy solution to appear—England
and Greece, hand in hand, like Punch and Judy, bowing and
smiling to the public and expressing an undying affection for one
another against which all these hot misunderstandings would fade
and give place to a new era of blissful Union. But among the
intellectuals in the Gymnasium common-room the temper had
grown much uglier and the tone of public opinion was slowly
beginning to follow suit. As if to match this new sharpness the
voice of the moderates raised itself to a new key of apprehension
asking us 'not to let things go too far'—though none could
specify where they might end, perhaps because none dared to
contemplate such an end calmly.

From the cockpit of my office I had another, by no means
reassuring angle of sight, for from here the international position
of the case seemed to be deteriorating rapidly. Turkish feelings
both in the island and outside had been roused and one began to
see, as if sketched in outline upon the peaceful landscapes of
the island, the silhouette of communal disorders whose roots,
embedded so deeply in the medieval compost of religious
hatreds, might easily be revived by the accidental shedding of
blood.

In December troops opened fire at Limassol, under severe provocation, and wounded three youths—an incident, though trivial, which straddled the front pages of the Sunday press in London and convinced the Government that such tactics were politically expensive and should be abandoned. I was heartily grateful, for the effect of this shooting in Cyprus itself was great and caused an instant sharpening of antagonism, and a disgust which was shared by moderate and extremist alike. The situation was becoming envenomed by neglect, inflamed alike by the hysteria of the apprentices and the schools and the poison of the Athens broadcasts. It was clear, too, that the available police forces could barely contain a determined demonstration composed of bottle-throwing schoolgirls, let alone a band of rough Paphiot youths, or members of the Union of Bricklayers. Troops would have the invidious task of turning out to restore order where the law could not.

But the restoration of order was only one aspect, the public aspect, of our duties; behind it there lay another task of greater magnitude, the tranquillization of the public mind which was now a prey to conflicting hysterias and in a state likely to be ignited by rumour or challenging speech. The climate of affairs was altering subtly, and those who had charge of their direction, now began to feel the tug of pressures for which they themselves had not been prepared. Slowly but distinctly we had begun to slide upon that treacherous surface of rhetoric and passion which for so long had expressed itself in a void of empty gestures, and still there was no sign from London of the urgent approaches such happenings should foreshadow. 'Something is going wrong,' said a Greek journalist. 'I feel as if I were no longer in control of my arms and legs. We are becoming marionettes, you dancing to London and we to Athens.' There seemed to be no retreat possible from the extreme positions which had been taken up by everyone, and if we the satraps prayed in the direction of London like devout Moslems facing Mecca, our prayers were echoed not less fervently by the vanguard of the Enotists, who were themselves in the grip of forces both domestic and foreign. A strange feeling of vertigo was in the air—as of sleepwalkers suddenly being awakened to find themselves poised on a steep cliff above a raging sea.

To all the opposing tensions there was only one answer—inaction—until such time as the reforms we considered necessary should be 'implemented', to use the delicious phraseology of the schoolmen. But if a renovated Public Relations department was to take me six months to build how much longer would it take, for example, to build a police force? It was not simply that it had to be recruited and trained, and its terms of service reformed: there was nowhere even to *house* the hypothetical body of the force. Decades of masterly inaction had reduced the common amenities of the island to an almost Turkish state of desuetude; the telephone system for instance was hopelessly out of date. We could not equip hotels with telephones: how then were the police to expand their communications network—by heliograph? Wherever one turned one came up against some insuperable obstacle of the kind which only the determination of a Hannibal could have shifted; but the regulations precluded our use of dynamite though our adversaries later were to labour under no such limitation.

Walking about at dusk in the iron parallelogram of Famagusta, these thoughts became absurdly mixed with evocations of past history, no less cruel and turbulent than the times in which we lived. Treading the deserted and grass-grown turrets of Othello's tower one could gaze down at the ships unloading in deceptive peacefulness, or turn and remark along the shallow coastline the white scar of Salamis, whose bony ruins also testified to the inexorable pressures of time and history which every hero has thought to suspend by some finite perfect action. Always it ended in something limited and grotesque like the skin of Bragadino, stuffed with straw: a dusty relic whose origin the Venetian worshipper no longer remembered, but which was still perpetuated here in this ruined fortress the invader had attacked—had eaten the heart out of like a cheese. These fat pompous military walls had sheltered one of the richest mercantile communities in the world. One hundred and fifty acres of grass-grown desolation. 'There still exist traces of some twenty churches of which all but two are in utter ruin. There is also a wretched konak and prison, a barrack-yard, with piles of stone cannon-balls, a small bazaar, and here and there among the ruins the huts of about a hundred Turkish families, whose chief subsistence is obtained from patches of garden-land which they have cleared of stones. All else is utter, absolute ruin—vast heaps of stone, enough to build a modern town. Imagine a city bombarded until all its buildings (save those of exceptional strength) were destroyed, and add to this the effects of an earthquake. Except for the absence of the slain, the present scene differs little from that witnessed by the victorious Turks as they entered the city under Lala Moustapha on the 5th of August 1571, after nearly a twelve-months' siege. Were Famagusta altogether without inhabitants it would be less impressive in its desolation than it now is as seen in the twilight —nothing stirring but the owl and the bat, and perhaps here and there, haunting like ghosts the narrow lanes, a few pale fever-stricken women in their Turkish veils and long white mantles, who might well be taken for the last survivors of a city where war, famine and plague had done their worst.' So writes the modest engineer Samuel Brown in 1879.

The fever and the veils have gone, of course, but little else has changed today except that the grass is greener, and young saplings crowd the huge moat, and the liners moo like cattle beyond the reefs. It is still the most haunting town in Cyprus, saturated with the memory of its past—a windmill turning rustily against a cornflower-coloured sea. The cries of children bathing in the shallow sea outside the famous, useless monuments to a military glory which silted up here in the Levant, generation by generation, only to decline and perish abruptly at the bidding of history —whose cruel shoals and whirlpools were once again at work sapping the age we had inherited from those forgotten captains and merchants: we also children of a sea-born power whose many bridgeheads were being slowly invested by the sea we had tamed and yoked.

The old Gothic cathedral wearing its uncouth horns of min-arets glowed softly in the fading light, amber as a honey-cell against the peacock's eye of sea. It was the ideal place in which to reflect upon the vanity of human affairs. I used to walk about its grassy galleries with my friends or duty-companions, enjoying the silence which grows up between sentences uttered among the ruins of time; and conscious that one day our history must touch and marry its own, to join the great confluence of tides which meet forever at the point where present meets the past in a death-embrace.

But our own present was forever tugging at one like a hound which nothing could quiet, and racing along the firm straight arrow of road towards the capital I would once more become aware of the thousand preoccupations of office waiting for me, and the noisy contentions of demagogues and illiterates which had begun to fill the empty theatre of world affairs with the shrill waspish voice of the times—nationalism. I would apprehend too the cobweb of lies and half-truths which were beginning to manufacture themselves in minds which, twelve months ago, would not have recognized the island's name.

Back across the Mesaoria, the hot barren plain with the single fortress lying in the middle—its roads radiating out from all directions, starfish-wise, Nicosia was merely a crude echo of the sea-dazzling city we had left; and its current associations so qualified its own very different beauties that I had often to refresh myself in the knowledge of it by taking solitary walks along the ancient bastions or through the crowded markets. Sitting in the long grass among the spiked and abandoned British guns on the Kyrenia wall, I would watch the Turkish children flying their coloured kites in the quick fresh evening wind which ushers in the summer twilights of the capital. Or sitting on the leads of Saint Sophia watch the black well of darkness slowly flicker into light, candle by candle, like Easter worshippers in some immense dark cathedral greeting the risen Christ.

Events now were drawing in, closing in upon us, and hardly a day went by without the arrival of some new visitor or some new and disturbing fragment of news. 'And to think that all this,' said a Greek journalist, 'comes about from a coolness between Eden and Papagos.' This was the latest Athenian explanation of our state —for no Greek can interpret policy in anything but personal terms. 'So Papagos was mortified. So Papagos says: "By God, here we Greeks have been walking about on tip-toe with our bladders bursting with the Cyprus question for thirty years, not daring to relieve ourselves because of the affection we have for England . . . why should we contain ourselves a moment longer?" So he goes to UNO because he knows that you will have trouble here.'

Rumours, disturbing in their implications, had begun to scuttle about the fents and warrens of the old town—the labyrinth of streets which lay within the Venetian walls. Rumours of landings, of the training of saboteurs, of resistance. But as yet they remained without substance and the disturbances of civil life pursued their refractory course in dreary demonstrations, riots and bottle-throwings which the good-natured and exasperated soldiery and police alike countered with shields and staves, with gas shells and arrests.

Everyone was new to the game, was an amateur. The foreground of the picture was still crowded with the kind of detail which made such a success of the early Keystone comedies— elaborate games of cops and robbers across the moat. The Girls' Sixth, led by Aphrodite, charging across the bridge to pelt the police with Coca-Cola bottles; benighted police auxiliaries defending themselves behind extraordinary shields (specially run up for them by the Public Works, no doubt) which resembled Woolworth fire-screens. The headmaster of the Gymnasium being beaten up by his own sixth form for showing lack of patriotism— and being forced to appeal for the restoration of order to the very authorities he had sworn to overturn. Perplexing conferences at Government House, nestling among the green lawns and carefully tended beds of English flowers, where these scenes of apparent frivolity and ludicrousness (who ever heard of a revolution of schoolchildren?) were gravely evaluated. So few were the broken heads and so many the broken bottles that the whole atmosphere was charged with an inadvertent air of carnival. 'You see,' explained the very school-teacher who had grasped the air before him to show how well-controlled the gymnasia were, 'you see, we can't control them. I'm afraid to go to class any more. The big boys are really ugly. Can't the Government do something?' This conversation was conducted behind the counter of a haberdasher's shop in Ledra Street to the background orchestration of broken glass and yelling as Aphrodite led another desperate charge of the Girls' Sixth against the thinly held bridgehead which spanned the moat. The whole street was ankle-deep in bottles. Across the road, on the periphery of the battle-field, the British Institute remained obstinately open, its director quietly watching from a balcony. From time to time a breathless student who had tired of throwing bottles or sprained an arm would slip into the library for a quiet spell of study as if nothing in the world were amiss. The crowds moved roaring up and down the streets, screaming for liberty like maddened bulls. An English spinster mounted rather precariously on a bicycle, however, rode straight through them; they parted, cheering, and when she dropped a parcel, a dozen members of Epsilon Alpha dived for the honour of picking it up and restoring it to her. 'I've never seen anything quite like this,' said a newspaper correspondent, running for his life along the moat, pursued by the Girls' Sixth. There were brilliant scenes rich in all the unrehearsed comedy of Latin life; as when the police experimenting with the new and exciting weapon they had been given—the gas shell—filled their own headquarters with tear-gas and had to evacuate it until the wind changed. 'They don't mean any harm,' said a Greek grocer dodging adroitly as a brickbat whizzed past him into a shop-window. 'It is just the people expressing themselves.' Then getting down under a counter he added, 'They are very polite people really, but they want self-determination.'

Across this pantomime world, however, there stalked a spectre which took no account of the clamourings of schoolchildren or the counsels of moderation which were being directed at the troubled world from every side, like hoses at a fire—the spectre of insurrection.

It was after dark when my telephone rang and the quiet voice of the Colonial Secretary ordered me to hurry to his office. The Secretariat was dark as I drove in under the magnificent euca- lyptus tree which spanned the hollow square upon which the building was constructed, and, leaving my car, climbed the worm-eaten old staircase which led to his office. With the same amused composure with which he greeted every turn and twist of events he now told me that information had been received that a caique loaded with arms and ammunition had set off for Cyprus, for a landfall near Paphos. We sat in silence for a moment while he lit his pipe and settled the papers on his desk. The fire crackled in the old-fashioned grate, and from somewhere in the middle distance came the pecking of a typewriter with its grotesque insistence on a world where there were still reports to be made and papers to be filed. I sighed. There was no comment to be made on something which we had expected and feared for so long. 'We must try and intercept it,' he said at last, and I could see that he too was thinking of that long bare coastline with its cliffs and bays deserted under the moon which stretches down from the horn of Cape Arnauti to Paphos. A thousand possible points of entry for the resolute smuggler. . . .

Point of No Return

'What they are they were; and what they were they are—an indolent, careless and mimetic people, but without a spark of Turkish fire, without a touch of Grecian taste. With neither beauty of body nor sense of beauty in mind—with neither personal restlessness nor pride of origin —with neither large aspirations nor practical dexterity of hand, they live on in a limpid state, like creatures of the lower types clinging to life for life's own sake; voluptuaries of the sun and sea; holding on by simple animal tenacity through tempests which have wrecked the nobler races of mankind.'

(*British Cyprus* by W. HEPWORTH DIXON, 1887)

I t was not by a smugglers' moon that we travelled westward towards Paphos, for we were in search of something less exciting than lawbreakers, but the knowledge that somewhere along that spectral coast a landing was to be attempted, filled the journey with an excitement it would not otherwise have had. Though the wind was icy the high-riding moon in a clear sky give one the illusion that spring had broken as we followed the loops and gradients of the coastal road, leaving Lapithos drowsing among her lemon-trees and climbing slowly towards the bare saddle on which Myrtou lies, the car's pale headlights tempering the steely grey of olive-trees with chalky yellows and mauves, pencilling in the empty roads and the sleeping villages as we flashed through them. The air smelt of snow and lemon-blossom, and old Panos beside me huddled gratefully in the duffle coat I had loaned him, talked quietly and methodically of the vine which he was going to select for the balcony from a special vineyard near Kuklia. We had set off by night upon an impulse, taking with us some wine and biscuits to sustain us for the three hours' drive; it would be perhaps the last chance Panos would get before the school term began again to visit the obscure holding which had once belonged to his grandfather, and where the famous vine of his choice still grew.

I was glad of the journey for other reasons; I wanted to study and memorize this desolate and unvisited coast-line of the Paphos district which as yet I hardly knew, though I had made several swift journeys along the coast road by day. By high moonlight it was eerie and full of a monochrome beauty which grew out of indistinctness, shadows emptied and splashed everywhere along the inclines of the night. At Morphou the broad gleaming bay unrolled itself in a salver of silver floccus under that perfect sky. We passed a camel-train awkwardly lurching along the road under the carobs, loaded with grain-sacks with men asleep on them, rocking by moonlight towards Nicosia. For a moment the soft thudding of their pads and the groans of the baby camels swam into sound-focus above the waspish drone of the car and the hiss of wind at the screens. Then they were swallowed and we were moving down into the valley to pick up the coast road, gleaming diamond-hard and polished with light.

We spent an hour shivering among the windy ruins of Vouni and drinking our wine, while my companion watched the sea boiling and fretting below us under the moon—its ruffled silver feathers flying in the windy tides which beat up from Turkey to shatter themselves on those forbidding headlands and capes, and rumble among the subterranean caves. The coast had become more desolate now and the road wound along it within sight and sound of the troubled waters; every bend was a hairpin cut into the grey mulch of a limestone whose coarse dirty thatch lay damp and inert, heavy with seashells. Once or twice we thought we saw the shadow of a man on the cliffs or among the olive trees and I pulled up, expecting a challenge, for I knew that troops were being moved into this area to support the police, but each time we were mistaken. The whole network of cliffs and promontories lay deserted under an empty sky. Kato Pyrgos, Limonias, Mansoura; we passed slatternly villages tousled in sleep, deserted farms, deserted fishing nets hanging out to dry on scaffoldings of wooden spokes. The headlights picked up only the flaring legends which decorated the crumbling white walls of the towns, ENOSIS, DEATH TO ARMITAGE, THE BRITISH MUST GO. 'These are somewhat new,' said Panos reflectively, 'but then the Paphiots were always extremists. But look at this one.' In red paint, not in blue this time, the words WE WILL SHED BLOOD written athwart a coffee-house wall. Panos sighed and nibbled at a biscuit. . . . 'There's something in the air,' he said in his dry academic voice, 'which makes me wonder.'

The moon had grown old and feeble by the time we reached Polis and a thin severe dawn threatened us from the east, draining the sea of light and freezing the sky to a bloodless white. My companion had been dozing fitfully and now he woke and suggested that we visit the stone of Romeos, Aphrodite's beach, before motoring on to the hot breakfast we had promised ourselves in the hotel at Paphos. It was a good idea to surprise the dawn at this forgotten point in history—the hollow curved beach with its great finger of rock raised in patient admonition—and to listen for a while to the oldest sound in European history, the sighing of the waves as they thickened into roundels of foam and hissed upon that carpet of discoloured sand.

In the fragile membranes of light which separate like yolks upon the cold meniscus of the sea when the first rays of the sun come through, the bay looked haunted by the desolate and meaningless centuries which had passed over it since first the foam-born miracle occurred. With the same obsessive rhythms it beat and beat again on that soft eroded point with its charred-looking sand: it had gone on from the beginning, never losing momentum, never hurrying, reaching out and subsiding with a sigh.

We walked down towards the water together in silence, and were abruptly halted by a sight which, though unremarkable enough in itself, somehow acquired a legendary quality, enacted as it was upon that deserted strip of sand, which still echoed, as it were, in our ears with all the vibrations of a forgotten music. A sea-turtle lay dead upon the beach (some disturbing memory here—was it Orpheus' lyre?) and a lean dog was digging out and feasting upon its decomposed entrails, closely watched by a scabby vulture from a heft of rock hard by. The vulture chuckled and gurgled and ruffled its feathers with hunger, and from time to time, overcome perhaps by the horrible slobbering noises of the dog as it ate, it hopped down and started to share the repast, jabbing and pulling at the turtle with its great beak. At each sortie the dog, trembling with hunger and rage, would turn aside and attack the vulture, which leaped nimbly into the air with a great beat of its wings, and retired to its rock again, crooning and mumbling protestingly.

We drove both dog and vulture off and buried the great creature in a sand-dune. Its shell was as heavy as a paving-stone. And then rubbing our cold hands walked slowly back to the car to feel the first thin rays of the sun upon us, by whose light we finished the last of our wine and biscuits while Panos expounded the meaning of Aphrodite's legend which he believed had been misinterpreted by the historians. She was a symbol, he said dryly, not of licence and sensuousness, but of the dual nature of man—the proposition which lay at the heart of the ancient religions from which she had been derived, and to which her legend itself was the most enduring and poetic of European illustrations. She belonged to a world of innocence outside the scope of the barren sensualities which are ascribed to her cult; she was an Indian.

His words came back to me with redoubled force later that morning when I stood before the leaning black pillar against which Paul had been chained to receive the brutal thrashing which he no doubt endured with the soundless indomitable fever of his kind. It lies in a nettle-grown depression surrounded by dense greenery and buzzing with flies, a desolate and abandoned place—but then the whole of Paphos rings with desolation and decay; mean villages squatting out history among their fly-blown coffee-shops, deaf to the pulse of legend. Paul's truth is not mine—and indeed here in Cyprus one is aware, as in no other place, that Christianity is but a brilliant mosaic of half-truths. Is it perhaps based upon some elaborate misunderstanding of the original message which the long boats of Asoka brought from the East; a message grasped for a while in Syria and Phoenicia, but soon lost in the gabbling of the scholiasts and mystagogues, shivered into a million bright pieces under the fanaticisms and self-seeking of religious gymnasts? Here and there a moving spirit like Julian's apprehended that the vital kernel had been lost, he did not know what, but for the most part the muddy river ran on, swallowing the rainbow. . . .

And then for a brief moment an Order like the Templars was irradiated by the light of the message—their defection from Christendom is one of the most fascinating of episodes; by what strange chance did it come about here in Cyprus, informed perhaps by what new sympathies those iron men had formed among the deserted temples and abandoned shrines? We only know that they were charged with assimilating Eastern rites and superstitions. . . . But there is an interesting and highly suggestive passage in the pages of Mrs. Lewis which comes to mind here. 'Paphos is still called Baffo, and adoration was paid of old to a stone, called by some of the Roman historians a *meta*, or mill-stone from its shape. . . . Now the Templars were accused of worshipping an idol, or whatever the object was, which was called by them Baffometus; and all sorts of rather far-fetched explanations of the name have been brought forward. . . . But what if it simply meant "The Stone of Paphos"? The Templars' headquarters were within a day's ride of Baffo.' And what if the stone itself were the black navel-stone which was later found here—perhaps the very same one which now lies in the Nicosia Museum, gathering dust: an unobtrusive witness to a truth which no longer has power to move us?

These thoughts, so appropriate to time and place, could not long endure the pressure of more worldly things: for I had promised myself to investigate the coffee-shops while Panos was busy up at the farm from which he hoped to select his vine. I tried three and in each was served my coffee with a taciturn coolness which in Greeks could be counted as a slight. Radio Athens blared and rasped out its parrot-like imprecations. Hostile dark eyes surrounded me, their spite only lit by a momentary gleam when I said something in Greek. In the third shop I said that I was a German archaeological student and at once the tension went out of the air. 'Hitler,' said the waiter, with a knowing air, as if he knew all about him. 'How are things there now?' 'Not too bad,' I said. 'How are they here?' His eyes became sly and

hooded, and a crooked smile came to his lips. 'Bad,' he said, and
shut up, at the same time abruptly switching off the radio in the
back of the shop. In the silence our unspoken questions and
answers hovered like bats. Yet the discourtesy, the reserve, was
somehow not in the people only—it was in the air. The silent
groups of young men with their piercing black eyes and shaggy
hair had a look of alertness—of enthusiasm tempered by despair.

I met Panos at the hotel and we set off homeward together
after reverently placing his newspaper-swaddled vine-shoots in
the back of the car. He seemed preoccupied as he smoked and
watched the mellow winelands spread away on both sides of the
road under the brilliant afternoon sun. 'What is it?' I said at last,
and he put a hand on my arm. 'They are saying very bad things
—even untrue things—anything that comes into their heads.'
'It's very Greek,' I said. 'But not very Cypriot, my friend.' He
sighed once more and threw his stub out of the window. 'I am
trusting in the traditional good sense of the British,' he said. 'It
hasn't failed before. They are slow, of course, exasperatingly
slow; but they must have realized by now that while we don't
want Enosis we want to have the *right* to vote for it. Eh?' We
tackled the long steep high road eastward, curling in and out of
the vine-holdings, still dotted with the smashed remains of the
great earthquake which had so mercifully missed the Kyrenia
range—though it had passed through Bellapaix with a roar like an
express train, shaking even the Abbey. Panos had brought some
of the black biting Stroumbi wine with him, and he opened the
bottle to sip it as we went along. 'You see,' he said, 'even I, who
have been for so long a faithful servant of the Government—and
they have treated me well—even I, who don't want the British to
leave, feel that I must have the *right* to decide the future; I confess I feel annoyed at the way we are being played with. It is not
fair, my friend. Behind it I see some of the traditional contempt
for us which I know you—not you—feel, and which makes
Cypriots angry. If they let things go on this way you will drive
our young men—you know how headstrong they are—into
actions which everyone will regret, the Cypriots most of all.'

But even he did not envisage anything as dire as the fears I was secretly entertaining—for he too, like the satraps, was thinking in terms of a serious riot or two which would be quelled as the riots of '31 had been; the unnecessary injustice of it was what upset him. Like many Cypriots he seemed to be almost indifferent to the Athenian factor—perhaps because his view was a parochial one, based on the little community in which he lived. 'What does baffle me,' he went on, 'is the English newspaper, because it shows me that the Government has not grasped the most elementary fact about the problem. It speaks always about a small band of fanatics incited by self-seeking priests; but if Makarios were really self-seeking how much better off he would be in staying quiet, head of an autocephalous church? If Enosis came he would be a nobody, like the Archbishop of Crete. No, whatever else you think about us surely you understand that Enosis will ruin us financially? Do you think it is gain we are after?' His plaintive weary old voice went on, articulating the questions which so many Cypriot Greeks must have been putting to themselves at this time, without rancour or venom: coloured indeed by sorrow to see such misunderstandings grow up about facts which seemed self-evident. How to explain them?

After all, self-determination was an article of faith for the Commonwealth, was it not? If India and the Sudan could claim it, could not the Greeks of Cyprus? 'I ask myself,' he said sadly. 'And because it may be inconvenient now we are prepared to wait —to wait for years if necessary—on the bare assurance that one day we can vote,' and he added with a smile, 'against Enosis probably—who can tell? Many of us are doubtful about a change. But the *right*, the bare *right*—you would win the island by granting us that.'

We reached Kyrenia at dusk and despite our weariness elected to have one glass of wine with Clito before bedtime. Here we were joined by Loizus 'the Bear' and Andreas 'the Seafarer' who were both waiting for the bus up to the village. 'The Bear' had been buying wood for the balcony window-frames upstairs and was pleased with his expedition. His tongue loosened under the influence of the white wine and he unbent enough to make a few gentle little jokes. But then the news came on the radio and the talk drifted round to the one subject which nagged the public mind like a toothache. 'I'm so sick of Enosis, I really am,' said an old beggar in the back of the shop. 'What will we do with it when we get it?' Loizus smiled and said: 'Gently now. It is for our children. But there is no hurry, even the Archbishop says so; besides the British are our friends' (touching my arm) 'and they will see that we get a square deal.'

Afterwards we drove up through the shadow-dappled glades towards the Abbey while Andreas sang a melancholy little song in a small tuneless voice and Loizus hugged his purchases like a child with Christmas presents. The evening was very still, and the cool silence of 'The Tree of Idleness' engulfed us like a mountain pool. Sabri was up there, sitting under the leaves contemplating a black coffee, waiting for me with particular information about carob-wood—he had saved me a special load. 'Sit, my dear,' he said gravely, and I sat beside him, soaking up the silence with its sheer blissful weight. The sea was calm. (Somewhere out of sight and sound the caique *Saint George*, loaded with arms and some ten thousand sticks of dynamite, was beating up the craggy coast by Cape Arnauti, making for a rendezvous near Paphos.) 'It is so peaceful here,' said my friend, sipping his coffee. 'But for these bloody Greeks Cyprus would be peaceful; but we Turks haven't opened our mouths yet. We will never be ruled by Greece here; I would take to the mountains and fight them if Enosis came!' O dear!

The next morning I presented the Government with a brief political report in which I tried to condense the fragments of all these conversations into something which might interest the policy-makers. The conclusions I had reached were roughly these: the present situation might be captured yet and manipulated while it was still in its operatic phase, so to speak, and capable of being turned to advantage with fair words. There was a good chance of our gaining perhaps fifteen or twenty years on the bare promise of a democratic referendum. This would be a valuable gain—indeed an inestimable one—for it would give us time to overhaul the entire administrative machinery as well as the police; neither was fit to take the strain of a modern emergency. And while (*pace* Potter) I was prepared to believe that the Cypriots were cowards and would never show fight I was gravely alarmed at the thought of Cretans or Rhodians coming in to show them how; I had seen something of them, and in the present state of the police I wasn't sure that public opinion, as yet sluggish and inert, couldn't be roused by example. The state of our unpreparedness for any real crisis was frightening.

Outside all this, of course, our moral and legal title to the island was unassailable, though it would be a psychological error to lie back upon it. The same went for the Turks, whose reaction to Enosis could be counted upon to remain hostile. But while one must deeply sympathize with anyone not wanting to be administered by Greeks it was impossible not to recognize that the Turks were a minority—while their actual influence in the island as traders, business men, industrialists was very small—their life being almost entirely agricultural. Besides there was a certain hollowness about their case—though it was supposed to rest upon a desire for Union with Turkey. It was not, in fact, a desire for change but an understandable desire for the *status quo*. It was difficult to see how they could expect more than the most complete minority safeguards in the case of Enosis. But with fifteen years in hand anything might happen—and I myself would be prepared to believe that, if the present Anglo-Greek amity prevailed, a referendum might even give us the Cypriot vote outright.

Of course, the island could always be held by military force—but nowadays, with wobbling electorates at home unable to stand bloodshed and terrified of force, could one hold a Mediterranean colony if the measures one had to take in order to do so overstepped the bounds of ordinary police procedure? I doubted it. Besides all this, too, the secondary effects of the Cyprus issue might impinge on the solidity of the Balkan Pact and NATO.

I have no idea whether such propositions sounded at all convincing; in the dusty purlieus of the Secretariat they perhaps read like the ravings of some unhinged temporary civil servant. Yet they were opinions which I had tested over and over again in conversation—not only among the peasantry but among people of different political persuasions, even among people like the secretary of the Archbishop.

Throughout all these tiresome months of tergiversation the Ethnarchy itself had become alarmed by the difficulties it was facing. The swollen tides of public opinion in Greece and Cyprus were pressing upon the walls of the slender dam—the Archbishop's personal prestige, which alone kept events captive. He too had his difficulties; not merely from Balkan fanatics pressing for trouble, but also from a fair-sized Communist party. 'He who rides a tiger fears to get down,' says the Chinese proverb. There was almost a note of anguish in the Ethnarchy appeals for some issue to the problem.

We could not provide it—only London could—and the wires were silent while the omens gathered about us. 'In default of a policy try a bread poultice' seemed to be the general attitude, and indeed seen from Whitehall Cyprus itself looks absurdly small—a pink spot the size of a fingernail on the fretted map of the tragi-comic landscape of the Near East. Disappointed as I was, I calculated that it would take London perhaps six months to see the truth, for certainly the rising discontents in the Balkans would alert the Foreign Office. The reports from Athens and Ankara would show how quickly the tide was rising, and how necessary it was to think about Cyprus instead of taking cover behind indifference or petulance.

Ten days later Wren's small force brought off a well-planned *coup*, capturing the caique *Saint George* with all its cargo and the crew of five Greek nationals, together with the reception party of eight Cypriots, on the desolate beaches near Khlorakas. The prime mover appeared to be Socrates Loizides, expelled from Cyprus in 1950 for his seditious activities. A document which he obligingly brought with him revealed the existence of a 'well-armed and organized secret revolutionary organization EMAK, which was to overthrow the Cyprus Government'. He had apparently been working on his preliminary manifesto when Wren gave the order to close in, for it was unfinished though full of the usual rhetorical flourishes which I had heard in every coffee-house of the capital during the past year; he also carried on this operation—a typically

Cypriot touch, this—an English grammar: he had, it seems, been brushing up his irregular verbs during his non-revolutionary spare time. (He is still studying hard, I learn, in the Central Prison at Nicosia and nobody need show surprise if he takes his Matric. by correspondence at some time during the next ten years.) All tragedy is founded in human comedy, and even here, at the turning-point in our affairs, the spirit of the irrational which always hovers over the Greek scene kept brushing us with its wings; it was impossible at Paphos, when the trial opened, not to be amused by the gallery of desperadoes who sat in the dock, so perfectly did they symbolize the ignorant and lovable peasantry of those islands where so many thousand Commonwealth troops were given shelter after the collapse in Greece. Paddy Leigh Fermor reappeared briefly to cover their trial and together we sat in the narrow little dock-house at Paphos, while the mob howled and banged outside the courthouse, and fragmented the learned exchanges of lawyers with the sound of breaking glass and characteristic ululations. Of course they were all mad by logical standards; worse, blissfully unaware of the *moral guilt* of their position in law as felons. This was what shocked the jurists. They showed absolutely no sense of civic conscience—nor for that matter very much revolutionary bite. The whole thing had the air of a good-natured farce—it belonged to that operatic world of fictions based in the Greek attitude to modern history. Loizides himself, a painfully shy man, awkwardly constructed and of spiderish aspect, who wore glasses of a high magnification, conducted himself like a schoolboy convicted of roasting an aunt. He carried his black little Japanese head low; but the others revelled in the limelight—the Cypriots were particularly good types, easy to replace imaginatively by any of my villagers. They beamed when the sentences were passed and cocked an appreciative ear to the hubbub outside. They felt themselves to be heroes and martyrs.

We for our part were filled with a quite unjustifiable elation at the trimness and expertise of Wren's little operation; it proved that the Police Force, though small, could be used efficiently—and indeed it was to accomplish marvels for its size and state of hopeless disrepair throughout that stormy year.

'Still in the operatic phase': the phrase has much to commend it. 'But what happens,' asked my brother idly, 'when in the middle of the opera a real shot rings out and an actor falls dead?'

'It will never reach that pitch,' I said.

'I wish I could be sure,' he said.

So did I but I could not say so.

The Feast of Unreason

'Branches of orange, lovely with flowers;
Seven are the Bridesmaids who sew the bed.'
'Into the Bride's hall flew two nightingales;
They came to bring her English needles.'

(Cypriot Greek bridal song)

'Whenever a separation is made between liberty and justice neither is in my opinion safe.'

(EDMUND BURKE)

———◦◦◦———

Was the choice of the 1st of April fortuitous? I do not know. It was not inappropriate. We had spent the long tranquil evening walking upon the battlements of old Nicosia, watching the palms flicker in the twilight wind which the dusk brings across the bony Mesaoria. The ravens creaked home on weary wings to the tall trees by the Turkish Athletic Association, where nobody ever smiled.

My brother was due to leave, and as a tribute to him and the noisome menagerie he was taking back with him, we had friends in to drink his health, and to stare (holding their noses) into the crates and cardboard boxes which housed his catch, and which temporarily occupied my spare bedroom. Afterwards we dined by candlelight and talked, and were on the point of going to bed when the silence of the little town began to ripple and bulge all round us. Parcels of steel plates began dropping from heaven on to paving-stones, while pieces of solid air compressed themselves against the window frames making them jingle. Something appeared to walk up the garden path and lean against the front door, something of immense weight—a mammoth perhaps. The door burst open to reveal the dark garden and the heads of flowers tossing in the idle night wind. Then something appeared to go off between our teeth. 'I take it you are trying to say good-bye to me appropriately,' said my brother. 'Believe me, I am honoured.'

A string of dull bumps now, from many different quarters at once—as of small geological faults opening in the earth somewhere along the battlements of the fortress. We ran down the steps and along the unlit gravel road to where the main road joined it. A few bewildered-looking civilians stood dazed in the shadows of the trees. 'Over there,' said a man. He pointed in the direction of the Secretariat building which was about two hundred yards down the road. The street lamps were so few that we ran in and out of pools of darkness on the fringes of the unpavemented highway. We came round the last corner abreast and walked into a wall of solid yellow fog smelling strongly of something—cordite? In the vagueness figures walked about, aimlessly, with detached curiosity, uncertain whether to go or stay. They did not seem to have any more business there than we did. There was a tidy rent in the wall of the Secretariat out of which smoke poured as if from a steam engine. 'Dust,' said my brother grimly, 'from under the administrators' chairs.' But there was no time for jests; somewhere a siren began to wail in the direction of Wren's headquarters. A lorry load of police materialized vaguely out of the yellow coils of fog. And then another series of isolated bangs and, after an interval, a deeper growl which was followed by a sudden small contortion of the still night air. 'The whole bloody issue is going up,' said my brother fretfully; he had been peevish all evening about the failure of his film which had run into difficulties, he said, due to a sudden wave of non-co-operation which followed hard upon a visit by the parish priest to his actors. 'Wherever I go there's a bloody revolution.' He had just come back from Paraguay where they had revolted under him, so to speak. A bang nearer at hand lent wings to our purpose. 'I must get back to my animals,' he said. 'The owls have to be fed.'

But I felt the tug of other duties. I took the car, ignoring the fretful pealing of the telephone in that silent, book-lumbered hall with its dripping candles, and raced down to the Police Headquarters at Paphos Gate. It had a forlorn deserted air, and was, apart from one sleepy unarmed duty sergeant, unguarded as far as I could judge. In the operations room on the top floor the

Colonial Secretary sat at a desk tapping a pencil against his teeth; he was wearing a college blazer and trousers over his pyjamas, and a silk scarf. Behind him the two clerks crouched in an alcove beside the receiving set which scratched out a string of crackling messages in Doric English. 'Famagusta . . . a bomb in the garden of . . . Larnaca an attack on . . . a bomb thrown at a house in Limassol. . . .' He glanced at the signal pads as they were hurriedly brought in and placed before him. He was composing a message to the Secretary of State. He looked up quietly and said: 'I suppose this is the sort of thing you meant?' 'Yes, sir.' 'The worst thing so far is the radio station. Five masked men tied up the watchman and blew it up.'

By now the press had begun to block the meagre lines and I diverted them to an outer office where I dealt with them as faithfully as I could; but police reports were very slow in coming in and in many cases the Agencies were hours ahead of us. (They were to remain so for many a long month to come.)

The radio station was indeed badly blitzed, but it was lucky in the possession of an engineering staff which had been eating its heart out for a chance like this; by two o'clock the engineers had crawled into the wreckage and produced a fairly detailed report on the damage and the welcome information that one of the transmitters had escaped, which would allow of some sort of programme going out next day, on reduced power.

By the time I got home again to the importunities of the telephone—which thenceforward was to ring on an average every six minutes, night and day—the picture was clearing and becoming coherent. The attacks had been island-wide and synchronized. Leaflets, scattered in the street of the capital, spoke of an organization calling itself EOKA (ETHNIKI ORGANOSIS KYPRION AGONISTON), which had decided to begin the 'struggle for liberty'. They were signed DIGHENIS, an ominous enough name which, to the Greek mind, rings the same sort of bell as Robin Hood does to our schoolboys. He is a hero who belongs to a cycle of medieval folk songs; his battles are famous and he fears no one, not even old Charon, Death. Did he not, in the course of one of them, leap across from Asia Minor and leave his fingerprints on Pentadactylos, in Cyprus, before recovering his balance and leaping back?

Next morning the swollen-eyed headlines covered the front pages of the world press and in fits and starts the power-lines grew heavy with questions and answers, with telegrams and messages, the idle flickerings of the world's frontal brain; and the press corps began to swell.

Yet the morning, like some perfect deception, dawned fine, and nobody walking about the calm streets of the town, watching the shopkeepers taking down their shutters and sipping their morning coffee, could have told that some decisive and irrevocable action had taken place in the night; a piece of the land had broken away, had slid noiselessly into the sea. In a sense now there was no more thinking to be done. We had reached a frontier. From now it would be a question of hanging on. Such solutions as those we had dreamed about were all thrown into relief by the ugly shadow of impending insurrection. And yet everywhere there were doubts. The ordinary people of Cyprus went about their work with the same friendly good-manners, many of them genuinely shocked by the work of 'hotheads' and genuinely grateful when the Governor described them as 'law-abiding'. I concluded that EOKA must consist of a small body of revolutionaries, unknown to the general public. Wren did not share this view. 'What would you say,' he said dryly, 'if every sixth-form boy in every public school in England had signed this oath?' His agents had brought in a new document.

YOUTH ORGANIZATION OF EOKA

Oath

I swear in the name of the Holy Trinity that:
(1) I shall work with all my power for the liberation of Cyprus from the British yoke, sacrificing for this even my life.
(2) I shall perform without question all the instructions of the organization which may be entrusted to me and I shall not bring any objection, however difficult and dangerous these may be.
(3) I shall not abandon the struggle unless I receive instructions

from the leader of the organization and after our aim has been accomplished.

(4) I shall never reveal to anyone any secret of our organization neither the names of my chiefs nor those of the other members of the organization even if I am caught and tortured.

(5) I shall not reveal any of the instructions which may be given me even to my fellow combatants.

If I disobey my oath I shall be worthy of every punishment as a traitor and may eternal contempt cover me.

Signed

EOKA

'Moreover,' he went on, 'there appeared to be plenty of bombs to go round—we're scooping the stuff up all over the island. They seem mostly home-made; the village smithies appear to have been working overtime. It rather makes nonsense of your theory about innocent old rustics with straw in their hair toasting the queen. You can't organize these things overnight, you know.' He was right, of course, and events bore him out. As the nights shook and rumbled to the crash of grenades it became clear that, despite the amateurishness of execution (there was more broken glass than anything at first), the whole thing was part of a design. Situated as we were at the frail centre of the cobweb, we held our breaths and praised heaven for the inefficiency of these mosquito raids. They succeeded overwhelmingly in one thing, however, and that was the undermining of public morale. Here and there, too, among a hundred incidents of juvenile futility there was one which bore the pug-marks of something uglier—the trained hand. Evidence began to come in of Cypriots having received para-military instruction somewhere outside the island—in Greece. Rumour spoke of 'phased' operations which would be directed against the police to begin with, and added under its breath the words 'like Palestine'.

To the disorder and alarm of the night-hours were added further demonstrations and riots organized by the schools which were dealt with crisply enough—but it was obvious that the police could not work right round the clock, chasing bombardiers all night and louts all day. The field of operations, too, lent itself to these harrowing tactics, for the labyrinth of warrens in the old town could hide a veritable army of bomb-throwers—even military estimates indicated that it would take practically a Brigade to search it thoroughly in one operation. When it was cordoned off, piece by piece, malefactors could easily slip over from the Famagusta Gate to the Turkish Konak in a matter of minutes.

The public, too, always timorous and in this case deliberately sympathetic to the trouble-makers, became deaf and blind, prejudicing the course of justice by its silence—which in the end could only lead to sterner measures by which the public itself would suffer. The perversion of justice was perhaps the most serious factor from the point of view of administration; Wren found it impossible to secure convictions against people unless caught *in flagrante delicto*. And then, the age groups to which these youthful terrorists belonged struck us as alarming. Moreover the moral pressure exercised by Athens radio, which went into raptures at every evidence of what it described as an open insurrection, was backed up by the local clergy whose public utterances reached new heights of bloodcurdling ferocity. The legal apparatus found itself grappling with new and disturbing formulations. Repressive measures would have to be taken; in what light would they be regarded by a world press already critical of our attitude to the question?

And then the police—always the police; Wren's calm and measured assessments had been committed to paper and sent on their way; but how could they be 'implemented'—with the best will in the world? And if things got worse would they not fall short of the requirements he now thought necessary?

The nights became stretched and tense, punctuated by the sullen crack of grenades and the roar of police traffic as Wren's forces raced to the incident in the vain hope of a capture. To the customary home-made grenades and Molotov cocktails was now added a new unpleasantness—a bomb fitted with a time-pencil: a soul-destroying weapon in its effects on the morale of peaceful civilians. These at least were not home-made.

'Freedom is acquired only by blood,' shrilled Athens radio. But whose blood? A bomb placed in a letter-box at the entrance to Nicosia Central Police Station went off while the street was still crowded with market-visitors and killed a Greek outright; sprawling among the wreckage on the sidewalk were thirteen injured Turks and Armenians. The shadow of communal reprisals grew bigger as the leader of the Turkish National Party warned the Greek community against any further outrage in the Turkish quarter. Bars, private houses, restaurants, graveyards— a bewildering succession of pointless targets came up. The military sent in supporting patrols by night now to help Wren; roadblocks and searches began to mark off familiar thoroughfares. The patient taciturn soldiery now began to stop cars and lorries on the main roads to hunt for arms. . . .

And as if to echo the disorders of the towns the sleeping countryside now began to wake sporadically with intimations of more serious, more considered, operations conducted by bands which were both more informed and more resolute than the juveniles. It became clear that there were two sorts of enemy, a vast amorphous mass of secondary schoolboys whose task was bombing and pamphleteering and supporting public disorder— and a group of mountain bandits whose task was to raid police stations, organize ambushes and operate against the net of roads and telegraph wires which constituted the nervous system of the administration. They were dryly classified by Wren as the 'Junior and Senior Leagues'. To these he was later to add a third and final category—'The Killers', which could not have numbered above twenty or thirty, to judge by the later ballistics evidence which could point to one gun, say, as having been responsible for upwards of ten street killings. But all this was buried in futurity, still covered by the deceptive mask of a perfect spring, smothered in wild flowers and rejoicing in those long hours of perfect calm which persuaded all but the satraps that the nightmare had faded. The shopping centres would be deserted for half a day after an incident; and then people would slowly creep out again, wistfully breathing in the silent air, like animals snuffing the wind; and reassured, they would start to go about the hundred trivial tasks of the day which the automatism of ordinary life had made endearing, comprehensible—containing no element of prediction.

The Feast of Unreason

So they would open shutters, set out chairs, dust, combine and recombine their wares in familiar patterns, or simply sighing, bend vulpine features to the loved and familiar Turkish coffee which came swinging towards them on the little pendulum-trays of the waiters. And in these same daylight hours blond and brown soldiers walked the streets, chaffing their acquaintances among the townsmen and being chaffed in return—and their wives rolled perambulators full of rosy children, about the market greeted everywhere by smiles and customary attentions. It was unreal. One has seen rabbits scatter like this at the report of a gun, only to re-emerge after half an hour and timidly come out to grass again—unaware that the hunter is still there, still watching. Civilians have no memory. Each new event comes to them on a fresh wave of time, pristine and newly delivered, with all its wonder and horror brimming with novelty. Only in dull offices with electric light burning by day the seekers sat, doggedly listing events in order to study their pattern, to relate past and present, so that like stargazers they might peer a little way into the darkening future.

The village was no less deceptive in its complete smiling calm —the flowering cyclamen and the rows of glorious roses which Kollis tended so carefully; once more, as the engine died and the silence swelled up round me, my friends detached themselves one by one from the knots of coffee-drinkers under the great tree, to bring me messages whose familiarity restored in a moment the pattern in things which already Nicosia was slowly breaking down and dispersing; talk of carob-wood, lemon-trees, silk-worms, a new wine. Of the crisis hardly a word was said, save by the *muktar* whose responsibilities weighed so heavily upon him that he felt permitted to ignore the laws of tact. 'Aren't you afraid to come up here?' he said. 'Why should I be?' 'Are you armed?' 'No.' He sighed. 'I will lend you a gun.' 'Against who —Andreas or Mr. Honey?' He laughed heartily at this. 'No. None of us would harm you. But people come here sometimes from outside, at night, in cars. Look!' On the wall under the Tree of Idleness' was written in blue paint: SLAVES BREAK YOUR CHAINS: LIBERTY OR DEATH. It seemed a poor place to choose for a recruiting centre, to judge by the statuesque devotees of indolence who sat there quietly enjoying a professional idleness. 'They came up in a car and painted it under the headlights. I heard them. Michaelis' son saw them and said they were masked.'

Up at the house everything was quiet save for the puffing and blowing of Xenu who was clearing up after my family's departure. At the spring, filling his water-bottle, stood old Morais, who catching sight of me, took a step down and shook my hand with warm agitation. 'Before God,' he said hoarsely, 'I do not want all these things to happen.' 'Nor I.' He stood for a long moment in deep perplexity, at a loss for words—but he had said everything; nobody wanted these things to happen, but they were happening. They prejudiced everything that could have been built out of the firm rough clasp of the old man's hand. He turned abruptly, almost angrily and stamped up the hill to his little house, muttering under his breath.

As week followed week I returned to the village less frequently, though I would have been glad to live out there if I had been able to persuade the authorities to install a telephone in Dmitri's wine-shop—but I am forgetting. To the normal hours of a standard office routine I was now forced to add hours of alertness at night, dealing with the routine questions of the press which poured in from every side. But though the corps had swollen and multiplied the work there were compensations in the form of friends whom I had not seen for some time; and my dinner-table such as it was always had a face or two I was glad to remember: Ralph Izzard, with his gentle and civilized air, Stephen Barber, boisterous and serious at once, Richard Williams whose companionable laughter and sly wit made time pass delightfully. And young Richard Lumley, who came for a week-end and stayed nearly six months, sharing the house and everything that went with it—sudden invasions of friends or visitors: telephone calls: alarms in the night: and blessed laughter (Shan Sedgwick borne through the door on gales of his own laughter with a live turkey under his arm). The crisis brought me people I might never have met again for many years.

The worlds I lived in now were like three separate ice floes gradually drifting apart on the Gulf Stream; the world of Government House or the Colonial Secretary's lodge—a world of fairy lights gleaming on well-tended flower-beds under the great stone lion and unicorn; a world where groups of well-groomed men and women tasted the rational enjoyments life had to offer to slow music, pacing upon freshly laundered grass as green as any England can show, outside time. Then the world of the office with its stereotyped routines and worries. Lastly the village, composed around the Abbey as around the echo of a quotation from Virgil, in which an amputated present was enough and the future nobody's direct concern. Once or twice I thought I remarked a trifling frigidity among the villagers which might have indicated a change of tone; but I was wrong. If anything they had become less rather than more critical of foreigners. There was something else underneath it, too, like the pressure of a wound, a pain which they carried about with them like a load. If the situation met with any response here it met only with a sad reproach from the dark eyes of the old men. They had stopped saying, 'Hey, Englishman,' in the old jaunty cocky way, but they had not yet abandoned the word 'neighbour'—only it was beginning to feel weighty, impregnated with sadness. These things are hard to analyse.

In the midst of this deepening sense of crisis there came a welcome relief in the form of a policy statement from London, convoking a Three-Power Conference to study the 'political and defence questions affecting the Eastern Mediterranean,' a means of offering the issues of Cyprus at least a safety-valve if not a solution. In my usual optimistic way I thought I saw in it a possible solution to things which might halt the deathward drift of affairs in the island. Alas! it was to prove only a brief respite. By now, of course, we had become inured to the nightly gauntlet of grenades and the running fire of telephone calls; nevertheless the news was welcome, and events seemed to be smiling upon us after so long a time of waiting.

The mosquito raids went on unremittingly of course; you cannot turn Greeks on and off like a tap. The Governor had narrowly escaped being killed by an exploding time-bomb in May—literally by moments—for the bomb, placed in a cinema and fused to go off during a charity performance, exploded as the hall had emptied but while the foyer was still full of people. The raids on the police stations too went on, while almost daily the police uncovered some new hoard of arms or ammunition.

Wren's deceptive composure covered many things—not least the realization that the task he was setting himself was an impossible one: for a police force is not merely a collection of arms and legs, and cannot be numbered by heads like a trayful of cabbages. Its animating force is intelligence, and here was the gap which could not be filled by the multiplication-table. It was fantastic in an island where everyone was related to everyone else, in an area so circumscribed, how little general intelligence was coming in. Usually in Cyprus gossip penetrated everywhere; if you blew your nose loudly in Larnaca before driving at speed to Limassol you would certainly meet someone on arrival who had already heard of the fact. Partly the silence was due to fear of reprisals; but mostly because the sympathies of the general public were engaged, and even the non-combatant's door was always open to shelter a bomb-thrower. Paddy Leigh Fermor had once remarked how completely sabotage operations depended upon the sympathies of the general public, adding: 'After all, in Crete there were only about five of us, each with a very small band of chaps, and we kept a number of German divisions sprawling and pinned down for years.' Were we to risk a repetition of the same thing in Cyprus? It was hard to decide, but on balance it did not seem that the Cypriots themselves would have the stamina to last out a long siege. I myself might have agreed with this proposition had I not felt that Greece was able to supply what was lacking in men, materials or moral support; and I knew that the island could not be effectively sealed off by sea and air.

Mine was not a widely shared view, at least among the foreign community. General opinion here suggested that tough tactics and economic reprisals could be effective against the middle classes who would not long withstand a direct assault upon their pockets, and indeed would if pressed hard surrender from their midst the few active terrorists among them. This showed a frightening political ignorance, both about the nature of revolutions in general and about the animating spirit of the present discontents. It was clear even at this time that the intellectuals regarded EOKA as having behind it the irresistible momentum of modern Greek history; Cyprus was simply a repetition of Macedonia. Crete had, after all, been cleared in this way; and the only tragedy of the whole affair was that the war was directed against a traditional and much-beloved friend whose lack of historical understanding was incomprehensible. . . .

It was easy to talk in bars about tough tactics ('One touch of the stockwhip, old boy, I've seen it before' and 'We must squeeze the Cyps till they squeak') but these were lines of thought which were politically unfruitful; for the stockwhip might fall upon innocent shoulders, and unwittingly cause a resentment which would provide recruits for EOKA rather than informers for the Government. There was a village proverb which said: 'He couldn't catch the mule so he gave the saddle a good thrashing.' This was what we were gradually being compelled to do by the pressure of events, though at this early time, with a Conference coming up at which our problems might all be rationalized, there seemed no undue cause for despondency. Indeed as far as could be judged the general public enjoyed a widespread feeling of relief that at last Cyprus was going to be submitted to the arbitration of the mind, and not allowed to rot slowly like a gangrened limb.

My own luck, too, was in; for I was offered a three days' visit to Athens and London for duty consultations, an opportunity I grasped eagerly. I also snatched a night alone at the Bellapaix house during this slight lull among the tensions of politics, glad to recreate with deliberation the routine of last year—which already seemed remote and unrecapturable; rising at four, I mean, and cooking my breakfast by rosy candlelight and writing a letter or two, to far-away Marie or my daughter, before clambering down the dark street with Frangos and his cattle, to watch the dawn breaking behind the gaunt spars of the Abbey. Clusters of gold and citron, stretched taut as a violin string, upon bass

Gregorian blues and greys. Then to climb the range with the light, spoke by spoke, to where the dawn spilled and spread on the bare cardboard plain with its two spikes of minaret rising out of the indistinctness, the car falling like a swallow towards the table-land of the Mesaoria. . . . I had come to love Cyprus very much by now, I realized, even its ugliness, its untidy sprawling vistas of dust and damp cloud, its hideous incongruities.

Then up over the Cyclades, into a different weightless world inhabited by the music of gulls and surf breaking upon deserted beaches, covered now in a green fleecy mist which allowed an island to become visible from time to time, tenuous as a promise. The edges of the sea lime-green, cobalt, emerald. . . .

Athens was recognizably beautiful still, as a woman who has had her face lifted may still be beautiful; but she had become a capital now, full of vast avenues and towering buildings. She had lost her grubby and endearing provinciality—had moved a step nearer towards the featureless modern problem town. It was hot, and everyone was away in the islands. The few friends I could find writhed over the Cyprus question like worms halved by the ploughshare—hardly able to believe their own eyes and minds. I was able to spend one memorable afternoon forgetting Cyprus however, with old George Katsimbalis in a favourite *taverna* under the Acropolis; and a whole day recalling Belgrade with Sir Charles Peake, who had been my Ambassador there, and who was now grappling with the thankless task of representing us in Greece: a Greece changed out of all recognition by the Enosis problem.

On the quiet terrace at his summer villa, near Kavouri, I recaptured some of the old illusion of timeless peace as I watched the sky darken at his shoulder, and the smooth black polish of that magnificent bay become slowly encrusted with lights, sweeping and slithering upwards into the sky, the hot black sky of Attica. Here and there a green eye or a red glowed and smouldered, marking a ship. But sea and land had become indistinguishable.

He spoke with gentle affection of Greece and of his hopes for the coming Conference which might find a resolution for things and bring us all a more breathable air; and I echoed them. It was hard to say good-bye, though, and leave that delightful villa, to drive back through the dry scented starlight to Athens; harder still to watch the Acropolis from a thousand feet fade and diminish in the dawn-light, all its nacreous marbles glowing at the sky.

London with its drooping grey mist and unemphatic tones awaited me. Coming out of the Colonial Office I knew at once that the Empire was all right by the animation of the three African dignitaries who shared the lift with me, and who walked to the bus stop talking like a trio of 'cellos. They gave off overpowering waves of Chanel Number 5—as if they had hosed themselves down with it after breakfast like genial elephants, before starting out on a round of official calls. I pitied the occupants of the bus they hailed with yells and waved umbrellas.

I attended as best I could to the wants of my office, but was completely unprepared for the honour of a personal interview with the Secretary of State, to whose office I was summoned on my third day. His intimidating height and good looks would have marked him out as extraordinary in any company; but to these were added the charm and liberal disposition of an eighteenth-century gentleman—great style completely untouched by affectation, and a broad cutting mind which was sophisticated in the true sense. And humour. There was no room for timidities and attitudes in his presence—his simplicity and directness would have riddled them. I told him what was in my mind; how great were the hopes to be reposed in the coming Conference. I added that while sharp Turkish reactions were to be expected, and the Turkish support of our case might seem on the face of it politically expedient, it would be unwise to shelter behind it. We should face the self-determination issue squarely if we wished to achieve a lasting settlement which would mobilize the general goodwill of the people without which even a heavily defended base would be simply an enclave in a bitterly hostile area. Cyprus seemed to me one case where sovereignty and security were not necessarily compatible; and within a planned time-limit of twenty years (which I believed might be acceptable) we might achieve a great deal. The present situation was containable indefinitely by force, of course, even if it grew worse; the one dangerous aspect was the police picture in the island. . . . I can put these points down since I made a note of them immediately after this talk.

He listened to me gravely and sympathetically, and I knew why. He himself knew the island well, had lived in Pearce's lovely house and walked the lemon-glades of Lapithos, or taken coffee with the villagers. He knew every inch of the sinuous Gothic range with its tiny hospitable villages. For him too the present situation was painful, crowded with associations, and full of thorns. He could tell me little, however, as the Cabinet was still debating the affairs of the island.

From the vantage-point of Whitehall, too, the angle of vision changed, for here in London Cyprus was not only Cyprus; it was part of a fragile chain of telecommunication centres and ports, the skeletal backbone of an Empire striving to resist the encroachments of time. If Cyprus were to be frivolously wished away then what of Hong Kong, Malta, Gibraltar, the Falklands, Aden—all troubled but stable islands in the great pattern? Palestine and Suez had been questions of foreign sovereignty; they had never been Crown possessions. Cyprus belonged, from the point of view of geography and politics, to the Empire's very backbone. Must it not, then, be held at all costs?

I could not find my way forward among all these mutually contradictory propositions; it seemed to me that everybody was right and everybody wrong. Yet a peaceful solution must be there to be won if only we could provide a formula. But the Conference would perhaps do that for us.

While I was busy with these brain-wrenching considerations I was told that the Secretary of State had decided to visit Cyprus the next day, and that I must return to my post forthwith. Arrangements had been made for me to travel back in his private plane.

The take-off was scheduled for five the next day, but frequent telephone calls were necessary to check this; we would fly all night, touching down only at Naples for refuelling.

At four that afternoon I found the sleek old-fashioned C.O.I. cars drawn up outside the private office, together with the Secretary of State's own gleaming Rolls. There still remained hurried last-minute dispositions to be made and my car was told off to pick up the personal bodyguard and Sir John Martin who was to travel out with us.

In the shady portals of New Scotland Yard we picked up a ruddy-faced, white-whiskered man in well-cut clothes, who combined the air of being a regular colonel with something else, an indefinable sense of having seen the seamy side of life; he joked slyly as his luggage was loaded. No, he did not carry machine-guns about him on assignments like these, he said. 'I manage with a good eye and a very small Colt.' One had the impression that anything larger would show a bulge in that well-cut suit. He had a novel and a set of pocket-chess with him, and proposed to spend the night working on a problem.

Now we swept across London, halting only to pick up Sir John and his suitcase. He was armed, more appropriately, with a copy of the *Iliad* which sorted well with his gentle and scholarly manner.

Rain was falling over London but by the time we reached Northolt the sky was clear and full of larks spiralling up from the grass of the airfield. I was impressed by the V.I.P. Lounge, which I was not likely to see, I thought, again in this life, and enjoyed the passport and customs formalities which were so cursory as to make me feel rather like the Aga Khan. Such are the pleasures of travelling in a great man's entourage. The old Valetta, however, had rather a second-hand air, and the Secretary of State inspected the guard of honour briefly. His wife and children were there to see him off, and he embraced them warmly and naturally in a way that would have touched old Frangos. The red dispatch cases were loaded and we climbed aboard and seated ourselves, while the pilot gave us a sharp talk about life-jackets, adding with a twinkle, 'This is a well-victualled ship, and there won't be any closing time once we are airborne.'

This however did not seem as easy as it sounded; twice we were recalled from the tarmac just as we were about to make our run, by telephone calls from the Prime Minister, and twice the Secretary of State made a good-humoured journey back to the telephone in the lounge.

Then at last we were up, in slow swerves and gyres, into a soft magical sunset over England. There was a general settling down and taking off of coats. 'Whisky and soda?' Sir John posed his *Iliad* strategically on the port-hole as he accepted the offering. Our ears began to tune themselves to the hum and whistle of the machine; smiles and gestures to replace words. The pilot came forward, stood to attention, and saluted smartly as he handed the Secretary of State a piece of paper. 'It's just come through, sir,' he shouted. 'I thought you might like to see it.' I thought this must be some thrilling communication from the P.M. and was quite alarmed when the Secretary of State groaned in anguish and clutched his head. What did this portend? War, perhaps, had broken out. 'England all out for 155,' he cried passing the paper to Sir John who pursed his lips and looked vaguely at it, unable to respond to the news with quite the same wholeheartedness. 'What a rotten show.'

After an hour of acclimatization and rest the food and drink disappeared and the red dispatch cases were brought forward and their contents spread out upon the table. The party fell to work with a will and carried on through the darkness until I began to doze myself.

We refuelled at Naples on a deserted field full of hollow darkened buildings with here and there a flare picking up the rounded flanks of some great charter aircraft. Cyprus with its problems did not swim up at us until about nine the next morning, brown and misty and framed by the singing sea. Regretfully the *Iliad* was put aside, the dream surrendered for the reality; my own paper-backed P. G. Wodehouse had lain untouched in my coat pocket. (I had been too ashamed to bring it out in such distinguished company. We highbrow poets have our pride.)

For the next two days there were conferences and meetings, indecisive in themselves perhaps, but valuable in giving the Secretary of State a chance to meet the personalities whose different attitudes made up the jig-saw of the Cyprus problem. I was amused too by the consternation in the Secretariat when the great man disappeared at dawn one morning. It appeared that he had gone to Lapithos for an early bathe, and to drink a coffee with some peasant cronies at the little tavern; a typical and delightful touch in the middle of so much boring work. He was back by 9.30.

That morning a time-bomb blew up the Income Tax Office harming no one; there was great dismay when it was learned that all the Income Tax returns for the year had not been blown up with the office. Another and later bomb at the Land Registry Office was discovered in time and rendered harmless. In this atmosphere of tiresome hazard the consultations continued, and more and more the question of self-determination emerged as the key factor to the political aspect of things—though of course this was now only another way of saying Enosis, since the Greeks were in a majority of five to one.

The Tripartite Conference was everywhere rumoured to be a trap, baited by an unacceptable constitution with no safeguards for a future freedom of suffrage on the Union issue; the Arch-bishop flew the short leg to Athens to keep the uneasy Papagos on the white line. Athens now seemed to have become quite uncertain of itself, for the question had begun to threaten the internal stability of Greece, and the stability of the very faction we had assisted into power and helped to fight the Communists. We were in danger now of letting the Right wing founder in Greece—and this process was being blissfully helped by the Cypriot Greeks who had never had any experience of foreign relations and who pressed for firmer international action. By now, of course, public opinion in Greece was in a very excitable state and anything smelling of moderation sounded 'unpatriotic'. Greek cabinets depend on the state of public opinion for their stability in a way that no other government does. Tail was wagging dog, Nicosia was wagging Athens. And behind it all a thundercloud was gathering over Greek-Turkish relations. These were urgent, indeed pre-eminent considerations; against them, it seemed to me, a bomb or two in Cyprus was a mere secondary feature. It was a relief to know that the Greek Government had accepted the invitation to London without asking for the conditions demanded by both the Archbishop and the Communists. It was a measure of the urgency with which the situation was viewed from Athens. They were in a nasty jam; but then so were we in Cyprus.

Meanwhile things were hardening up domestically; if terrorists could not be brought to justice they could at least be penned out of harm's way. In early July the Detention Laws were promulgated, making Wren's task a bit easier, and indirectly I suppose saving a number of lives among the apprentices and schoolboys who were locked up summarily when they could not, for lack of witnesses, be charged. This touched off a series of attacks by Athens radio, which accused us of 'Fascism' and even 'Genocide'. The living conditions of the detainees became a staple for commentaries and hysterical knife-twisting, and the conditions of life within Kyrenia castle were hotly debated. 'We again challenge the Public Information Officer to answer the following question on behalf of the Cypriot people: are there or are there not latrines at the castle? And if there are no latrines, what is the substitute? And one more question: Is it or is it not true that the contents of the metal buckets, used as horrible substitutes for latrines, are emptied at a very short distance from the castle, thereby endangering the health of the detainees? It must be true, Mr. Durrell, unless our sense of sight and smell, as well as the swarms of flies and other filthy insects, deceive us.' This seemed to be going a bit far; I was tempted to ask the Greek Ministry of Information a few choice questions about the general state of sanitation in Greece—which has to be experienced to be believed —but I spared him; Philhellenism dies hard. 'Nevertheless,' said the Colonial Secretary, 'you'd better go up yourself and have a look, and arrange to have the press taken round to show that though we may be Fascist beasts our sanitation is still sound.' I reluctantly agreed to do so.

The camp had now been moved from the castle to Kokkinotrimithia, and here on the harsh bare unlovely table-land the sappers had run up a few huts and a great wire pen. It looked from far off like an abandoned turkey farm. I rode up with

Foster who spoke despairingly of the lack of reason the prisoners showed, of their absolute contempt of law, of civic morality. 'About two-thirds of them could be indicted on serious offences,' he repeated with fussy solicitude, 'the little bastards! And they throw clods at visitors and shout "Fascist" at us. Us, Fascists, I ask you!'

It was a sad place; like one of those soulless transit camps near the western desert. The inmates looked a somewhat chastened and bedraggled lot—and a number were by no means infants. I kept an eye cocked for my students. On past form I was convinced I should find the whole of Epsilon Alpha behind bars, but I was relieved to recognize only two, the fat ruffian Joanides and Paul. Joanides was a grocer's son, and a natural comedian of such talent that I had been forced to expel him at the beginning of almost every lesson, much to my regret as his sallies (which were all in *patois*) were very funny indeed. He had spent his English hour walking up and down the corridors whistling tunelessly and pretending, when the headmaster was on the prowl, that he was going to the lavatory. He set up a great whoop when he saw me and said: 'So they got you at last, Mr. Durrell? I told you you were too friendly with the Greeks. Now they've nobbled you.' For a moment I think he really believed it. We entered the pen and he fairly romped up to me. 'What are you doing here?' I said with severity, 'fool that you are. This is where your folly has brought you, Imbecile.' I asked Foster what he had been doing, and the boy shifted uneasily from one fat calf to the other. His round face fell. 'He had a bomb on him,' said Foster sighing with grandmotherly despair. 'I ask you, a grenade.' Joanides looked from Foster to me and then back again. He was sad to find us so severe. 'Ach! Mr. Durrell,' he said, 'it was just a *little* bomb,' extending his index fingers and holding them three inches apart. I passed him by in silence.

Living conditions were cramped but not bad. Probably less hard than they are for many a National Service youth. We toured the huts, examined the food and hot-water facilities. To judge by the books on most of the window-sills and beds a number of the terrorists must have been intellectuals. I saw Myrivilis' *Life*

Entombed and the rare Athens edition of Cavafy; Seferis' poems and *Aeolia* by Venezis with my own preface which had been lovingly translated from the English edition. These things hurt me, as I realized for the first time that the appeal of EOKA was not to wrongdoers, congenital felons, but precisely to the most spirited and idealistic element among the youth. They would be the ones to suffer at the dictates of the ringmasters.

Paul was standing in a window, looking pointedly away across that cruel and barren no man's land of red sandstone. He gave no sign and I did not wish to intrude upon him. I hesitated, and then joined Foster to make a slow circuit of the room, picking up here and there an exercise book or a newspaper. At last I went up to him and put my hand on his shoulder. 'Why are you here?' I said.

He was not far from tears, but the face that he turned to me tried to be composed, impassive. He did not speak but stared at me with a look of furious anguish—as if indeed a wolf were gnawing at his vitals. 'He had a bomb too,' said Foster wearily. 'Bloody little fools! What do they think they gain by it? He threw it in the churchyard by the cross-roads. I suppose he thought he'd scare us all out of our wits.'

'Are you in EOKA?' I asked.

'We are all EOKA. All Cyprus,' he said in a low controlled voice. 'If he wants to know why I threw it in the churchyard tell him because I was a coward. I am unworthy. But the others are not like me. They are not afraid.' I saw suddenly that what I had mistaken for hatred of my presence, my person, was really something else—shame. 'Why are you a coward?' He moved a whole step nearer to tears and swallowed quickly. 'I was supposed to throw it in a house but there were small children playing in the garden. I could not. I threw it in the churchyard.'

Superb egotism of youth! He had been worried about his own inability to obey orders. It is, of course, not easy for youths raised in a Christian society, to turn themselves into terrorists overnight —and in a sense his problem was the problem of all the Cypriot Greeks. If Frangos had been given a pistol to shoot me I am convinced that he would not have been able to pull the trigger. 'So you are sorry because you didn't kill two children?' I said. 'What a twisted brain, what a twisted stick you must be as well as a fool!' He winced and his eyes flashed. 'War is war,' he said. I left him without another word.

I interviewed two committees, each consisting of a group of three elected youths, whose duty it was to be responsible for the opinions of their pen. They had little to complain of, though they complained hotly and manfully about everything. I heard them out, wore them down, and at last listed their grounds for complaint—the most serious of which was that the crowded conditions prevented them from studying for their examinations! Most of them were due to take G.C.E. this year. When I told Foster this he took both hands off the steering wheel and put them over his ears. 'Don't,' he pleaded in anguish. 'Don't tell me any more. They are *mad*. I can't take it. First they throw a bomb, then they want to pass their School Cert., and I'm a Fascist because they can't!' He moaned and rocked from side to side. 'It's like being a male nurse in an institution. Are all the Greeks as mad as this lot?'

The answer, of course, was yes. 'Well, I'm out of my depth,' said Foster, 'and the sooner I get back to U.K. the better.' I must say I sympathized with him.

The days passed in purposeless riots and the screaming of demagogues and commentators; and the nights were busy with the crash of broken glass and the spiteful detonation of small grenades. The Turks began to get restive. Sabri's eyes darkened and flashed as he spoke of the situation. I had driven over on Sunday to collect some wood for the house. 'How much longer are they going to tolerate these Greeks?' he demanded. The day before there had been a serious riot and he himself had turned back a mob of Turks bent upon setting fire to the Bishopric. (Sabri was a very gallant man: I once saw him dive fully clothed into Kyrenia harbour to rescue a Greek fisherman's child in difficulties.) 'We Turks would not tolerate it,' he said as he sat, unmoving among his perambulators. 'You must take sterner measures. Fines. Severe sentences. I know these people. I was born here. They will come to heel. We Turks know the way.'

But of course the methods of 1821 were hardly possible to contemplate today, and the Greeks knew it. If we had been Russians or Germans the Enosis problem would have been solved in half an hour—by a series of mass murders and deportations. No democracy could think along these lines.

And then, how recognizable were the Cypriots of today from those of yesterday? That evening a Dutch journalist repeated to me a conversation he had had with a Greek consular official in which the latter said: 'To be honest *we* never thought the bastards would show fight. We never dreamed all this trouble would come about. We backed them up morally because we think their claim was just; but never materially. It's entirely a Cypriot show, and it has astonished us. Cyprus is like a man who has been told he is impotent for generations; suddenly he finds himself in bed with a lovely girl and discovers that he isn't—he can actually make love! We thought it would be all over in a month, but now we think it will really go on.' He had forgotten, he said, that the quality of obstinacy was something which the Cypriots did not share with metropolitan Greeks. . . . And so on. True or false?

From all these fragmented pieces of the original life of Cyprus —the quietness and certainty of ordered ways and familiar rhythms—it was impossible now to assemble a coherent picture, even up at the Abbey where the coffee drinkers still sat, drenched in the Gothic silence and coolness of those idle afternoons, against a wall with its livid cartoons which urged them to throw off their imprisoning web of sleep and act.

But the shots which rang out on the afternoon before the London Conference opened should have dispelled any hopes I entertained of a dramatic and satisfactory solution to our troubles. The death of P.C. Poullis in the open street after a Communist rally, not only virtually put Wren's Special Branch out of commission, but later provided the Greeks with the first of the Enosis martyrs in the person of Karaolis, a mild well-mannered youth in the Income Tax department of the Government. The grotesque, the unreal, was rapidly becoming the normal. The hush of Cyprus, which had, for so many generations, been the calm unemphatic hush of an island living outside time but within the boundaries of a cherished order, had changed: the hush of a new fear had gripped it, and the air was darkened with the vague shapes and phantoms of a terror which the Government could no longer dispel or hold at bay. The political liberty of the subject was a secondary consideration where one could not offer bare security of person in the open street. We were penetrated at every point; Security in the professional police sense had become as vague a term as the personal security of the subject. The six thousand civil servants themselves now began to feel the squeeze of the terror; an invisible pistol dogged them. There was no question of loyalties—for everyone was loyal. But no informer could pass the barrier without being discovered and that meant death; conversely not to obey a terrorist command might also mean death. What was the position of a secondary schoolboy who had signed the EOKA oath and who one day found himself in a small room with three masked men who ordered him to place a time-bomb or commit a murder—*or else pay the price*? The police depended upon Cypriots for intelligence; they were penetrated. In the administration it was the same. The Colonial Secretary himself had a Cypriot secretary—devoted and loyal as she was. Secure confidence was everywhere prejudiced, and everywhere there grew the sensation of the walls closing in upon us.

But the key was finally turned upon Cyprus by the London Conference, where the Turkish attitude, which had now become as hard as a rock, could not be shifted by a degree; nor was anyone disposed to imitate Hannibal and try a little vinegar. My worst fears were realized, though here again I was guilty of misjudgement, for the Turkish case was not merely politically expedient to follow; it linked itself in other ways to pacts and agreements outside Cyprus, affecting the Arab world. Could one afford to cross Turkey? Either way we were confronted by a hedge of thorns. We had undermined the stability of Athens and indeed our whole Balkan position by an earlier refusal to take the Greek case on Cyprus seriously; we might, in any late attempt to unwind the spools of policy back to that point, unsettle the Turkish alliance, and prejudice the whole complex of Middle Eastern affairs in which this great Moslem power played such an important part. We had allowed too much time to pass, and Turkish public opinion was now in the grip of a hysteria which, though less justified, was as strong as that which was gripping Athens. The Turkish case, as such, did not of course carry as much weight as the Greek though one could sympathize with the Turks of Cyprus. Nevertheless it was difficult to understand how a hypothetically Greek Cyprus could constitute a graver military threat to Turkey than did Rhodes or Thasos; and the two hundred thousand Turks in Thrace do not seem to find life harder than the corresponding number of Greeks living in Turkey. . . . But national hysteria makes a poor counsellor, and the shocking riots which followed in September in Turkey made the argument seem hollower than ever, and revived in a flash the ancient barbaric animosities which lie buried in the hearts of Turks and Greeks, and which both until now believed dead for ever.

But the fruitless Conference had cut the frail cord which held us still attached, however tenuously, to reason and measure. So long an orphan administratively, Cyprus was now cut adrift, a political orphan, to float slowly down the melancholy *couloirs* of Middle Eastern history, blown hither and thither by the chance winds of prejudice and passion.

I still visited Panos whenever I could, to sit and drink his heavy sweet Commanderia on the terrace under the Church of the Archangel Michael. He had changed, had aged. Did all our faces reflect, as his did, the helpless forebodings we all felt for the future? I wondered. He spoke gently and temperately still of the situation, but obviously the failure of the Conference had been a blow to him. 'There is no way forward now,' he said. 'It is too late to go back to the point where you missed the catch. Things are going to get worse.' He was not deceived by my false assurance and empty optimisms. 'No,' he said. 'This marks a definite point. The Government will have to drop palliatives and act; that will be unpleasant for us. Then we shall have to react as firmly. He mourned, as so many Greeks did, the lost opportunity when the Foreign Office refused to substitute the word 'postponed' for 'closed' upon the Cyprus file. Everything, he thought, had followed from that. His view of the future was not reassuring, but then neither was mine. Only the village with its calms and quiet airs lulled my fears. But here, too, the invisible thread was shortening. 'I feel uneasy about you coming up here,' said the *muktar* quietly. 'Have you any reason to?' 'None. But we hardly know what's going on inside ourselves any more.' Old Michaelis was in good form still, and still told stories with his old flair over the red wine. He hardly ever spoke of politics, and then in a low apologetic voice, as if he feared to be overheard. Once he said with a regretful sigh: 'Ach, neighbour, we were happy enough before these things happened.' And raising his glass added: 'That we pass beyond them.' We drank to the idea of a peaceful Cyprus—an idea which day by day receded like a mirage before a thirsty man. 'You know,' he said, 'I was told of a telegram which Napoleon Zervas sent to Churchill saying "Old man, be wise: Cyprus promised to Greece is thrice British."' He grinned and put a finger to his temple. 'Note carefully he said "promised" not "given" *There* is the matter! Yesterday the promise would have been enough. Today . . .' He made a monkey-face to suggest a lot of people all talking simultaneously. It was an admirable illustration of the situation.

It was some time during that month that I myself nearly fell a victim to gunmen, though whether by design or at a hazard I do not know. It was my own fault. The nights were worn threadbare by telephone calls or bomb alerts, and sleep was impossible until the small hours. Happily there was a small bar called the Cosmopolitan almost opposite the house on the main road, and here one could have a drink and meet journalists after filing time. I used to go along there every night at eleven or thereabouts, where I was usually joined by one or other of my friends or accompanied by Richard Lumley. I usually sat, too, in the same place, to be near enough to gossip to Cyril the barkeeper and his delightful French wife. One night the dog started barking, and Lazarus the waiter went out of the back door to see why. The whole place was surrounded by dense and gloomy vegetation, thick untrimmed bushes and trees which gave it a desolate air. The waiter came back white as a sheet and almost fainting, stammering: 'Get away from the window.' He had seen three masked men levelling something from a bush outside. I had a heavy torch, and Cyril and I, impressed by the man's very real fear but not really believing him, went out to have a look. Reluctantly Lazarus came to the balcony and pointed out the place. It was in a thick bush. The grass did look a bit trampled. But not ten paces away, between two trees, was a lighted window which I recognized as the window of the bar. 'Lazarus,' said Cyril, and he too now sounded scared, 'go and sit in the seat of the Kurios.' The waiter obeyed, to appear a moment later, lit and framed ('like a photograph' said Cyril grimly), in the window. We returned thoughtfully to the bar where the shaking Lazarus was pouring himself a brandy, and interrogated him further. He had come out on the balcony, he said, and found the dog barking at a bush behind which there were three men in masks. They had some sort of weapon—from his description it sounded like a Sten; they stared at him for a moment and then 'sank into the ground'. The whole of the little knoll was densely wooded and offered an easy escape. The episode was most alarming.

It was an eerie feeling too to walk back to the house alone that night down that corridor of darkness with only here and there a frail puddle of light from the street-lamps. The whole quarter was deserted, and my usual companions had not appeared. Doubtless the press corps had hurried off to the scene of some new incident. As I turned off the tarmac on to the gravel I was even more alarmed to hear footsteps behind me, following me at a leisurely pace. Now the whole front of my little house was lighted, and offered an even better firing position than the bar-window might have done, surrounded as it was with scrub and orange-trees. I felt it wiser to face a possible attacker in the darkness of the lane, consoling myself with the reflection that even if I was unarmed he would not know it and would assume I was. And I had the powerful torch. I stopped now, and the footsteps stopped too in the darkness. Frightened as I was, I felt absurdly glad that my heart was not beating faster than normal—thanks to the excellent double brandy Cyril had given me. I held my right arm as far away from me as possible and started running back the way I had come, towards the invisible man; after five paces I switched on and picked him up, shouting: 'Hands up.' He had nothing in his hands and was smiling good-naturedly. 'Mr. Durrell,' he said reproachfully. As I came up and searched him I recognized him, though by now I had forgotten his name; he was the taxi driver who had driven me across the island when first I arrived, the cousin of Basil the priest. He seemed surprised and delighted. Apparently he did not know me by my name either. 'I am guarding you, sir,' he said.

'Guarding me?'

'My taxi is behind the Cosmopolitan at the taxi rank. Cyril told me that you were leaving, and that some men had been after you. He told me to be answerable for your safety, so I was following you to see you came to no harm.'

It was a great relief. I took him back to the house and we drank a whisky by the fire before saying good night.

The next day I borrowed a pistol from a kindly Scots major in the police. It was both a consolation and an obscenity but it symbolized the trend of events perfectly, for Cyprus was now no longer a political problem so much as an operational one—and its cares were soon to be confided to someone who was a match for the hazards it presented.

September was another milestone on the road. 'Since UNO has excluded any other means to regain our liberty,' read an EOKA pamphlet, distributed in Larnaca, 'we have nothing else to do but to shed blood, and this will be the blood of English and Americans.'

The attacks on police stations sharpened. Rioting and the hoisting of Greek flags everywhere kept the police busy. The first terrorist murderer (Karaolis) was arrested and charged. The Executive Council sustained an irreplaceable loss in the resignation of Sir Paul Pavlides, whose good offices and un-self-seeking counsel had been invaluable up to now. He too could see no way forward. Achilles was nearly murdered by two armed men one morning as he drove to work; they opened up on him from either side of the car at a range of three feet, while he was stuck in the driving-seat unable to draw his Browning. It was a lucky escape. Renos Wideson's father, a magnificent and uncompromising old man who alone dared to say publicly what so many people thought—that Enosis was all very well but could wait—was nearly murdered by a gunman. (In all, three attacks were made on him to which he responded with great spirit. The fourth time he was shot dead at point-blank range.)

To the alarms of the night were added the daylight terrors of the open street, where small groups of students patrolled on bicycles, suddenly opening fire with pistols. And yet between these incidents the calm, the good nature, of everyday life was restored as if from some fathomless source of goodwill, banishing the fear these incidents had created. The sun still shone; and in perfect September sunshine the yachts fluttered across the harbour-bar at Kyrenia, the groups of drinkers sat around the cafés in idle conversation. The whole thing had the air of some breathtaking deception. There was no way of matching the newspaper pictures of bodies lying in their own blood upon pavements crowded with shattered chairs and glass, with the serene blue of the Levant sky, the friendly sea rubbing its head upon the beaches like a sheep-dog. The casual visitor was always surprised to see men bathing now under the protection of rifles. *Autres temps autres moeurs*. I could not help reflecting wryly that had we been honest enough to admit the Greek nature of Cyprus at the beginning, it might never have been necessary to abandon the island or to fight for it. Now, it was too late!

The Vanishing Landmarks

'There is no borrowing a sword in war time.'

'The Clergyman's son is the Devil's grandson.'

'Every gypsy praises his own basket.'

(Cypriot Greek proverbs)

———◦———

With the political issues irremediably landlocked by the implacability of Turkish opinion, both metropolitan and domestic, the island was now to be turned upon another course, away from the academic exchanges of the council chamber towards crueller extremes. From the problem child of the politicians it was to become the field of operations of the soldier. The replacement of Sir Robert had not been unforeseen, though it was misinterpreted by those who did not yet realize how fundamentally the whole problem had been altered by the failure of the London Conference.

By now, terrorism and disorder could no longer be met by appeals to sweet reason, and the hopes that international decisions might obviate the sort of measures which the state of things demanded. Extremes must now meet if the whole structure of civic life and administrative order were not to be prejudiced for ever; and on this sharp wind Sir John flew in to take over. 'Fly' is the word, too, for he had all the deftness and dispatch of a francolin, and the keen clear bird-mind of one trained to decisions based in a trained power of the will. His little hovering aircraft aptly symbolized the powers of this visitant from outer space.

Small of person as Lawrence was, though perfectly proportioned, he had the graces of a courtier combined with the repose and mildness of a family sage. Up at the Abbey, Kollis showed me

with great excitement the schoolboy's autograph album in which
the new Governor had written his name, plain 'John Harding' in
a hand which showed not only the firm uncomplicated lines of his
character but some of the unselfish and enthusiastic zeal of a
child. 'Why,' said my friend, and this was to become an echo
everywhere (even repeated by Makarios), 'did they not send us
such a man a long time ago?' Why indeed!

Upon the disorder and dishevelment of an administration still
wallowing in shortages and indecisions he turned the pure direct
eye of a soldier with a simple brief—the restoration of public
order, the meeting of force with force; and he was followed
swiftly by his soldiers, whose splendid professional bearing and
brown faces—still smiling and kindly—brought a fresh atmosphere to dusty purlieus of the five towns. Skilfully and smoothly
the chessboard was altered, the pieces rearranged. The new
Governor, in a series of swift flights, took in all there was to be
seen in the five towns, gathered what he could of information and
counsel from the administration, and made his dispositions with
the speed of long practice. With one hand, so to speak, he re-
opened negotiations with the Ethnarch (for it would be folly not
to appeal to whatever goodwill and reason remained, and there
was plenty); with the other he completely underpinned Wren's
force with his Commandos, offering them a much-needed support until such time as they could be brought up to strength and
made the effective guardians of civil security. The old-fashioned
administrative scheme of the Secretariat went by the board at
once to keep pace with the times and eventualities. To the tele-
communications cobweb which now covered Cyprus he added an
operational H.Q. inside the rusty wires of the old Government
building which was directly in touch with his office in Government House. These were the terms in which the next stages of
the game were to be played.

If no agreement could be reached on a Constitution we should
be forced to sit down and sweat the lead out of our skins. I must
confess to having had misgivings about the talks, for it was clear
that the Turks had effectively blocked the light of day, and would
never be persuaded to accede to any constitutional demands

which the Greeks found acceptable. But it was necessary to keep the door open, even if it was not wide open, and here the Field Marshal performed a feat which would have done credit to a master among diplomatists. That his efforts to persuade the Ethnarchy to accept a constitution met with failure is not surprising. He had nothing to offer—indeed he was cumbered by formulations so abounding in double negatives, in triple-dyed reservations, that anyone—not merely a Greek—might feel that they had been designed to make a fool of him; moreover they invited the Archbishop to take up a position which would not only have been immediately repudiated by every other Greek and Cypriot as prejudicing the future of suffrage on Enosis, but which did not even guarantee an elected majority in the legislature without the permission of the Turks! The Turkish position by this time was so well known that the talks could hardly do anything but break down, as they did. But one's heart went out to the patient and truly lion-hearted little man who had undertaken once more to rake about in the dirty dustbins of politics for fragments which might be joined together before they were irretrievably thrown out and lost. It was a peaceable task for a soldier, and he performed it with the same swift lucidity and perfection of timing that characterized his professional duties in the craft to which he had been bred. Neither failure nor success can move such spirits whose sense of duty is their only religion.

But the rest now belonged to the slow and hideous annals of siegecraft—for with the coming of the soldiers the spirit of resistance itself gradually spread, igniting the sleeping villages one by one. They had once been passive and uncommitted to the struggle imposed on them by the political ringmasters, though their sentiments had always lain with the rebels. It had become necessary to rake out the hot ashes in search of the embers still capable of setting fire to the rickety and worm-eaten old house which Cyprus was and still is. In default of police intelligence this could only be done by the massive methods of saturation—to literally soak up the fire-power of resistance as blotting-paper soaks up ink.

(I am condensing the impressions not merely of days, but of

months—for though the administrative shuffle and reshuffle had now become a daily feature of life ('worm cut in half and wriggling') I did not feel that I had any further effective place in the scheme of things. We had long since passed the shoals and narrows of policy where special knowledge or statecraft could avail us, and were heading for the open sea.)

The long roads to the coast became swollen with army transport as the bathing parties went down to the beaches, reminding one of the transport-jammed trails leading up to the Western Desert. Red berets and green now added their blobs of primary colour to a landscape once dominated by Greek sky-blue and Turkish magenta. The deserted beaches around Kyrenia and Famagusta were full of the brown bodies of soldiers at rest, swimming away their leisure.

The life of the towns endured the new climate of affairs with the same deceptive normality—the smiles and gestures of impenitent friendliness were fewer, but they were still there, the last fragile handclasp of parting. Only my little village lay obstinately outside the frame of things, saturated by the smoke of wood fires in an early autumn, its inhabitants drowsing away the noons at their spindles. But they were no longer talking village affairs, weddings, baptisms, for the radio bulletins poured in upon them, drenching them with news they might never have known of searches and curfews and killings in the various quarters of the island. Then, too, masked men had visited them to collect arms, frightening the wits out of them. 'I thought they were Easter mummers,' said Anthemos, 'and then I became afraid of the firelight shining on their masks. They said: "Dighenis wants all the shotguns." They were armed. What could we do? We handed them over—all except Petro who had hidden his. They were not from here, you know. Nobody recognized them. They came in a car and left it on the threshing-floor.'

I met Andreas sitting in a corner of Clito's little cave, hunched up over his drink and silent. At my greeting he turned a vacant weary face to me and tried to smile. He looked shrunk up and all of a sudden much older. He said in a whisper: 'The boy has gone. Said he was going to the mountains. I tried to keep hold on him

—what could I do? There are no schools, and always this business of strikes and riots. He has changed very much. You know, I was going to come in to your office and ask you if you couldn't get him arrested as a terrorist—put away somewhere safely. But Dmitri's bus wasn't going. Anyway I didn't have the money. And also I was torn, you understand, trying to understand if I was right or wrong. Now they will catch him and kill him.' Tears came into his eyes. He swallowed them down and smiled as Clito came over with a bottle of brandy. He had told nobody, it seemed, and telling me was in its way a relief. He cheered up a little after a couple of brandies, and we walked down the little twisted streets to the harbour arm-in-arm.

'How different it was,' he said, seeing the long row of parked lorries and the crowded spit of sand which was all Kyrenia had in the way of a beach. 'But praise be, the village is still the same, neighbour. It hasn't changed. And even you can come there and find everything quiet.' But for how long, I wondered?

Christmas came with its cloudy skies and the skirling rain, bringing new tones to the Gothic range, making us forget the long painful nights of tedium with their sporadic excitements and alarms. The gradually growing pressures upon the terrorists began to react upon the civil population, upon industry, business and entertainment. Curfews plunged the old town in darkness no less than the bloody incidents which were now an almost daily feature of our lives. Road-blocks with their laborious searches began to fragment the clumsy road haulage systems upon which local industry relied to feed the villages and the ports. Tourism flickered fitfully for a while, and then went out. Stage by stage the island became an armed camp, spreading the sense of suffocation in restricted movement, passes and permits, limitations on traffic; and in the wake of the bonny soldiers came the contract police— big heads, big feet, and big appetites. Pistols became part of the *tenue de ville*—what every well-dressed man must wear; bulging like pouter pigeons, sagging at the buttocks, dragging at the shape of coat-pockets and trousers. Bulpit, Gorge and Piles; Dubbin, Bulk and Shove; we laid our pistols on the bar of the Homer Palace and called for a double with the air of bing-bing artists in a

Western. Visitors from Kenya and Malaya, and those who pined for the Mandate, found themselves breathing familiar air. There was nothing left to recognize in Nicosia now—the old town shuttered, dark and dead, the joints outside its walls swollen with new faces. Most of the poppy-shallow cabaret girls had gone, too, and those who remained only did so presumably because they could not resist the thrill of feeling a pistol pressed against them as they danced.

Outside all this hubbub, secure in the mastery of his craft, the Field Marshal sat before the great wall map in Government House—its loose leaves covering the first yellowing field survey of the island by that other soldier of fame—Kitchener. Absolutely composed, contained, with his eye (that fresh francolin's eye) upon the invisible enemy in the mountains. Of his three handsome A.D.C.'s the third was now Richard Lumley, basking in the unexpected glory of an appointment he so well deserved. But one could not visit the Governor in his cockpit at Government House without being impressed by that matchless concentration based in repose.

In the whipping rain upon the blank promontory where Marie's half-finished house stood, I walked by the thundering sea mentally recreating those long lamp-lit evenings of calm argument over Clito's wine, or those walks by high moonlight to the lonely mosque of the Seven Sleepers whose history nobody knew, but who slumbered under the green holiness of their flags in the bubble-domed mosque, conscious perhaps of the moonlight (so dense was it) as it soaked through the white plaster to their very bones.

It was time to leave Cyprus, I knew, for most of the swallows had gone, and the new times with their harsher climates were not ours to endure. My contract still had several months to run, however, and it would be wiser to let it lapse than to hurry away and perhaps give the Greek press grounds for believing that I had resigned on policy grounds, which would have been unfair to my masters. But Maurice was leaving soon and Sarah—and the precious circle of friends which had composed and framed my own personal picture of the island, had given it density and beauty.

Austen and Pearce came and went at their swallow-like tasks of house-building in other, more favourable climates. Freya came through for a few days on her way to Turkey. And Sir Harry, to whom the island meant more than it could to any Cypriot, bound up as it was with his own youth. We lunched quietly on a deserted beach to the west of Kyrenia, drinking the good red wine labelled incongruously 'Ace of Hearts', and eating a *moussaka* for old time's sake while the old unchanging sea rushed and hissed upon the pebbled shore. How could he find the times through which we were passing anything but incomprehensible and inexpressibly painful? In his memory he was still sitting upon the famous keep at Famagusta, watching the sea uncurl and flex itself, yawn and stretch like a heraldic lion of Saint Mark, in the year 1918. What could I tell him that would afford him any comfort? His mind's eye was still full of a forgotten sleepy Cyprus with its old-fashioned kindnesses and haunting white villages. The island that he knew so intimately and loved so much was soon going to pass through the eye of a needle—with no Kingdom of Heaven waiting for it on the other side.

They came and went, and much of the old magic was still there for them to experience—for there were still lulls, empty days, full moons which were bombless. One needs about a month to catch the particular flavour of terrorism which is made up of quite intangible fears—feet running down a road at midnight, a silent man in a white shirt standing at a street-corner holding a bicycle too small for him, a parked car with no lights, a factory door ajar, the flick of a torch in a field. Terrorism infects the normal trans-actions of life. The horror of deliberate murder, of ambush or grenade, is at least purging—the pity and the terror are in them, and the conciseness of actions which can be met. But the evil genius of terrorism is suspicion—the man who stops and asks for a light, a cart with a broken axle signalling for help, a forester standing alone among trees, three youths walking back to a village after sundown, a shepherd shouting something indistinctly heard by moonlight, the sudden pealing of a doorbell in the night. The slender chain of trust upon which all human relations are based is broken—and this the terrorist knows and sharpens his claws precisely here; for his primary objective is not battle. It is to bring down upon the community in general a reprisal for his wrongs, in the hope that the fury and resentment roused by punishment meted out to the innocent will gradually swell the ranks of those from whom he will draw further recruits. Here is the dangerous ground, for the margin of effect is a narrow one; the theory of collective responsibility worked out in terms of fines, arrests, curfews, can only run for a length of time, and will build up opposing pressures to match those applied to a situation. In other words, the use of force might prove as sterile for us as the political expedients we had tried in the past, building up before the bows of the Government a heavier ånd heavier wave of opposition with each succeeding drive forward. I could not judge the truth of this for myself, I hoped it would not be so; but it seemed that the great danger in the measures I foresaw our having to take might be, precisely, the creation of Greeks where before there had only been Cypriot Greeks—for if we were not fighting Greece itself we were certainly fighting the spirit of Greece. And in this I did not foresee an easy resolution, with Athens so near and symbolized so vividly by the very type of insurrection which the Cypriots had planned and were executing. Lulls, yes, and fair periods—perhaps even lasting for years; but finally the obstinate problem would reassert itself in one form or another. And there was no political solution offering more than half of what each of the three nations wanted! Cyprus had really become a dangerously weak spot in the NATO alliance.

There was, in a sense, no novelty in the steady progression of events from this point forward, though the details impacted forcefully on the dramatic world of the press, full of vivid and confused colouring: as with bacteria the slide must be stained if one is to see the object under the microscope—but perhaps I have used the wrong metaphor. It would have been better to borrow one from the techniques photographers use to 'blow up' a negative. But seen objectively, from the other end of the corridor—from the Cyprus which I had known two years before—the image changed. The outlines of all that we know as civic life grew hazy with the Habeas Corpus Act lying suspended, Communist and

Enotist alike behind bars, and the press under restriction; this was a state at war with itself.

Terrorism itself began to spread rather than to diminish—an ominous clue to the temper of things; and to the nauseating foulness of the street-murder of soldiers and policeman was added the disgusting, and typically Balkan, murder of civilians suspected of being traitors. Apart from this of course there was many an old score settled in the name of Enosis. The black mask was protection enough. 'When you give a chap a mask and a pistol,' said Wren thoughtfully, showing that by now he was fully abreast of the Mediterranean temperament, 'the first thing he does is bump someone he owes money to before getting on with more ethnic business.' He had become—we had all become—bitter.

But this disgraceful hunt for unarmed civilians who were shot down like rabbits in church, at the coffee-house, even in hospital, drove the last effective wedge between myself and my villagers whose obstinate and unwavering friendship had not faltered. It did not even now. With the old Cypriot obstinacy they still walked to Kyrenia to post me a wedding-invitation—I had on an average one a week—lest I should think that anything had changed. But now it was I who did not dare to go, for informers were everywhere and I could not bear to think of Andreas or Frangos or fat Anthemos having to answer for 'treachery'. Yet still the invitations came, there came flowers and mandarins and bulbs; and still Andreas the 'Seafarer' came to discuss the merits of concrete brick, though the balcony was finished. Wherever I met a villager I was welcomed with a cry and a handshake—even on a lonely road beyond Famagusta which was an eerie enough place for a Greek to be seen talking to a foreigner in a car. And then Panos was shot dead. He had walked out for a breath of air at dusk, through the winding narrow streets near the harbour. The walls around wore the familiar autograph of Dighenis though I doubt if Dighenis himself pressed the trigger of the pistol which killed him.

Two days before we had spent the day together out at Marie's headland at his own request; he was anxious to study the ambitious tree-planting programme she had begun, and I for my part was glad of advice as I did not quite trust her factotum Janis, and made a point, while she was away, of keeping an eye on the trees. It was a warm cloudless morning, and we set off in high good spirits for there had been a full two-day lull in bomb-incidents and killings and the warm lassitude of the island had begun, as always, to fill one with the illusion of a peace which now lay far back in memory, in a prehistoric era of the consciousness it seemed, yet was always ready to be revived by such a lull in operations. Clito had loaned us a wicker-covered demijohn full of white wine, while Panos' own salad-garden had provided lettuce and cucumber and slender shallots. A loaf of the rough brown peasant wholemeal and some slices of cold beef topped off the supply which we calculated would last us all day. With this provender loaded we tanked up the car and set off through the silvery olive-groves to Saint Epictetus, across the peaceful green flanks of the Gothic range, now drowsing in the warm sunlight of a spring morning, and crisply etching its delicate outlines upon a clear blue sky. The great cliffs which crowned the range gleamed brown-gold as loaves. 'Where to?' I said, for I had promised him a private visit or two before we made our way down to the head-land. 'Klepini,' he said. 'My calendar tells me the cyclamen will be starting.' Panos had his own favourite nooks and corners of the range, familiar from years of walking about it—just as a lover will have favourite places in which to plant an expected kiss—the nape of the neck, or the curve of a pectoral muscle; moreover he carried in his head a veritable flower-calendar which told him, almost to the day, that the almond-blossom would be out in Carmi, or the dog-roses above Lapithos. In his memory he carried a living flower-map of the range, and knew where best to go for his anemones and cyclamens, his ranunculuses and marigolds. Nor was he ever wrong.

As a concession to the sunshine he wore an open-necked shirt; but nothing, not even an August heat-wave, could have persuaded him to wear anything but his rusty old black suit with its chalk marked sleeves. As we rolled along the coast-road he exclaimed delightedly at every glimpse of the sea through the carobs and olives, puffing at his cigarette, his spectacles gleaming. 'Today we shall forget everything—even the situation, eh?' he smiled, settling himself firmly in the front seat with the air of a man determined upon pleasure, whatever it may cost. I did not tell him that I had a small radio under the front seat, and that I would have to keep in touch with the news bulletins to see whether or not there might be a sudden call for my services which would send me racing back to the capital. The dreadful tug of my work was still there—yet in this benignly slumbering morning we seemed to be far from the bondage of politics or war. The little pistol itself seemed an anachronism in all this pastoral blue and yellow—the young barley struggling to its feet upon the tobacco-coloured winter fields. We ran on round the loops and curls of the road, the sea marching bravely with us, until we came to the little village dedicated by its name to a saint about whom nobody knew anything. Epictetus the philosopher might have been intended, but the ascription is doubtful; it is more likely that some rock hermit with the same temperamental predisposition as Saint Hilarion had lived and died there, bequeathing in the memory of his name something of the austerity and pain of a solitary life to which the villager could cling as a symbol for holiness.

The narrow streets of the little village were empty and most of the shops closed, save for the coffee-house in the main square where half a dozen farmers sat before their morning coffee idly scanning the newspapers of yesterday. This peaceful and traditional scene was only belied by the heavily sandbagged police station with its stalwart Commando guarding the front door, his keen blue eyes in a brown face turned towards us in hostile curiosity, one finger on the trigger of his Sten. His alertness was comforting; when I waved at him he smiled and waved his hand back at me, comforted perhaps by a familiarly English face among so many dark ones. 'How I wish,' said Panos, turning an admiring eye upon the young soldier, 'things were normal. But they won't be.' He shook his head and sighed deeply. 'For a long time yet, my friend, unless . . . unless . . .' But he shook his head. 'They won't take us seriously until the hotheads gain control. Look, oleanders. It is too early for snakes is it not? I thought I caught a glimpse of one.'

A few miles beyond the village, after a series of vertiginous loops and dips of the road, one finds great bunkers of sand shored up against the road—a quarter of a mile from the beach. The carobs and olives hereabout stand a couple of feet deep in the drifts which year by year move inland, smothering the light scrub and holm-oak in brown suffocating dunes. The whole great Pachyammos beach is marching inland, though precisely why I cannot tell. But these dunes athwart the road are a godsend for builders who send out lorries to collect the sand for use in Kyrenia; and here we came upon Sabri, sitting unmoved under a carob in a red shirt and grey trousers, while a grunting team of young Turks filled a lorry for him. We stopped and he came delightedly across to talk to us. Panos and he were old familiars, if not actually cronies, and it was warming to see the genuine friendliness between them. They were co-villagers first, and the link of the village was stronger here, on neutral ground, so to speak, than any differences of race or belief. 'Are you buying more houses?' he asked, and the smiling Panos answered for me. 'Never without your help. No, we are going to gather wild flowers.' Sabri said: 'I am gathering money,' nodding towards his little team of workers in their coloured head-cloths. 'We poor men,' he added wryly, 'cannot take the day off when we wish.' He was busy building a big house for an English lady, he added. 'It is not arty like yours, my dear, but rather *posh*, as you say.' I knew exactly what he meant. It would be called 'Auchinlech'.

We sat for a while in the warm sand under the ancient carob tree, trading a sip of our wine against a couple of rosy pomegranates which he had stolen from a wall in Kasaphani, while the sunny morning began to make the foothills glow and tremble in the humidity, and the old grey crocodile-skin of Buffavento turned to violet. The moon was still in the sky, pale and bloodless. Somewhere in the thin blue beyond the range of eyesight a plane cracked and re-cracked the sound-barrier and sent a wave of thunder flowing over the hills. 'Bombs?' said Sabri comfortably —in the warmth and contentment of that perfect morning it was impossible to make such a word sound any different from the word 'lizards' or 'wildflowers'. Panos turned and yawned. Our own silence surrounded us like a cocoon, softly woven by the briny air which climbed the hot dunes to stir the breathing shadows under the carobs. 'Summer is beginning,' said a Turkish youth, wiping the sweat from his dark brows with the end of a coloured headcloth. It was quite an effort to tear ourselves away from these warm dunes and follow the little signpost which said 'Klepini', but Panos' thirst for cyclamens was not to be denied, and so we reluctantly turned the little car off the main road and began the slow ascent upon the less kindly surface of the village road.

Though it was only a few hundred feet up we had moved into different air. The faint luminous tremble of damp had gone from the sky, and the sea which rolled below us among the silver-fretted screen of olives was green now, green as a Homeric adjective. The foothills began here, and the village itself lay higher up on a platform of reddish sandstone, remote and smiling. And here were the cyclamens and anemones we sought—sheets and sheets of them glittering like young snow, their shallow heads moving this way and that in the sea-wind so that the fields appeared at first sight to be populated by a million butterflies.

'What did I tell you?' said Panos, catching his breath with pleasure as we breasted the slope and rolled down the shady inclines among the trees to come to rest noiselessly on the thick felt of green. We sat with the engine switched off, listening to the wind among the trees, silent. Reality was so far in excess of expectation that we were suddenly deprived of all desire to pick the flowers which dusted these quiet terraces to a starscape—thick as the Milky Way. One could not walk among them without doing them damage. Panos sighed deeply and puffed his cigarette, indulging the relish of his eyes as they travelled across the enchanted slopes whose familiarity had never once staled for him in fifteen years of repetition. 'Embroidery,' he said under his breath in Greek, and with his hand followed the soft contour of the hills, as one might run one's hand affectionately over the flanks of a favourite horse. 'I knew that last thunderstorm would do the trick.'

We unpacked our hamper, placing it on a great smooth stone,

and walked slowly to the edge of the cliff, to look down the coast towards Akanthou with its brilliant yellows and sere browns where the corn and barley grew wave upon wave. And as we walked across the carpet of flowers their slender stalks snapped and pulled around our boots as if they wished to pull us down into the Underworld from which they had sprung, nourished by the tears and wounds of the immortals. Here the trees perched upon the clear rock walls which their roots had penetrated, over-hanging the valleys where the rooks turned and cawed in the wind, ruffled by the slightest air current. And beneath it all, drawn in long quivering strokes across the middle distance, swam the green sea, the opiate and legend of Europe, drawing itself like a bow back and forth upon the steely Taurus which flanked our horizon in and bound the earth to the sky in tempering the mag-nificence of both.

My companion was silent now, as he climbed into the branches of a tree to look down with delight upon the rolling relief map below with its bearded curves of lowland falling downwards at one corner to the sea-line, and then climbing and sweeping away towards the sky-blue edges of the world where the Karpass threw up its snouts of stone, and the boundaries of the peninsula were marked by the crash of water on stone and the plumes of spray turning in the air. 'I shall be sixty next year,' said Panos, 'what a pleasure it is to get old.'

The white wine tasted sharp and good and as he raised his glass Panos gave me the toast of the day: 'That we may pass beyond' (i.e. the present troubles) 'and that we might emerge once more in the forgotten Cyprus—as if through a looking-glass.' In a way, too, he was toasting a dying affection which might never be revived—one of those bright dreams of deathless friendship which schoolboys still believed in, of an England and Greece which were bondsmen in the spirit.

How stupid such figments sound to the politicians and how vital they are to young nations!

'You know,' said Panos quietly, 'I received a threatening letter from EOKA—a second-grade letter.'

'How do you mean—second-grade?'

'There are different types. First there is just a warning letter. Then there is a letter with a black dagger and a definite death-threat, which encloses a razor-blade. That is what I got. I expect one of my pupils decided to get his own back by trying to frighten me.'

'What would they have against you?'

Panos poured himself another glass of wine and watched his cigarette-smoke disperse in the still air. He was still absently smiling with his eyes, as if at the memory of our first glimpse of Klepini with its petal-starred glades. 'My dear fellow, how should I know? In these situations everyone informs on everyone else. There is no circumstance of my private life not open to view.'

'Perhaps because I stayed with you—though I haven't visited you more than once since the serious trouble started.'

'I know. I guessed why and I was grateful.'

'Then why did you come out today?'

He stood up and dusted the chalk-marks off his sleeve.. He heaved a long sigh. 'Because I wanted to. Life is going to be intolerable enough with all these curfews and fines and strikes; it would be unendurable if one had to obey the dictates of the hot-heads. And besides, I am only one of dozens who have received such letters, and nothing has happened to them.'

'But I am a Government Official.'

'Yes, that is true.'

'They might suspect you of giving information.'

'What do I know? Nothing. It is true I am not as patriotic as most people, though I believe that Enosis is right and must one day come; I am a Greek, after all, and Cyprus is as Greek as . . . Vouni. But of course I shrink from violence though I see that it will certainly bring Enosis sooner than polite talk will.'

'How do you mean?' He stretched himself upon the rock now, face downward, and thrust out his hands until his fingers were buried in the dense clumps of anemones. 'O Lord!' he said, 'I promised myself not to talk politics. But sometimes you ask such silly questions. Can't you see? First there was no Cyprus problem. Then a few bangs followed and you agreed there was a problem, but that it couldn't be solved ever. More bangs followed. Then you agree to try and solve it, but in fact only to bedevil it further. Meanwhile however EOKA has seen that a few bombs could change your inflexible "Never" to "Sometime"; now they feel they have a right to provoke an answer to the question "When?" They are not politically as stupid as the authorities believe them to be. They have, in fact, very much shaken the British position and they realize it. The peasants of your village have two little proverbs which illustrate the present state of Cyprus perfectly. Of a stupid man they say "He thought he could beat his wife without the neighbours hearing." In this case the neighbours are your own Labour Party, UNO, and many others; we are provoking you to beat us so that our cries reach their ears. Then, from another point of view, your operations against the terrorists must be conducted across the body of the Cyprus people—like a man who has to hit an opponent through the body of the referee. As you say in Bellapaix, "He can't gather the honey without killing the bees." How, then, can you gather the honey of a peaceful Cyprus?'

We began to gather great bunches of the flowers now and stow them in the wicker basket; and while I carefully dug out the bulbs I needed for my garden Panos contented himself more easily, winding his cool wet stems about with the broad leaves of the arum lily. 'We could go on like this for weeks,' he said, 'and even today if we worked at it we couldn't make any impression on the field.' He was walking about from point to point as he picked his flowers, matching the various shades as he did so, composing each handful with a skill that showed practice. I could already see them glowing in the blue Lapithos vases which decorated a shelf in the kitchen, strategically placed beyond the reach of his children. After they had gone to bed he would take the flowers down and place them before him as he fell to work upon the great piles of grey copy-books with their school essays in spidery Greek straggling over the pages; and sighing, pause for a moment to refresh the 'eyes of his mind', as he said, with a glimpse, in them, of the Klepini groves.

We picked and picked until the back of the car was brimming

with flowers—'like a village marriage' as Panos said—and then sank back upon our thrones of granite to unpack the bread and the meat.

The sun was approaching mid-heaven and the great lion pads of rock among the foothills were already throwing forward their reflections of shadow. Panos put away his spectacles and fell to cutting up the coarse brown loaf, saying as he did so: 'On days like this, in places like these, what does it all matter? Nationality, language, race? These are the invention of the big nations. Look below you and repeat the names of all the kings who have reigned over the kingdoms of Cyprus; of all the conquerors who have set foot here—even the few of whom written records exist! What does it matter that *we* are now alive, and *they* dead—we have been pushed forward to take our place in the limelight for a moment, to enjoy these flowers and this spring breeze which . . . am I imagining it? . . . tastes of lemons, of lemon-blossom.'

As he spoke there came the sound of a shot among the olive-groves, the echoes of which rolled about for a while on the range, sinking and diminishing as if they described the contours of the land in sound; then the silence closed in again, and everything was still save for the rustling foliage in the trees around us. We looked at each other for a long second. 'I thought the shot-guns were all in,' I said; he smiled and relaxed his pose as he lit a cigarette. 'It was a shot-gun all right,' he said, 'and quite near.' With a sudden soughing of wings three jackdaws passed over our heads, as if alarmed by something in the valley beneath. 'Last year one would not have turned one's head,' said Panos with a chuckle, 'and look at us. It's some poor fellow shooting at crows to keep them off his fields.'

A small foreshortened figure now appeared at the cliff-edge and stood looking down the slope towards us. He had a shot-gun under one arm, and he appeared to be listening as he watched us. I said nothing, and without his spectacles Panos 'had no horizons' as he always said in Greek. 'There is a man,' I said quietly, and as I spoke the figure started to stroll towards us at a leisurely pace, holding his uncocked gun in the crook of his arm. As he came nearer I saw that he was dressed in the conventional rig of a village farmer and wore a game-bag at his belt. His heavy brown snake-boots with their corded tops made no sound in the deep grass. Through the open neck of his shirt I caught a glimpse of the heavy flannel sweat-shirt that all peasants made a point of wearing, summer or winter. He walked slowly towards us across the glade at a deliberate and unhurried pace, only stopping for a few seconds every ten paces, the better to eye us. 'He is coming this way,' I said. Panos did not put on his spectacles, but propped his chin with his hands, and began to swear under his breath. I had never heard him use bad language before. 'I swear,' he explained, 'at the humiliation of having to feel afraid in the presence of an unknown man—a sensation so foreign to Cyprus as to be quite frightening in itself, the very idea of it. God! what have we come to?'

I did not answer, for the strange man was standing still, indulging in one of his regular little pauses. He had a large square head with a thatch of greying hair upon it. The wide wings of his black moustache were swept back and up from his mouth. He cocked a barrel of his shot-gun now with a clumsy sort of gesture, intended no doubt to be unobtrusive. The sound of the hammer clicking back was quite audible—like someone cracking his knuckle-bones. 'Measure for measure,' I said, and slipped the little pistol under the napkin on my knee, consoled by the cold butt under my fingers and at the same time disgusted—for Panos' sake. He observed the gesture and made a wry mouth. 'That won't be much use,' he said. I went on eating my sandwich and watching the newcomer lazily out of the corner of my eye. He had stopped now and stood undecidedly beside the trunk of a carob tree. 'Ho there,' he called in a deep hoarse voice, and I knew at once from his tone that we had nothing to fear. Sticking the pistol still wrapped in the napkin back into the basket I raised the demi-john of wine and gave him the traditional Cypriot greeting. 'Kopiaste—sit down and join us.' He relaxed at once, uncocked his gun, and stood it against the tree before walking over to us.

'Why Sir Teacher,' he said reproachfully as he took Panos' hand. 'Why did you not say it was you?' Then he turned his dark curious eye upon me and explained gruffly, 'The Sir Teacher stood godfather to my second son.' Panos was now sitting up and putting on his glasses the better to enter into the spirit of recognition. 'Why Dmitri Lambros,' he said. 'What are you doing here?'

'I've been shooting crows,' replied the newcomer, with a flash of white teeth in a face as dark as a plum cake. 'I know it's forbidden,' he added as if to forestall an inevitable question. 'But up here . . .' he waved a hand in the direction of the mountain, 'we are so far away. You can hear a car as it turns off the highroad at the bottom of the hill. Plenty of time to put it away.' He winked and with a brief word of thanks raised his glass with a friendly nod at me before drinking deeply and exhaling his breath in a rapturous 'Ah! that was good.' He wiped his rough brown hands with their ragged nails on his thighs before accepting the hunk of bread and meat which Panos offered him, asking as he did so, the dozen conventional questions which, like the opening moves of a game, must be made before any real conversation can begin in peasant Greek. His naturalness and the frank roughness of his glance were pleasing, and I could see from Panos' expression that he held the man in good esteem. In his game-bag reposed three bedraggled and crumpled corpses of the jackdaws against which he had been waging war, and these he showed us with some pride. 'I've got a good eye,' he explained.

'How are things up at the village?' asked Panos, and I was not surprised to hear him answer 'Quiet as the grave,' for the village was far more secluded among the foothills even than my own. 'Of course,' he added after a moment, 'we've got one or two of Them. They watch us. But so far there has been nothing. But of course if the English hang this boy Karaolis. . . .' Panos interrupted him gravely to say: 'The Kurios is English,' and Lambros turned upon me a pair of dark sweet eyes, full of a sort of bravado. 'I guessed—in fact I have seen him down at the land where the Desposini Maria is building a house, have I not? And her man Janis is my cousin. So you see, nothing can be hidden in Cyprus!' He lit a cigarette swiftly and deftly and sat back on his haunches blowing out the smoke with a long exhalation of rare pleasure. 'Why is there so much feeling about Karaolis,' I said, 'since everyone knows he was guilty?' He looked thoughtfully at the ground and then raised his face to mine, gazing earnestly into my eyes. 'Guilty but not culpable,' he said. 'What he did was for Enosis not for gain. He is a good boy.' I sighed: 'This is word-play. Suppose a Turk Hassan killed someone on behalf of Volkan and then said it was for Enosis.' He stroked his moustache with the backs of his fingers. 'The Turks are cowards,' he said. Panos sighed. 'Don't be a twisted stick, Dmitri, it is true what the Kurios says. Crime is crime whatever the motive.' The man shook his head slowly from side to side like a bull and gazed up through lowered eyebrows. His mind refused the jump; Karaolis was a young hero. Once again I could not help remarking how absent was any conception of abstract guilt—abstract justice. Who could discern in the thought-processes of a modern Greek the exercise of a logic which was Socratic? They thought like Persian women, capriciously, waywardly, moving from impulse to impulse, completely under the domination of mood. Had Karaolis been killed outright he would still have been canonized as a martyr but everyone would have accepted the fact and shrugged it off—to get shot is part of the penalty for shooting. A martyr no less, his death would have been accepted as part of the hazard of ordinary life. But the long-winded processes of the European juridical system were an intolerable bore, an incompre-hensible rigmarole to a people which valued action first and the pallid reflections thrown by its moral values afterwards. Here, they thought, comes the old hypocritical Anglo-Saxon mania for trying to justify injustice. The boy was a hero, and they were trying to slip a noose about his heroism. 'We know the truth,' he said, setting his jaw obstinately, and Panos glanced at me with a twinkle and an expression which said: 'Argument on this topic is useless.' I knew it was.

We changed the subject now before it bred a taciturnity and ill-nature which would have been foreign to this chance meeting among the carob trees, and spoke about village affairs which were nearer to his heart. Helen and Maria, the daughters of the school-master, had married last week, and their wedding was the most sumptuous they had had in the village for years. The wine flowed like a canal. 'Even now after five days my head rings with the wine,' he said smiling, rubbing his chin with a tanned hand. It had been like old times. And in the afternoon some English people had come to look at the church; at first the children shouted 'EOKA' and were inclined to throw stones, but when they found the strangers spoke a little Greek and were 'gentle' everyone felt rather ashamed. So while they were in the church the children gathered flowers for the lady and they left with bundles of them in their arms, smiling. 'Such are the children of my village,' he said proudly, thrilling at the mere thought of hospitality upheld in the face of intense antagonism. Then he added, turning to me: 'Such are the Greeks.' I knew this too.

The sun was in mid-heaven now, and the wine low. It seemed a crime to leave the cool deep grass and the shady trees; but if Panos was to see Marie's land we should be on the move. 'Dmitri,' said Panos, whose mind was still busy with his flower-calendar, 'there is a favour I must ask of you.' The man smiled delightedly. 'Anything, Sir Teacher,' he said, pronouncing the most revered title in vernacular Greek with pride. 'You know the little ruined mill above the village? There is a glade there by the stream where the mushrooms grow. Set some of your famous children to pick me a basketful and bring them when next you come to Kyrenia, will you? And tell them I will send them sweets in exchange.' 'With the greatest pleasure,' said Lambros standing up and pitching away his cigarette.

I turned the car while Panos packed the food away in the hamper and gazed ruefully at the demijohn. 'It's amazing,' he said. 'We've drunk nearly half. Let us have one more glass for the parting.' We stood in a circle under the great carob and raised our glasses. 'Health,' cried Lambros, and we echoed him; and then, as if anxious to provide a phrase which would bridge the unhappy gap between himself and the hated-loved foreigner, he stuck out his hand to take mine and said, 'All will be well one day.' 'All will be well,' I echoed.

He retrieved his gun and stood in full sunlight to watch us go, one hand raised in salutation. I let in the clutch and the car rolled smoothly down the gradient towards the sea, its tyres crunching on the bony gravels and ribbed stones of the village road. It was quite hot now and the mountains had turned pale and feathery as the ground-mists reached them from the damp plain. At the last hump before we joined the main road I paused for a minute to watch the long carved coastline stretch away into the haze, trembling and altering in the bluish afternoon as the light of a star will. Saint Epictetus lay below us with its white belfries and cubist houses; just beyond the long stone tongue of land on which Marie's house had already begun to grow up, gleamed fitfully.

Sabri was still smoking under his carob on the main road. He waved to us and shouted: 'There's a search on down the road. In Saint Epictetus.'

'They will be looking for arms,' said Panos quietly. This also had become a feature of our lives, an expected and normal part of the daily routine.

We rolled on down the green and sinuous roads while Panos peered into the dry beds of torrents to spot flowering hibiscus and oleander below the dusty culverts. After so many years he undoubtedly knew every bush, every individual clump of lentisk or sage, so that our journey was sharpened at every turn by the expectations of his memory. On the last curve but one before the little village, which lies among flowering trees, secretively folded in upon itself, we saw the first soldier. High on a bluff above us, standing lazily against the sun, with his Sten slung loosely in the crook of his arm and his red beret gleaming like a cherry among the silver olives. I raised a thumb in racial recognition and he smiled, jerking his own laconic thumb in the direction of the village and then patting the air lightly as if to say 'Go slowly.' Panos took a childish delight in soldiers and unerringly recognized him as a Parachutist. 'The new Kingdoms of Cyprus,' he said, 'are made up of principalities where berets of different colours rule—green for the mountains, red and black for the Gothic range. We are getting used to them.' The idea gave him pleasure. Nor was he disposed to be peevish when we came upon a road-block in the shape of a barbed-wire hurdle manned by a couple of stalwart children who did not look above eighteen; one stood by with a rifle while the other came forward and saluting politely took my identification papers. His broad southern accent and shock of yellow hair were pleasing characteristics to happen upon so far from England. A self-conscious moustache was trying to attach itself to his upper lip. He read my papers carefully, moving his lips slowly, and then handed them back and saluted again. 'Is the gentleman with you a local, sir?' he asked, and Panos nudged me delightedly. 'Did you hear—he called me a gentleman,' he said in a whisper; and leaning out he said: 'I am Grik schoolmaster.' He never allowed an opportunity of prac-tising his English to slip by. The young soldier looked grave and frowned. 'Well, I'll have to search you, 'op out,' he said, trying desperately to sound unkind. Panos was delighted. It was obvious that he adored being searched. 'Yes, Yes,' he said eagerly. 'Search me.' And stepped into the road to be frisked by the two youths, and to turn his wallet inside out at their behest. I must say they were efficient as well as thoughtful. They made a note of the time and of the car's number. 'Okay, Dennis,' said the large one, 'let them in.' Then he turned to me and said wistfully, 'Lovely lot of flowers you got there, sir,' his English eye resting gloatingly upon the back seat of the car piled high with blossom. Panos' spectacles gleamed. 'Yes. You wish? I give you some,' and before the young soldier could say any more he found himself, to his embarrassment, holding several great bunches of Klepini ane-mones. He made a vague gesture of handing them back, saying: 'I'm on duty now, sir,' but I had already let in the clutch and we were rolling down among the trees to the village, leaving him alone with his problem and the smiles of his companion.

There were brown military lorries parked in the little square by the church and the main street was full of an unwonted animation, the red berets glimmering in the sunshine until the cobbled streets looked like a strawberry bed. Pens of barbed wire were being run up and the villagers slowly and patiently gathered into them for searching. Little groups stood about everywhere, look-ing on and chattering, for all the world as if they were watching the hucksters set up their stalls in preparation for some familiar village fête. Nor could they conceal their admiration for the physique of the brown Commandos who strolled among them, tugging and pushing good-naturedly at the fringes of the crowd like sheep-dogs at a trial, still smiling and patient. The whole operation was being conducted in a leisurely fashion with an air of awkward kindness. The village priest, awaiting his turn to be penned with the rest, 'like turkeys' as Panos said, had ordered a coffee and a newspaper, and sat firmly on the balcony above the road, with his spectacles on his nose, reading, while at the same table sat two Commando officers, lounging like panthers, waiting perhaps for him to finish before politely shepherding him 'into the bag'. Panos looked about him with the greatest interest, his commiseration for the villagers tinged with amusement. 'There is Renos,' he said. 'He is being pushed. I'm so glad. If ever a man needed a push it was him. How funny. But these Parachutists are like gods tumbled out of heaven. How did they get so big? They are grown in special earth perhaps?'

The crowd eddied and swirled in one corner about a group of youths, and the soldiers pressed in firmly shouting in the unconscious accents of the world's most famous policeman. 'Pass along there, please, cut it out. Move along there, please.'

There were several lorries full of troops standing by at ease, wreathed in grins. They set up a ragged whistle as we passed and in answer to my gesture extended a forest of grubby thumbs. A lot of them had roses pinned to their berets. 'I can see,' said Panos, 'that they have been pinching flowers from Sabri's rose garden and from Kollis.' 'Is that considered looting?' I asked, and he giggled. 'But what is all that?' he asked as we passed a lorry piled with pick helves and the awkward old-fashioned riot shields which belonged to the past era of wholesale street rioting. Indeed a couple of the youths were playing grotesquely at a game of gladiators, clad in the steel helmets and wielding what some wag had long ago christened 'the Armitage patent anti-Coca-Cola-bottle shield'. They made clumsy passes at each other with pick helves as they circled round and round, their boots striking sparks from the tarmac. Enthusiastic applause came from inside the covered lorries where dozens of pairs of eyes took in this gratuitous piece of clowning. Panos was consumed with interest.

'Do they really use that equipment—so like a gardening set?' He had never seen a full-blown riot, and knew nothing of the counter-measures the administration had taken. He listened with great interest as I explained: 'The Governor has made a rule that there is to be no shooting unless the troops are shot at. For ordinary riots they use pick helves; for ambushes and anything more military, their professional equipment. But as they never know when they set off for an incident just what sort of incident it is going to be they have to take everything along. Last month outside Paphos they faced bombs and shot-guns. Last week in Larnaca they faced schoolchildren. In Lapithos two days ago they had to clear a road-block of fallen trees and face up to two hundred villagers throwing stones.' Panos gazed at me with wonder and admiration at such spirited planning. 'They take everything into account,' he said.

We were through the barriers now and on the last crown of the hill from which we could glimpse the little barrel-vaulted church of Saint George which marked the landward end of Marie's pro-perty; the spring gushed from the rock below the village, and here several old ladies were doing their washing with complete composure, though the troops were in full view. A baffling air of sleepy normality hung over everything. Birds sang in the hedges, and the first lizards scrambled among the thickets, teased by these sunny premonitions of the summer to come. Panos sighed and settled himself more comfortably after this interlude with its crowded human panorama and liveliness, so foreign to the slow dragging tempo of this spring day. The road looped and coiled twice like a snake and then suddenly untied itself to run, straight as a die, between the carob-groves; and here, marked by a single tall cypress tree, was the turning which led off towards the sea, and the desolate headland where the great house ('Fortuna' it had been christened) was to stand. We chose to leave the car somewhere near the main road and walk down the soft dust path-way between the trees which would lead us, after many a curve and twist, to the headland where the charming little toy church of Saint George stood, glittering white against the backcloth of blue sea. Early lizards scuttered among the stones and the rank grass beside the road was full of the busy clicking and scratching of anonymous insects, stretching down in a whispering wall of green to where the sound of the sea took over—racing blue and fair today, bursting among the grottoes and caves with dull explosions and filling the beaches with the passionate scrabbling of pebbles sucked back in the dark undertow. On the outward breastwork of the magnificent little bay stood the old Mosque where I had spent so many precious hours; Marie's house was to be built in such a way as to let the windows on the seaward side frame a view of it.

It lay now, folded inside its containing wall, like a gull resting on a stormy sea, the whole peninsula behind it with its tortured anfractuosities of white rock giving back the brilliant light like a mirror. I saw the small black spot which was the Hodja move antlike across the whiteness, followed by his cat, diminished by distance to a black pin-head. They were going to the spring. The bareness and purity of the place were as lucid as a theorem in Euclid—the little shrine of the seven forgotten generals or saints (opinions varied as to their origins and qualities), which had welded itself to the white headland, joining the white of plaster and limewash to the whiteness of the natural rock—picked clean as a bone by the winter sea. It was as if some animal or Titan of unimaginable size had eaten and excreted a mountain of seashells, translated into this calcareous rock, which stretched down into the sea, worn razor-sharp and bearded with weed which swayed and ruffled with the sea's breathing. The coast itself had been cut out with a fretsaw, idly and purposelessly whittled by a preoccupied god.

Yet the richness of limestone fed with fresh springs had crept down to each headland, giving it a fat scalp of good earth in which the young wheat could find a purchase less than a hundred yards from the barren sea-margins. Marie's house for example— a wheat field swept up to her back door, yet the front windows opened upon the bare stony promontory whipped by the waves.

The roofless house, with its promise of great cool rooms opening upon the water, stood empty now. The workmen had left early today, abandoning the desolate heaps of lime and sand and

pruned rocks out of which it would all be finished. Janis was at
the end of a field digging. He shouted and loped unevenly towards us like a camel across the furrowed earth, eager to unlock
the bamboo palisades which surrounded the little temporary huts
where Marie lived while she was waiting for 'Fortuna' to be completed. 'God be with you,' said Janis with delight, shaking hands
all round and exposing a mouth as devoid of teeth as an oyster in
a shapeless grin. I introduced my companion and told him that
we had come to study the arrangement of the trees, which seemed
to delight him even more. He jumped up and down in an ecstasy
of willingness to please, like a monkey on a chain. But first the
laws of hospitality must be observed strictly. He unlocked the
gate and led us into the little loggia with its fantastic palms where
the two peacocks talked in undertones, and setting chairs for us,
poured us glasses of sherbet—which in Greek still preserves a
haunting trace of Aphrodite's name, for it is called Aphros or
Foam. Drinking, we completed the politenesses due to conven-
tion before I told Panos that I would go and bathe while he did
his tour of inspection. 'I know it will be cold,' I said, 'but I have
only a few days left before I leave the island. Don't deny me the
pleasure.' Panos grinned. 'Pleasure or torture?' 'One partakes of
the other.' 'Good.' No Greek can resist aphorism; its form will
make him believe it to be true, even if it is false. 'Good,' he
repeated rising. 'Then I shall go off with Janis.' The old man
bobbed and curtseyed again. 'Willingly. Willingly.'

When they went off on their tour of inspection I lingered for a
while in the quietness of the loggia enjoying the distant boom of
the sea on the cliff-head and thinking how pleasant a place
Fortuna would one day be in a future empty of politics and the
shabby discontents and cruelties it engenders. Janis had unlocked
the rooms where Marie lived and idly I entered them to note how
dusty the bookshelves had become, and to tell over the various
treasures whose history I knew and which would one day find a
place in the great house: the Spanish chest, Moorish lattice,
Indian paintings and stuffs, Egyptian and Turkish lanterns, and
books everywhere piled up in heaps, the rare companions of a
solitude not self-imposed but sought. A mirror and comb from

Bali, a Tanagra, an iron statuette of Krishna, a *mandala* painting —these things had caught the hem of her dress on some speedy emphatic journey across the world and had come here to take up a lodgement in the cool rooms of her house. These are the sort of things which the writer carries about like talismans, to remind him of lost experiences which he must one day re-evoke and refashion in words. This dancer from Bali echoes the past with all the fidelity of a seashell held to the ear. . . . The sea-wind stirred the curtains, reminding me of the bathe I had promised myself.

I took a book from the shelf, copying her own habit though I knew I should not read, and unearthed my bathing slip. The path to her private beach led down through a small natural amphitheatre to a wall of rock which marked the sea-boundaries—and all along it the heavy screen of wattles which were to make a wind-break shuffled and scratched. Here stood the little bamboo hut which served both as a changing room and as a summer bedroom. A lizard lay asleep on the bamboo couch looking like a Greek politician waiting for an opening. As I undressed my eye noted the empty Chianti bottle, the red fan, and the gourd dippers—they echoed those improvident and happy afternoons of two years ago; a striped towel and a Penguin history of Architecture, stained and cockled with sea-damp, lay on a seat fashioned from the trunk of a palm tree. They repeated, more clearly than words could, the names: 'Pearce and Dante'. An empty bottle of Riesling with a sediment of oil in the bottom said: 'Paddy Leigh Fermor' (here during a tremendous freak thunderstorm we had sat, drinking wine and oiling ourselves against the sunlight we knew would follow it, while the rain slashed the slatted bamboo roof to ribbons and Paddy sang the trailing, ululating songs of the Cretan mountains, punctuating each strophe with a swig of Chianti). On a nail hung a tear-bottle. . . . But my movements had disturbed the lizard which abandoned the couch and retired to the roof.

Despite the high sea running the lagoon itself was calm save for a slight swell. The wind was north which meant that the western headland took the full force of the sea and sent down the smooth

lolling aftertow into the bay. The Spring water was cold and
pained one—as a drink of iced wine will hurt the back of the
throat—but it was delicious. I abandoned myself to the running
tide, not swimming, but simply keeping afloat, to be drawn
smoothly out into the bay from where the whole screen of luminous mountains was visible. The sun had cleared them now and
they were taking on that throbbing dark mauve which inhabits the
heart of a violet. The trees had turned silver and the slices of
corn-land to the east gleamed kingcup-yellow and shone like
bugles. I let myself be drawn slowly but surely towards the little
mosque, which glittered before me as if carved from rock-salt,
but veined by the winter damps in a dozen tones of grey and
yellow. The Hodja stood watching me from his balcony with his
cat in his arms—a patch of vivid black like a raven's wing. I raised
my hand in a salute and he answered it at once. Then he turned
and walked down the path to the seashore to wait for me as I
drifted unhurriedly towards the pitted and perforated shelf of
rock which prevented the full force of the sea from exploding on
the walls of the Mosque. Hereabouts it was as if some great rock-
carpenter had been busy, carving out shelf upon shelf of meta-
morphic limestone, and stepping them downwards to the sandy
bottom of the lagoon, three fathoms deep. Once jagged and
serrated like teeth, these tables had been ground smoothly down
and papered over with brilliant fucus and immense wigs of seaweed which stirred like gonfalons in the movements of the current. The top of this natural table was full of rock-pools, flushed
out by the lazy tides, and abounding in shrimp and crab and the
smaller varieties of fish. The capricious tides threw them up on
to these stone tables and fell back, to leave them marooned, and
here the barefoot shepherds roamed occasionally to see what they
might capture for the pot.

We were alone this afternoon, the Hodja and I, with only the
sea and sky for company. He divested himself of his festering
shoes (the simile from Rimbaud was not inappropriate in this
context) and hitched up his robe as he tiptoed across the slippery
weed-covered floor, carefully circumnavigating the rock-pools to
reach the edge of the shelf where I lay, arms and legs spread out

in sixty feet of emerald and fire opal. His huge head wobbled on its stalk, gleaming with sweat, like a toadstool. 'Welcome,' he said, raising his paws in the mouse-gesture. 'Will you stay tonight?'

'I can't,' I said sadly. 'I must go back.'

He ducked up and down, his head imitating the jogging motion of a camel, his underlip thrust out in commiseration. 'I have wine,' he said wistfully. I reached out and grasped the carpet of soft weed, and hanging for a long moment to adjust my body to the swing of the sea, hoisted myself dripping and panting on to the shelf beside him. We tiptoed back the way he had come, over the slippery shelves to the firm dry rock. 'I have some papers,' he said, 'which I wish you to see, to help me fill in.' I had a drink of fresh water from the spring and climbed the rock with him to the little white terrace, now brilliantly situated in the very eye of the sinking sun which had set fire to the misty slopes above Lapithos. The light flowed out from the horns of the mountain, squeezed out laterally now, in a shaft of thin pencils, touching in the unsubstantial silhouettes of the fortresses and capes with a dream-like unreality. The terrace with its whitewashed walls was a glittering sun-trap, and here the old man brought me a single uncomfortable chair to sit on, above the hushing of the sea and the faint tingle of wind which snatched at the old Turkish pennant, holding and releasing it, blowing and lapsing. The long dusk began to settle with a shiver, and one of the silver peaks began to nibble the disc of travelling light—throwing a deep cool penumbra of shade into the valleys. Soon the light evening wind would be rushing across the Mesaoria to set the windmills turning in Nicosia; the homing yachts would flutter and tremble outside the Kyrenia bar; and Sabri on his little balcony at the police mess would glance at his watch and incline his cheek to take the breath as he sat contemplating the hard enamel of the water and the Turkish mountains huddled in shadow like a flock of sheep.

Dusk began early on this side of the Gothic range for we lay in shadow while the mid-heaven still blazed with sunlight; it slanted downwards to us, refracted and diffused, pouring down not primary colours but the cool tones which shadows give to olive trees and barren rock, soaking up the light along the peaks like blotting paper. As the sun fell, darker and darker streaks would come to blur visibility with the soft ashen tone of charcoal-crayon rubbed into a drawing by the soft thumb of a draughtsman. Somewhere in the dark recesses of the smelly little room where he slept, the Hodja's radio gave out the muffled strains of a Turkish song, like the shrieks of a cat in a bag. Then he closed the door and the sea-silence fell once more. He joined me in the sunlight, walking with that histrionic shuffle in his benighted shoes. In his hand he clutched a large wad of papers which at first sight looked like Income Tax forms—though at a salary of ten pounds a year I could not see his having to pay Income Tax. 'I must fill these in,' he said, 'to get money.' He spoke in his gobbling Greek letting the reptilian lids of his eyes fall shyly.

They were Football Pool Coupons, flamboyantly printed. God knows—Allah alone knows—where he had got them from, or what thoughts passed through his muddled old head as he turned them over and over, crouching at his wood fire while the radio brayed. 'Money,' he croaked again, holding on to the main theme connected with them by a sheer effort of will. He rubbed horny thumb upon fingers to illustrate his meaning in Greek, repeating '*Parades . . . bolika*' ('Oodles of dough'). But alas I did not know how to fill them in for him, never having done one in my life. Worse, I could not explain how they worked when he pressed me —for his Greek consisted of a few rudimentary words which had to be supplemented by mimicry. Aware of the hopelessness of the task, I nevertheless kicked an imaginary football about the terrace for a moment, but he shook his head hopelessly, still croaking 'Money. Money,' like Poe's Raven, and then turned desolately away to shuffle back to his little room and replace them, no doubt, under his mattress, like talismans from the great incomprehensible world outside where people wrote cabalistic things in pencil on a paper and were suddenly, inexplicably enriched. Watching that magnificent sunset I thought how touching were these incongruities which overlapped each other so swiftly in the common life of the island.

The slanting light was now impacting on the sea to fling itself in a brilliant dazzle upwards at us. When the old man came to join me on the terrace his red turban threw a patch of dancing scarlet on the wall behind us. He crouched down beside me, motionless as a tortoise, unspeaking, and together we gazed into the heart of the darkness which had begun to overflow and trickle out of the valleys towards us. It was a blessed moment—a sunset which the Greeks and Romans knew—in which the swinging cradle-motion of the sea slowly copied itself into the consciousness, and made one's mind beat with the elemental rhythm of the earth itself. He said nothing and I said nothing; we simply sat there together as if bereft of the power of speech, watching the night encircle us.

Presently, on the headland opposite where the new house stood roofless as a ruin, in silhouette, a small black figure appeared and waved against the violet sky. Panos' hail came to us across the bay, diminished by distance and broken by the sea-rhythms on the rocks below. It was time to be going. I had decided to walk back to the house over the headland.

It was difficult to say good-bye to the Hodja who always appeared to be overwhelmed by his loneliness on this bare shore when one was leaving; he clung to one's hand, or to a corner of one's coat, a sleeve, a towel—anything, to put off the moment of parting, while he desperately racked his soft brain for a topic of conversation which would detain one. 'Will you come back to-morrow?' he asked anxiously. 'No.' He made a grimace and rolled his glaucous eyes. 'The next day?' I shook his hand firmly and dropped it—but it climbed up my arm to my elbow, like a vine, and clutched it. 'On Saturday,' I said, though I knew it to be a lie, for on Saturday I should have left Cyprus, perhaps forever. I had not the heart to tell him the truth.

'On Saturday,' he croaked. 'Good. Good. Bring a Turkish newspaper, effendi mine, a Turkish newspaper, please.' He bobbed and mimicked a premature thanks for this favour. 'I will,' I said, making a mental note to post him *Hur Soz* from my office. 'And so good-bye.' He took up his little cat, as if for consolation, and shuffled down with me to the spring, muttering under his breath.

I started to walk towards the sunset along that ivory sea-line while he stood, motionless as a lizard, watching me. The shadows came out to meet me, and with them the chill of the earth as it turned on its axis towards the darkness; the island was sinking into blueness as if into some great inkwell. But when I looked back the Mosque still blazed in sunlight, vertical and emphatic, echoing those ancient discoveries in space which still haunt our architecture—the cube, the sphere, the square, the cylinder. And still the little black figure stood, still as a statue, with the little tan cat in its arms, watching me.

By the time I reached the bamboo palisades Janis had lit a petrol lamp, whose blinding white light squashed out the evening around it and lit up the marble table-top with a crystal flare. They both sat there with their heads upon their hands, as if weighed down by an enormous fatigue, and something about their posture struck me; they were sitting so still and silent. Marie's little radio stood on the marble between them, and it had apparently just been turned off—of so recent a date seemed the silence which had just fallen, had opened between them like a chasm.

'Karaolis is to hang,' said Panos in a small choked voice, croaking as if with an enormous fatigue. Janis had tears in his eyes. There was nothing I could do but sit heavily silent between them, in the sympathetic silence one keeps for someone who has just suffered an irreparable bereavement. We had all known, and knew that this must happen; never for a moment was the objective logic and justice of the fact in any doubt. Their sorrow was the sorrow of people who had seen someone pursued by the Eumenides of ill-luck; a victim of events which could have turned out differently had they been differently conceived in the minds of those who had precipitated them. Panos lit a cigarette and looked at his own hands as they lay before him on the table. 'This is the end of something,' he said. 'We shall not be able to speak naturally, look each other in the eye, for a long time to come. O curse it!' Again it was not the injustice of the fact he questioned; the fault was in our stars. He stood up and for a moment his mildness dropped from him; he said, with disgust and fury: 'Why were you not honest in the beginning? If you had said,

"This is a Greek island but we are determined to stay in it, and will fight for it," do you think a single weapon would have been raised against you? Never! We know your legal title to the island is unquestionable. But that small lie is the seed from which all these monstrous things have grown and will continue to grow. Everything follows from it: *of course* Karaolis must hang. The Governor is right. I would do the same. . . .' He stubbed out his half-smoked cigarette on the table and with trembling hands drained his glass of wine. He stood up. 'But it is not Karaolis only who will be hanged; the deep bond between us will have been broken finally.' What he meant, I reflected, was that the image— the mythopoeic image of the Englishman which every Greek carried in his heart, and which was composed of so many fused and overlapping pictures—the poet, the lord, the quixotic and fearless defender of right, the just and freedom-loving Englishman—the image was at last thrown down and dashed into a thousand pieces, never again to be reassembled. In a paradoxical sort of way they were mourning, not Karaolis, but England.

We sat for a long time in silence while the violet evening gathered about us and the sea hushed upon the headland. The peacocks chuckled among the palms. The white harsh light, filtered by blueness, shone through the doors upon the rooms full of Marie's treasures.

The day before I had been to say good-bye to the francolin, walking in leisurely fashion up the narrow winding street of the little village which lies without the wooded knoll on which Government House now stands—the site of Coeur de Lion's first camp outside the then unwalled capital of the island; I was reflecting, as I walked, how different it had been a year before, sauntering up at dusk in a dinner-jacket through the unguarded gates with their heraldic lions and into the cold and pretentious portals of the great anodyne building. One might wander for half a day in the grounds without being challenged then; and the house itself with its warren of corridors seemed empty, tenantless, uninhabited even by servants. Today the scarlet-capped military police manned stout road-blocks. The barbed wire had been

renewed; and in a pit outside the front door crouched a red beret
with an automatic gun trained upon the house-gate.

When I thought of the relative unpreparedness of the year
before I marvelled that half a dozen resolute youths had not
broken into the place and blown it up ages before the military
took it in hand. Nor could I blame the soldiers who had seen our
condition for feeling that we, of the old political régime, were
somehow compromised, belonging as we did to that peaceful
world of 'jogging along', of *laissez faire*.

It was changed now; the billiard room was full of operational
maps and the impedimenta of the three smart secretaries who
manned the waiting-room outside the great study where the
Field Marshal worked.

He received me with the same wonderful warmth and composure and gentleness, unhurried in the midst of the hundred
pressures of a task which was both political and operational. I told
him of my plans, to take the four months' leave due to me, and to
visit Europe for a while before considering whether to return or
not. 'I think you should come back,' he said, 'when you feel like
it—after all this is over.' I regretted only that there had not been
time and opportunity to be his guide to Cyprus. 'I shall come
back for a holiday myself one day,' he smiled. 'And by the way,
do keep your eye open, and if you feel we're going wrong for
goodness' sake don't hesitate to tell us so.'

But what could I tell him? The very decisions which were
operationally necessary to the present situation were political
lunacy for whatever must follow upon the present. To try to
marry military and political considerations at this stage was like
trying to play a drum from a piano score. We had all of us been
made the clowns of shortsightedness at home, for now military
solutions precluded the political. (For example, the deportation
of the Archbishop which was operationally just was politically
nonsensical—as he was not only the one true representative of the
Greek community who could not be replaced, but his absence
left the field open to the extremists. Though his complicity in
EOKA was obvious, nevertheless he was the only brake to
terrorism and the only person who could curb it.) I could not

help reflecting what a sad waste of money and reputations the whole problem had been; and if the peace could only be kept with the help of twelve thousand armed men what security could the island enjoy as a base? . . .

But then much is a matter of destiny; if we were to sweat the lead out of Cyprus the Governor was the one person to achieve it. Moreover, given a few happy strokes of luck he might draw EOKA'S teeth in time, and genuinely win the peace he had been sent to keep. What he needed was not the counsels of specialists or the lucubrations of political wiseacres but something as clear and uncomplicated as his own direct vision of necessary expedients. He had not been sent to complete the wreckage of the Balkan Pact or shake nuts and bolts out of the frail skeleton of NATO. His mission was to police and hold a turbulent island, and all secondary consideration which we might produce at this stage could neither give him comfort nor do anything save contribute to infirmity of purpose. He needed, in fact, someone to wish him luck in a tedious and thorny task which offered neither the hope of peace nor the honours of war. And wish him luck I did on the old culverin with wooden wheels which stands under the lion and unicorn over the front door—a relic which Henry VIII had once sent to de L'Isle Adam, Grand Master of the Order of Saint John; another warrior like him who had propped the tottering fortunes of the Crusaders in their battle against the infidel. The soldier inhabits his own field of merits and his morals are founded in obedience to those for whom matters of life and death are not debatable issues, but must be acted upon. The francolin fitted warmly and naturally into the great gallery of human beings whose portraits made up the history and changing fortunes of this marginal place. That fine head belonged to the historical tapestry of Cyprus—very English in its warm colouring and lively composure. He belonged to that trace of forgotten captains whose sense of destiny had made them free men, committed to history; men who combined the power to turn perfect verses and in the same breath to order the pyre which was heaped about the feet of Saint Joan to be lit: if it was part of an operation whose enthralling science demanded that they disinherit pity.

But these thoughts had led me far from the two silent figures at the stone table, throbbing with the breathing whiteness of the petrol lamp. For them the foreground of this peaceful and happy place where they had lived so simply, drinking wine, picking wild flowers, marrying and burying—the whole had suddenly become darkened with the air itself, by blood.

'We must be going,' said Panos softly, at last. Janis too rose, throwing a sprawling shadow on the white walls. They sighed deeply and stood for a moment in deep thought before following me out. The sea burned in the eye of the night like an emerald. 'Good-bye,' said Janis, his old loving formality clouded now by the shadows which had gathered about us. 'Go with the good,' I responded as we moved out into the dense dusk carrying our own silhouette with us for a few yards before it was swallowed by the night which lay now, spilled everywhere about us in the cavernous shadows of olives and carobs. We left the rock-bound silence of the headland behind us and picked up the car which was already damp with the night dews.

Panos did not speak and I drove the four miles back to his village in a silence which I felt matched his mood. There was nothing resentful in it—it was the silence of profound sorrow.

I dropped him at the edge of the long flight of white stairs under the Church of Saint Michael, unaware that we should never meet again. He thanked me and placed his hand for a moment on mine; then, shaking his head sadly, he walked up the stairs bearing his great armful of flowers from Klepini. I had a glass of wine with Clito—who served me with tears in his eyes, but unspeaking; and then walked back to the seashore where I had left the car in the rich cool darkness of that perfect spring weather. All the sights and sounds of Kyrenia came to me with a new and poignant brilliance, as if experienced for the first time. The balconies spanning the conversational streets with their pattern of humble intimacies, now silent as the vines which climbed everywhere; fishermen mending nets by elf-light; a man hooping a barrel; a grey-headed man stringing a mandolin; a Turk in a wine-red fez; two boys playing hopscotch; children sleeping like sculptures below the bastion of the castle; a man blowing upon a tray of embers which was covered with sweetcorn; a little boy padding about with a thurible from which a wisp of laurel-smoke ascended—in Clito's the drinkers took a pinch of smoke with finger and thumb and made the sign of the cross with it; a coffee house sweet with the sound of cage-birds, where the *nargilehs* were piled in a rack like muskets in a magazine—you brought your own ebony mouthpiece before choosing your favourite one to smoke.

I walked down to the harbour where the still water was full of frozen lamplight from the houses round about it under a black rubber star-cancelled sky. It was very peaceful, yet all around us in the darkness now the island was slowly erupting in little spots of hate and the operational lines at the office would be scratching out their messages. 'A bomb at the Cinema in Larnaca . . . two men killed in a coffee-house . . . a bomb at a car-park in Paphos . . . a sentry murdered in Famagusta. . . .' Infinitesimally small flashes of hate like the spark of single matches struck here and there in the darkness of a field, none strong enough to ignite the whole, thank God, yet there, ever present, as a reminder of the sullen weight of the people's wish. My footsteps echoed softly upon the sea-wall. I was, I realized, very tired after this two years' spell as a servant of the Crown; and I had achieved nothing. It was good to be leaving.

A Pocketful of Sand

'If God had not made brown honey men would think figs much sweeter than they do.'

(XENOPHANES)

———◆———

I had to collect some books and papers from the house on the morning of the execution. A general strike had been declared in the capital, paralysing the ordinary transactions of life and creating a grim artificial holiday for us all. Such extensive precautions had been taken against civil violence that I did not fear a serious newsbreak or that my absence would be remarked. 'You are mad to go to your village today of all days,' said Achilles. Nevertheless time was so short that there was no other way to retrieve the papers I needed.

It was a beautiful ringing day and the curling streets were thick with almond and peach blossom. As I turned the last corner and came to rest under the belfries of the Abbey I saw that the whole village was there in the little square, the usual loafers sitting under the Tree of Idleness. The crowd was of Sunday proportions; nobody had gone to work. But as the engine fell silent I was aware of some altogether novel factor about the scene. It lacked all animation. The whiskered shepherds were all sitting in their accustomed places but nobody had ordered a coffee; the dusty packs of playing-cards lay on Dmitri's shelf untouched. It was like a hollow transcription of a known reality snapped by the camera's lens. To the matured resonance of the Abbey's silence the villagers had added, like an extra dimension, a silence of their own, hollow and profound. My footsteps echoed harshly on the gravel as I walked slowly across to the little café which was crowded but utterly silent. Everybody looked at the ground, awkwardly and with a shy clumsy disfavour. My good morning provoked a raised head and a nod here and there, but not the usual roar of response and the wave of brown hands. Dmitri stood behind his bar counter holding on to his apron as if for support, and swallowing. He had turned so white that he looked as if he were about to faint. He answered my greeting by moving his lips soundlessly. My mail lay on the counter before him. I took up the letters, feeling as if I should apologize for intruding upon a scene of such universal grief.

On the cobbled street up to the house the same faces bobbed curiously from the doors, but instead of chaff and the traditional greetings, 'Welcome, neighbour, Yasu Englishman,' there issued from the old-fashioned gates with their cable-pattern carvings and defaced armorial bearings only the same drugged silence. People ducked away into the gloomy corners, into the darkness, sliding away from speech and smiles like fish. Mr. Honey sat at his usual corner under the walnut tree by the bridge. It was customary for him to rise and grab inexpertly at the lapels of my coat as he bade me sit and drink with him. The gesture began involuntarily as he caught sight of me, and a smile darkened his dark face. He threw up his hands, made as if to rise unsteadily, and then subsided again with his chin on his breast. I passed him in silence.

The cool lower rooms of the house echoed with silence and the sunlight filtered through the bitter lemon trees in the garden outside. I did not dare to climb to the balcony, so sad was I to leave it all. Xenu the puffing maid was cleaning up the kitchen. She greeted me warmly enough but said in the same breath: 'Have you heard the news?' I nodded. 'The execution?' She puffed and swelled with sorrow. 'Why should they do such things?' I became angry. 'If you kill you must die,' I said; she raised her hand, as if to stop me. 'Not that. Not the execution. But they would not give his mother the body, or so they say. That is a terrible punishment, sir. For if you do not look upon your loved one dead you will never meet again in the other world.'

I busied myself in the little study, turning out a case of books. I found the old wicker basket which had accompanied me on all my journeys in Cyprus. It was full of fragments collected by my daughter, buried in a pocketful of sand which leaked slowly through the wicker mesh. I turned the whole thing out on to a sheet of newspaper, mentally recalling as I turned over the fragments in curious fingers where each had been acquired: Roman glass, blue and vitreous as the summer sea in deep places; handles of amphorae from Salamis with the hallmark thumb-printed in the soft clay; tiles from the floor of the villa near Paphos; *verde-antico* fragments; Venus' ear seashells; a Victorian penny; fragments of yellow mosaic from some Byzantine church; purple murex; desiccated sea-urchins and white chalk squid-bones; a tibia; fragments of a bird's egg; a green stone against the evil eye. . . . All in all a sort of record of our stay in Cyprus. 'Xenu, throw all this away,' I said.

Once more I walked down the main street to the car in the same heavy ominous silence, observed once more from many chinks and slits in those old houses, arousing no comment; and once more the village stared deeply at its shoes in silence under the great tree—frozen into immobility. The eyes which avoided mine, flickering shyly away from my glance 'like vernal butter-flies'—I cannot say that they were full of hate. No. It was simply that the sight of me pained them. The sight of an Englishman had become an obscenity on that clear honey-gold spring air.

I caught sight of a few of my friends, among them Michaelis and the Seafarer, sitting inside the café but I did not feel like intruding upon them with my good-byes.

The car started with a roar, fracturing the dense silence over-flowing from the Abbey no less than from those silent, uncompre-hending minds grouped about under the old tree. Nobody waved and nobody smiled.

I slipped down the empty street under the blossoming trees and out on to the crest of the hill. Frangos was on the threshing-floor looking out to sea; he turned his head as the car passed but did not wave. I lit a cigarette and was about to increase speed when my eye caught sight of a figure rushing down through the olive-groves towards the road with the obvious intention of head-ing me off, waving and shouting. I recognized the small brown agile Andreas, running for all his sixty years like a boy of sixteen. I drew up.

He came panting down the last terrace and gave a tremendous jump into the road, beaming and panting. 'Mr. Darling,' he cried, in his excitement using a version of my name which had once been current and which, under teasing, he had discarded. 'Thank God I caught you. I wanted to tell you that the boy came back! He did not join EOKA because he won a scholarship to London instead. The Government radio announced the names yesterday!' He expelled his breath in a great sigh of relief and crossed himself twice, emphatically, in the Orthodox fashion. 'God is great, and his wisdom hidden from us. The boy will go to London now. Will your mother look after him when he is in England—if you are not there? After all, neighbour, he is a kid still.' I could not look at his warm, merry kindly face without emotion. I got out into the road and we smoked a cigarette together while he talked with great excitement about London and of how much he had wanted to go there himself. 'Education is everything,' he said. 'How much we wished for it ourselves. Now perhaps our children can have it.' I felt bitterly ashamed of the neglect these people had endured—the poor Cyps. 'Of course we'll look after him,' I said. Andreas pressed my hand. 'And don't fear for the house,' he said, laying his hand upon his heart, 'I will keep it sound and clean, everything in place. And I shall look after the vine on the balcony for your daughter. You will have shade from it over the whole balcony when you return next year, neighbour.' We stamped out our cigarettes in the road and shook hands. 'And don't forget,' he said, 'to write to us, Loizus and Anthemos and the Seafarer—send us picture postcards of the London church—the big one with the clock.' I promised him that I would. 'Remember,' he called after me, quoting the village proverb which illustrates hope for the future. 'Next year's wine is the sweetest.'

'You see,' said the driver of the taxi which took me up by night to the heavily guarded airport, 'you see, the trouble with the Greeks is that we are really so pro-British.'

There had been two or more explosions in various parts of the town that evening, and doubtless there would be more. He drove with a certain elated caution across the deserted streets with their occasional patrol and their inadequate lighting. He was an elderly man with a grey moustache and a leisurely manner. His accent was a Paphos accent. 'I don't follow you,' I said absently, with one ear cocked for trouble along the dark roads, and only slightly reassured by the blue bead (talisman against the evil eye) which was tied to the dashboard. 'Even Dighenis,' he said thoughtfully, 'they say he himself is very pro-British.' It was one of those Greek conversations which carry with them a hallucinating sur-realist flavour—in the last two years I had endured several hundred of them. 'Yes,' he continued in the slow assured tones of a village wiseacre, 'yes, even Dighenis, though he fights the British, really loves them. But he will have to go on killing them—with regret, even with affection.'

BITTER LEMONS

In an island of bitter lemons
Where the moon's cool fevers burn
From the dark globes of the fruit,

And the dry grass underfoot
Tortures memory and revises
Habits half a lifetime dead

Better leave the rest unsaid,
Beauty, darkness, vehemence
Let the old sea-nurses keep

Their memorials of sleep
And the Greek sea's curly head
Keep its calms like tears unshed

Keep its calms like tears unshed.

LAWRENCE DURRELL

Select Bibliography

NEWMAN, PHILIP. *A Short History of Cyprus* (London, 1940). Handy, condensed history.

LUKE, H. C. *Cyprus under the Turks* (London, 1921). Information on the Turkish Period.

DIXON, W. HEPWORTH. *British Cyprus* (London, 1887).

LEWIS, MRS. *A Lady's Impressions of Cyprus* (1893).

BROWN, SAMUEL, M.I.C.E. *Three Months in Cyprus:* during the winter of 1878–9 (1879).

ORR, C. W. J. *Cyprus under British Rule* (London, 1918). Information on the British Period.

GUNNIS, RUPERT. *Historic Cyprus* (London, 1936). Comprehensive 'guide-book' to the antiquities.

COBHAM, C. D. *Excerpta Cypria:* Materials for a History of Cyprus (Cambridge, 1908). Selected extracts from books and travel-diaries on Cyprus, A.D. 23 to 1849. A unique compilation.

STORRS, SIR RONALD, and O'BRIEN, B. J. *The Handbook of Cyprus* (London, 1930). Detailed information on every aspect of the island.

HADJICOSTA, ISMENE. *Cyprus and its Life* (Nicosia, 1943).

BALFOUR, PATRICK. *The Orphaned Realm* (London, 1951).

Index

Index

Index